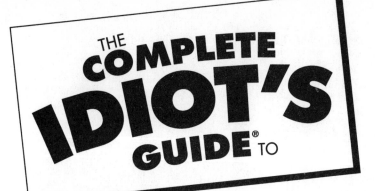

Technical Analysis

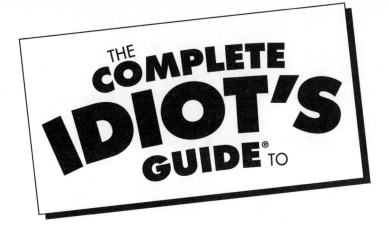

THE COMPLETE IDIOT'S GUIDE® TO

Technical Analysis

by Jan Arps

ALPHA

A member of Penguin Group (USA) Inc.

ALPHA BOOKS

Published by the Penguin Group

Penguin Group (USA) Inc., 375 Hudson Street, New York, New York 10014, USA

Penguin Group (Canada), 90 Eglinton Avenue East, Suite 700, Toronto, Ontario M4P 2Y3, Canada (a division of Pearson Penguin Canada Inc.)

Penguin Books Ltd., 80 Strand, London WC2R 0RL, England

Penguin Ireland, 25 St. Stephen's Green, Dublin 2, Ireland (a division of Penguin Books Ltd.)

Penguin Group (Australia), 250 Camberwell Road, Camberwell, Victoria 3124, Australia (a division of Pearson Australia Group Pty. Ltd.)

Penguin Books India Pvt. Ltd., 11 Community Centre, Panchsheel Park, New Delhi—110 017, India

Penguin Group (NZ), 67 Apollo Drive, Rosedale, North Shore, Auckland 1311, New Zealand (a division of Pearson New Zealand Ltd.)

Penguin Books (South Africa) (Pty.) Ltd., 24 Sturdee Avenue, Rosebank, Johannesburg 2196, South Africa

Penguin Books Ltd., Registered Offices: 80 Strand, London WC2R 0RL, England

Copyright © 2010 by Jan Arps

International Standard Book Number: 978-1-59257-901-3
Library of Congress Catalog Card Number: 2009932958

12 11 10   8 7 6 5 4 3 2 1

Interpretation of the printing code: The rightmost number of the first series of numbers is the year of the book's printing; the rightmost number of the second series of numbers is the number of the book's printing. For example, a printing code of 10-1 shows that the first printing occurred in 2010.

Printed in the United States of America

Note: This publication contains the opinions and ideas of its author. It is intended to provide helpful and informative material on the subject matter covered. It is sold with the understanding that the author and publisher are not engaged in rendering professional services in the book. If the reader requires personal assistance or advice, a competent professional should be consulted.

The author and publisher specifically disclaim any responsibility for any liability, loss, or risk, personal or otherwise, which is incurred as a consequence, directly or indirectly, of the use and application of any of the contents of this book.

Most Alpha books are available at special quantity discounts for bulk purchases for sales promotions, premiums, fundraising, or educational use. Special books, or book excerpts, can also be created to fit specific needs.

For details, write: Special Markets, Alpha Books, 375 Hudson Street, New York, NY 10014.

Publisher: *Marie Butler-Knight*
Editorial Director: *Mike Sanders*
Senior Managing Editor: *Billy Fields*
Senior Acquisitions Editor: *Paul Dinas*
Development Editor: *Nancy D. Lewis*
Production Editor: *Kayla Dugger*
Copy Editor: *Amy Lepore*

Cartoonist: *Steve Barr*
Cover Designer: *Kurt Owens*
Book Designer: *Trina Wurst*
Indexer: *Celia McCoy*
Layout: *Ayanna Lacey*
Proofreader: *Laura Caddell*

Contents at a Glance

Contents

Foreword

Trading is an occupation for many, a hobby for some, and a lifelong engagement for a dedicated few. As trading educators, trading is our focus and it is our purpose to educate traders so they can achieve success in a world that is difficult and enigmatic, a world that ebbs and flows to the rhythm of human emotions—specifically, fear and greed. It is a world that cries out for education to advance the effectiveness of hard workers and to enlighten the uninformed. Education is the key to succeeding as a trader, which means getting in and getting out of a trade with a profit. Ultimately, it is all about buying and selling, so the decisions you make regarding these two actions are paramount to success. Jan Arps understands that and writes this book to help you achieve that end.

One of the goals of this book is to show you how technical analysis can help you make more intelligent buying and selling decisions.

Like any good technician in any field, you need the most trustworthy tools, and more importantly, you have to know how to use them to achieve the best results. This is what Jan's book does for you: It gives you a toolbox full of technical analysis tools, and it teaches you how to use them.

Jan is an educator, and this book is educational. That is why I like it and why I want you to read it. If you are a beginning technical analyst, you will find virtually everything there is to know regarding technical analysis in this book. If you are an advanced technical analyst, I am certain a nugget or two awaits you in Jan's book. My mother once told me, "You don't know it all, mister." I consider that excellent advice.

To more than a few people, technical analysis is akin to reading tea leaves or following some guru on blind faith. Jan recognizes this, noting, "The uninitiated may view technical analysis as a bizarre cult obsessed with charts, graphs, and assorted diagrams." Another goal of the book is to dispel this notion, to put people at ease with technical analysis as a trading tool, and to tie technical analysis to the mathematical field of probability and the scientific field of behavioral psychology.

Technical analysis can't predict the future. However, it can help you identify the probability that a stock's price may change. This probability is determined by comparing different instances of similar patterns of behavior in the past. Technical analysis uses historical information of the past behavior of investments, as well as an understanding of human behavior, to make decisions about possible future price movements.

As an educator, I found the material in this book quite enlightening. Although I am not a master at technical analysis, the book inspired me to learn more about it, and so I have—and so will you, especially if you are just starting out and technical analysis is your chosen trading approach.

The technician doesn't focus on what the underlying company does or makes, nor does he focus on what the company's financials reveal—these are in the domain of fundamental analysis. The technician strictly pays attention to price movement and using various indicators or looking for price patterns that help him predict future price direction.

Traders rely on technical analysis more than fundamental analysis for short-term trading, at least that is our experience at my company, TraderPlanet, where our "networkers" constantly discuss some element of technical analysis in our forums, blogs, and columns. I suspect the reason is, in general, that technical analysis is for trading and fundamental analysis is for investing; although Jan and others would argue that fundamental analysis has a critical flaw that should turn all traders to technical analysis as the preferred analytical approach.

There is at least one major flaw in fundamental analysis. Some of the information can be highly suspect and unreliable to those of us who aren't in the know or aren't deep inside the company or on the floor of the stock and futures exchanges.

So if technical analysis is the most widely used and beneficial analytical approach to trading, then it makes sense that you should thoroughly understand and apply technical analysis to your trading. I don't imagine you will find another book out there that covers more ground on this topic, in more detail, and with more focus on the needs of the trader as a technical analyst.

To many, technical analysis seems complex and a "mind bender," if you will. True, it is complex (that's where this book can help), but so what? Like most things in life, hard work is the difference between success and failure. Returning to the well of my maternal sage once again, she also taught me, "If it's worth doing, it is worth doing well." Clearly, Jan gets this and directs the book to that end. Chapter after chapter teaches one to understand technical analysis and how to apply the "tools of the trade" to create success.

Equally important is the implicit message that threads its way through both the craft of technical analysis and this book: Successful traders find an edge and exploit it.

All you need is a well of knowledge, worthwhile practical experience, emotional discipline, and some faith in the technical tools you are using. Once you have these elements in place, you are a true technician, one who looks at the chart. "The truth is in the chart." This is the essence of technical analysis, and Jan's book will get you much closer to that needed edge.

Lane J. Mendelsohn,
Founder of www.TraderPlanet.com

Introduction

Have you ever wondered why a particular stock is on an upward trajectory, only to hit a seemingly invisible ceiling and reverse its course? After meandering downward for several sessions, the stock may bounce and resume its upward course.

If you knew when the stock's price was going to reverse direction (either up or down), you could make money by buying low and selling high—or, in the case of the short trader, selling high and buying low. Either way, there is power in information.

Technical analysis is about giving you a better idea of when a stock's price is going to reverse (or continue in the same direction). If you know in advance (or can make a well-educated guess) what the price of a stock will do and when, you can make some serious money.

Technical analysis provides you with the tools to make a highly educated guess regarding the direction of a stock's price. It does not predict the future or find you a compatible mate. However, if you master the basics of technical analysis, you have an advantage in the market. You'll have to solve the compatible mate problem yourself.

Your advantage is a reliable system that alerts you in advance when prices are going to change direction. Technical analysis includes tools that significantly increase your chances of investing success.

But isn't technical analysis, well, technical?

Yes, the logic and math behind technical analysis are indeed technical, however you don't need to be a math whiz to understand what technical analysis can do for your trading profits.

Most of technical analysis is reduced to easy-to-understand charts and graphs. Once you learn to read and recognize specific graph properties, you will be on the road to nailing down the profits that may have eluded you previously.

This book is not an encyclopedia of technical analysis. It is a broad view with enough detail so that you can understand the logic behind the most important technical analysis tools.

You will learn enough from this book to see the results for yourself. If you want to pursue technical analysis further, I've included a list of books, websites, and other resources to help you become a technical analysis master.

What to Expect

This book is an introduction to technical analysis. It covers some of the most common tools you'll use to help improve your trading profits. It is not a system guaranteed to make you rich. You still must learn and apply the tools of technical analysis—there are no free lunches.

The CD included with this book is invaluable in demonstrating with actual stock charts the patterns and indicators that tip savvy traders to when a stock's price may reverse direction.

Every type of investor and trader will find technical analysis to be an important part of their arsenal. A short-term trader uses technical analysis to signal when a stock's price has peaked or bottomed and is about to reverse direction. Long-term investors understand that buying a stock at the best price results in a greater profit opportunity.

How This Book Is Organized

The book is divided into four parts.

Part 1, "Introduction to Technical Analysis," defines the trading need for technical analysis and sets it in a proper context of today's markets.

Part 2, "Tools for Technical Analysis," describes the importance of key elements such as understanding charts and introducing price trends.

Part 3, "Time to Trade," suggests how you can begin to use technical analysis and what support (computers, software, and so on) you will need to be successful.

Part 4, "Trading Mechanics," walks you through the actual process of trading, including strategies to help you succeed.

Extras

Throughout each chapter, I've included the following sidebars, which add detail, specific tips, or cautions for the beginning technical analysis trader. Watch for these:

TA Intelligence
Guidance and wisdom from the experts.

 **def•i•ni•tion**

Important definitions of industry terms.

 Info/Tips

Lots of insider information on making the most of technical analysis.

 Heads Up

Warnings about the pitfalls and dangers facing technical analysts.

The Included CD

This book comes with a CD that contains many full-color versions of the charts in some chapters. You will find the discussion much more meaningful if you have access to the CD while reading the book. In addition to the chart examples themselves, I offer some additional details or tips for reading and understanding the charts.

 This icon indicates when the CD and its charts come into play.

Acknowledgments

First of all, I would like to thank my loving and supportive wife, Peggy, for encouraging me and tolerating the time I have spent wrapped in my own thoughts and away from her while writing this book. She has been my Rock of Gibraltar, my True North, and has been by my side in all my endeavors over our many years together.

I also want to acknowledge and thank my engineer father for having originally introduced me to the concept of market technical analysis over 50 years ago, when he taught me how to use an adding machine and a slide rule to calculate moving averages. Every weekend we would update our charts on the dozen or two stocks he was following back in the 1960s. I used to draw price charts and moving averages, based on prices published in *The Wall Street Journal,* by hand on graph paper purchased at the local blueprint store. Then I would draw trendlines with a colored pencil and a ruler. Technology has come a long way since then, Dad. I regret that you are no longer here to share it with me.

My brother, Ron Arps, Ph.D., a published author who recently retired as an honored research scientist at IBM Almaden Research Lab, has been my sounding board and confidante throughout my life, sharing ideas and trading concepts along with our life experiences. Thanks, Ron, for all the insights you have provided in our many bull sessions and brainstorming discussions about the market and technical analysis over these many years.

Craig (Hawk) Arps, one of my three brilliant sons, has recently begun sharing my lifelong interest in technical analysis and is rapidly becoming an accomplished technical analyst and trader in his own right. Welcome to the club, Hawk.

Thanks also go to the good folks at Bloomberg LLC, eSignal, and MultiCharts for having enough confidence in me and my unique technical analysis tools to have incorporated them directly as a part of their respective charting platforms.

Extra thanks should also go to the folks at TradeStation Securities, Inc., whose TradeStation charting and trading platform has been my principal technical analysis platform over the past 17 years. Most of the charts prepared for this book were created using the TradeStation charting platform.

I want to thank those who have worked with me in the preparation of this book: in particular, my editor at Penguin Books, Paul Dinas, who has made sure that I stayed on the straight and narrow, on target and on deadline, and Ken Little, who has assisted me with his authoring expertise in the writing and editing of this book in *The Complete Idiot's Guide* strict format.

Thanks also to those who contributed to the writing of select chapters in this book:

My hard-working assistant at Jan Arps' Traders' Toolbox, Keith Harris, who reviewed and edited my pearls of wisdom and contributed many of his own ideas in the writing of these chapters.

My good friend, Steve Woods at FloatCharts.com, who assisted me in the writing of the chapter on float analysis and the preparation of all the exhibits for that chapter. Also, a special thanks to the folks at StockSharePublishing.com, who created and continue to support the FloatCharts.com website, the only place where you can obtain official Woods float charts for most listed stocks.

Jay Dorger, my divergence expert, friend, and client, was responsible for much of the information in the chapter on price-oscillator divergence. His monographs, "The Wizard's Attic, a Closer Look at Jan Arps' Many Tools"; "The Junkyard Trader, 101 Ideas for Building a Trading System"; and "Nutshell, a Review of Some of the World's Best Trading Books," have been a staple in my library for many years.

Bear market and money management expert Paul Fribush of First Global Capital Managers contributed his expertise to the section on money management and has generously shared with me his research and trading knowledge over many years.

Trademarks

All terms mentioned in this book that are known to be or are suspected of being trademarks or service marks have been appropriately capitalized. Alpha Books and Penguin Group (USA) Inc. cannot attest to the accuracy of this information. Use of a term in this book should not be regarded as affecting the validity of any trademark or service mark.

Part 1

Introduction to Technical Analysis

Sometimes referred to as "behavioral finance," technical analysis can help you anticipate potential changes in the direction of market prices resulting from crowd behavior driven by the emotions of greed and fear. It can help you as well to develop more effective money management techniques that will improve the profitability of your investment funds and reduce your risk of loss.

Technical analysis provides rational and rule-based tools for trading almost any type of security. Unlike fundamental analysis, technical analysis focuses on price and volume as key indicators of future price direction.

Information Is Power

In This Chapter

- ◆ Technical analysis defined
- ◆ Understanding the difference between data and information
- ◆ The importance of price information for trading decisions
- ◆ Technical analysis versus fundamental analysis

If you knew today what IBM stock would sell for tomorrow, you could act on that information to your advantage. If I told you there is a method that will help you anticipate what IBM (or any other security) will likely sell for tomorrow, you might be interested in investing some of your time to learn how to use it. Best of all, it's completely legal.

Technical analysis can't predict the future; however, it can help you identify the probability that a stock's price may change. This probability is determined by comparing different instances of similar patterns of behavior in the past. Technical analysis is a tool used for hundreds of years to study and anticipate the price movement of securities.

The uninitiated may view technical analysis as a bizarre cult obsessed with charts, graphs, and assorted diagrams. But for those in the know, technical analysis is a tool that will help you make more money with any security you trade. Traders and investors from all over the world use technical analysis every day to help them make better buying and selling decisions. You can, too.

What Is Technical Analysis?

Technical analysis is a method of anticipating future price movements of securities. It is not a business of predictions, but one of probabilities based on past price history. Technical analysis uses historical information of the past behavior of investments, as well as an understanding of human behavior, to make decisions about possible future price movements. Like weather forecasting, technical analysis doesn't result in absolute predictions about the future. Instead, technical analysis can help investors anticipate what is "likely" to happen to prices over time.

Info/Tips

Although throughout this book we refer to the trading of stocks in the context of technical analysis, the same principles apply whether you are trading bonds, futures, foreign exchange, or any other tradable instrument in a public market.

Technical analysis depends on historical price and volume information to anticipate what a security's price may do in the future. The reason technical analysis works is because buying and selling decisions are based on human behavior, and humans tend to react in predictable patterns. The technical analyst or technician uses past price behavior to look for clues that will suggest what may happen next.

The technician doesn't focus on what the underlying company does or makes, nor does he or she focus on what the company's financials reveal—these are in the domain of fundamental analysis. The technician strictly pays attention to price movement, using various indicators or looking for price patterns that help him predict future price direction.

Data Is Not Information

It is important in our discussion of technical analysis to draw a distinction between data and information. When you look at a stock's price in the newspaper, you are seeing raw data. The prices listed for various securities in and of themselves tell you nothing of value. It is only when you put the numbers in context that they take on meaning. Most listings either in the newspaper or online provide some context, which is the beginning of technical analysis.

For example, the listing usually tells you whether the closing price was higher or lower than the previous close. This is helpful but hardly sufficient to make an informed decision. If the stock (or other security) closed up one dollar, what does that tell you? Not much more than the stock is selling for one dollar more today than it was yesterday. What can you do with that information? Not much.

However, if you combine that news with days, weeks, or months of previous price data for this security, you can begin to see patterns or trends. Since it is difficult to look at columns of numbers and make much out of them, technicians convert that data to chart and graph formats. When a large amount of data is displayed graphically, technicians are able to discern trends and characteristic patterns in price movement.

Technical analysis is the process of converting data (price movement) into information that reveals trends that can be used to make buy and sell decisions. Price information can be for any type of traded security. If you were to show detailed charts of any security's historical price movement, a technician would reach some conclusions about the future direction of the security's price. You don't have to specialize in stocks or bonds or futures contracts as you would in fundamental analysis. The key is the interpretation of the data.

Info/Tips

Almost no one draws charts by hand anymore. If you are serious about technical analysis, check out some of the charting programs available online. Many will let you use the software for free during a trial period.

Why Study Price Movement?

Price movement is a reflection of the market's reaction to supply and demand. The more demand, the higher the price. The lower the supply (often as a result of high demand), the higher the price. Conversely, if few investors are interested in buying a security, sellers will find lower prices. Factors such as how risky a security is perceived to be also affect its price. Investors will demand more return for a higher risk and are usually unwilling to pay a high price.

We could go on with other examples; however, the point is that price movement follows patterns or trends that are affected by supply and demand. When you study price movement, you are studying historical facts, not theories. Other means of analysis attempt to determine what a security should be worth—its intrinsic value. That determination is based on many assumptions, some of which can turn out to be incorrect.

Technical analysis starts with the assumption that we know exactly what the security was worth in the past because an exchange was made at that price between a buyer and a seller. There is no guessing or estimation. The price is what it is. The movement of prices, however, represents a pattern of behavior. Technical analysis seeks to identify those patterns of behavior and to interpret them.

The term "technical analysis" may be a bit misleading. Perhaps "price action analysis" or "supply,

TA Intelligence

Charles Dow, co-founder of Dow Jones, is credited with encouraging the development of modern technical analysis in the late nineteenth century.

demand, and reaction analysis" would be better. Nowadays, the term "behavioral finance" is emerging, and that is also a good description.

Technical Analysis vs. Fundamental Analysis

Maybe it's helpful to describe what technical analysis is by defining what it is not. It is not fundamental analysis, which is the other, and better understood, form of analyzing an investment opportunity. There are other methods, but these two are the predominant tools used by most investors. It is important to note that although each method takes a completely different approach to understanding an investment, the two are not incompatible. Many investors use both to one degree or another.

What Is Fundamental Analysis?

Fundamental analysis is the study of information about a company's operations, products, management, supply/demand balance, and finances, as well as rumors and news. The goal of fundamental analysis is to reach a consensus about the "fair value" of a company's stock. This conclusion is reached after an exhaustive examination of the company.

Investors who conclude that the company's stock is priced at less than the company is really worth might buy the security and hold it until the market agrees with their evaluation of price. This is known as "value investing," and its successful application has made many investors rich—Warren Buffett most notably.

An investor using fundamental analysis might conclude that a company is on a strong path of sustained growth and its stock should continue to rise. These growth stocks are often in high-growth industries such as technology. The investor will hold the stock as long as it continues to grow, but if growth stops or slows, the investor may decide to sell for a profit. When high-flying stocks suddenly come crashing down, it is often because growth rates have stumbled and investors sell their holdings, forcing the price down precipitously.

A Fundamental Flaw

There is at least one major flaw in fundamental analysis. Some of the information can be highly suspect and unreliable to those of us who aren't in the know or who aren't deep inside the company or on the floor of the stock and futures exchanges.

Consider this: if widely disseminated fundamental information were the primary driver of stock prices, you would think that every time a new piece of news was released, prices would react and then stabilize at a new perceived value in stair-step fashion and stay there until another piece of fundamental news caused the price to move up or down in reaction to that news. In reality, however, prices are constantly moving up and down in the absence of any new fundamental information. Why should that be? The answer is that prices move in response to supply and demand activity, which is, in turn, driven by the human emotions of fear and greed. Fear of suffering a loss is a powerful motivator of investment decisions, as is the desire to make extraordinary gains.

Heads Up

When your emotions enter the investment decision, good judgment departs. Technical analysts learn to trust the charts, which are based on facts.

Technical Analysis Is Different

There is a saying among practitioners of technical analysis that the truth is in the chart. The price bars on the chart are a reflection of people buying and selling. It doesn't matter what the company or commodity is. Whether it is Microsoft, General Motors, Exxon, pork bellies, gold, the euro, or bonds, they are all the same to the technical trader. People buying and selling are creating the patterns on the price charts. It is irrelevant whether the company is making cars or iPods, fried chicken or submarines.

It also doesn't matter what time frame we are looking at. Technicians might be looking at monthly, weekly, daily, hourly, 30-minute, or 5-minute time intervals. Patterns made on the charts are consistent through any time frame, so long as there is active trading. One of my favorite sayings is, "A chart is a chart is a chart." Charts are a reflection of human nature, and human nature is repetitive and predictable.

Acting on the What, Not the Why

Technical analysis starts with a chart of prices, based on the belief that the truth behind a stock, bond, or futures contract is in the chart or, better yet, the chart patterns. These patterns reflect supply and demand and the behavior of crowds. They reflect actual trades that occur when buyers and sellers have put their money where their collective mouths are.

In truth, almost every trader and investor uses some form of technical analysis. Many of the most reverent followers of market fundamentals are likely to glance at price charts before executing a trade.

Info/Tips

Traders and investors agree on one basic truth: knowing when to sell is as important as knowing when to buy. Technical analysis helps you with both decisions.

At their most basic level, price charts help traders determine ideal entry and exit points for a trade. Traders can look at a chart and know if they are buying at a fair price (based on the price history of a particular market), selling at a cyclical top, or perhaps throwing their capital into a choppy sideways market.

Technical Analysis Helps Decision Making

When it comes right down to it, if you are making buying and selling decisions about your investments, you are making technical analysis decisions. You are deciding what to buy, when to buy it, and when to sell it. You may be deciding to buy and sell based on the earnings and business prospects of a company (the fundamentals). Still, when you buy and when you sell is an individual decision that you alone must make, and every investor and trader makes that decision differently.

Some investors buy or sell a stock based on what they've heard, a newspaper article they read, or maybe a hot tip. A technical trader ignores these outside voices and focuses on the charts of price movement. Technical traders look at a chart and believe that what is really happening inside a company (commodity, mutual fund, investment vehicle) is reflected in the patterns of its past price behavior. These patterns reflect the human emotions that created them based on the information available at the time.

Market participants are emotional human beings. They have a tendency to behave in a similar manner given similar circumstances, so if we can figure out the circumstances through examining chart patterns and understanding crowd behavior based on sentiment and emotions, then we are well along the path in figuring out what they are likely to do next. After all, they've done it before.

A practitioner of technical analysis is looking for a signal in a price chart—a signal free of rumor, nonsense, outright lies, or information planted by insiders or con artists or pitchmen to manipulate the public and the average investor for their own purposes. A true technician doesn't want to know what people are saying. It only distracts him. The technician looks at the chart. The truth is in the chart.

Making Sense of Market Activity

One of the goals of this book is to show you how technical analysis can help you make more intelligent buying and selling decisions. Many times the market appears to react irrationally to current realities. Prices of individual securities seem to change for no logical reason. Technical analysis helps investors cut through the noise of daily market activity and focus on identifiable price trends.

In the following chapters, you will learn about analysis tools and techniques that …

- Signal a market turn.

- Signal a continuation in a trend.

- ◆ Signal an end to a trend and the beginning of another in the opposite direction.

- ◆ Signal just a brief correction in the trend.

- ◆ Signal the end of a stagnant period.

- ◆ Signal an end to a *pullback* and continuation of the original trend.

These are powerful tools that, when used correctly, can make you a more successful trader/investor.

def•i•ni•tion

A **pullback** is a retreat in price from a previous high. A pullback may be a brief pause, or it could signal a change in the trend's direction.

Are You a Trader or an Investor?

For the sake of clarity, it is helpful to divide market participants into two groups: investors and traders. It may seem like splitting hairs, but identifying investors and traders has a practical application in the understanding of technical analysis.

Investors and traders share a common goal—they want to make money with their investments. How each achieves this goal, in part, distinguishes investors and traders. It is not an issue that one is right and the other wrong. Nor are the terms mutually exclusive. Investors can, at times, be traders, and traders may choose to be investors under the right circumstances.

Admittedly, these definitions are somewhat arbitrary; however, most market professionals would agree with these broad attributes.

What Defines an Investor?

Most definitions of an investor focus on two attributes: the normal time to hold a security and the strategy employed to achieve success.

Investors are typically long-term traders. They plan on holding most securities for five or more years. It is not unusual for investors to hold on to a security until death and pass it on to their estate. There are strong historical reasons for long holding periods.

Countless studies have concluded that over the long term, stocks in particular have produced the best returns of any widely traded security. The key phrase here is "long term."

Info/Tips

Investors are more concerned with long-term growth; however, holding an investment for a lengthy period is no guarantee of success. Traders, on the other hand, don't follow a calendar but instead follow an investment's price movement to decide when to buy or sell.

One study noted that there has not been a single 20-year period when stocks lost money. In specific terms, this means that if you held a broadly diversified portfolio of stocks for any 20-year period, including the stock market crash of 1929, you would not have lost money.

A general rule of investing is that if you will need your money within five years, you should avoid putting it in stocks. Stocks can be very volatile, and over short periods you can lose a lot of money if you have to sell.

In addition to a traditionally long holding period, investors tend to rely heavily on fundamental analysis. The theory is that great companies will be successful over time, even if suffering short-term losses due to economic or market conditions. Warren Buffett is the only person to make the top five wealthiest people in America by virtue of his investing prowess. His strategy is to identify great companies with strong management and hold them for years.

Heads Up

Don't be confused by terms and labels since many are arbitrary. It is an individual's actions that determine whether he or she is an investor or trader or both.

The foundation for most investors' decisions is fundamental analysis. Despite its flaws, fundamental analysis continues to be the strategy of choice for most long-term investors. Nonetheless, it takes great intestinal fortitude to hold on to an investment position through huge drawdowns, as was seen in the recession that began in 2008.

Are You a Trader?

Traders generally do not have a specific holding period in mind when they buy a security. Their goal is to cut losses short and let profits run. This is the slogan of traders. They seek to buy a security at the correct moment and watch their profits increase. They will exit the trade when charts and indicators tell them a change is coming, which means their profits will erode. The period of profit gathering might be measured in seconds, minutes, hours, days, weeks, or months.

The technician is unconcerned with anything but what the charts are saying about price movement. His attention is focused on possible changes in direction that could signal a reversal of his profitable position. Good technicians don't trade on instinct, feelings, or any other subjective emotion. They simply ask, "What does the price behavior on the charts tell me that the market wants to do next?"

Of course, interpreting charts and patterns is part science and part art, especially when signals aren't clear. Technical analysis can't predict the future; however, it can suggest what is likely to happen based on a study of historical price movement. Technicians are also subject to being blindsided by events that change historical price patterns—a lawsuit, management changes, new competition, and so on. However, they are trained to react quickly when price patterns suddenly change for the better or worse.

The fundamental analyst is also at risk for the unpredictable. However, an investor who is really tuned to the company may anticipate some events and take precautions. What he doesn't typically see are abrupt price changes that are unrelated to the fundamentals but are driven by investor behavior. For example, when markets began to tumble in 2008, fundamentally strong stocks tumbled right along with the more speculative stocks when shareholders found themselves needing to dump them to meet cash needs.

The Least You Need to Know

- ◆ Technical analysis focuses on price behavior rather than fundamental information about individual companies.

- ◆ Technical analysts use historical price action to anticipate future changes in price.

- ◆ Technical analysis is the art of converting raw price and volume data into actionable information.

- ◆ Technicians analyze charts and historical data to make buy and sell decisions rather than relying on feelings, intuition, or guesses.

What Moves the Market?

In This Chapter

- ◆ The difference between market theory and practical guidance
- ◆ Why price matters
- ◆ The relationship between price history and the future
- ◆ Selling short when prices decline
- ◆ Why charts are important
- ◆ A historical view of technical analysis

It is said that the market moves because of economic news, interest rate changes, worries over inflation, and so on. Well, not exactly. The market moves when investors react to two basic emotions: fear and greed. Investors buy or sell when they believe doing so will earn a profit or prevent a loss. The problem is that many investors have no system for deciding when they can earn a profit or prevent a loss. The consequence of this is a reasonably predictable pattern of price changes that technicians can recognize and profit from.

Price changes are driven by supply and demand, and practitioners of technical analysis view these as the drivers of price trends. Armed with the knowledge that lets them see these trends, technicians can plot a strategy based on science and reality. Price patterns repeat themselves over and over again, and an investor or trader who can recognize these patterns is at a definite advantage.

Market Theory

You may hear many different theories or ideas about market movement that attempt to explain why prices change. Unfortunately, many of these theories and ideas provide very little concrete help in figuring out your next move (buy or sell?). What investors need is a way to predict possible price changes that they can profit from. Theories that explain past price changes are not very helpful unless one can act on them before the price changes.

Are Markets Really Efficient?

One of the most widely held theories of market movement is the efficient market hypothesis, which says that everything that is known about a company or commodity is automatically incorporated into its price. So if a company reports earnings that are different from what the market was expecting, that important information is instantly incorporated into its stock price. If this were true, it would be essentially impossible to beat the market. The efficient market hypothesis is highly regarded by many as the answer to market movement. However, there is ample evidence that contradicts the efficient market theory, and many successful investors have proven that you can "beat the market."

> **Info/Tips**
>
> The goal of technical analysis is to increase the probability that you can identify the beginning of a sustainable price trend and act on it to make money.

Practitioners of technical analysis also argue that the market is efficient, but not in a theoretical manner. Markets are efficient because they bring together a willing buyer and a willing seller at a price both can accept. As the supply and demand for an investment rises or falls, the price paid in the market changes. These changes may be rapid or slow, and they may go up or down.

The idea of fair value is conclusively settled with each completed transaction. Ultimately, an investment (or anything else that is bought and sold) is worth what a willing buyer and willing seller agree on as a price. That price may, and likely will, change often with changes in supply and demand.

Competing Ideas on Market Reality

Whether it is talking heads on television, workshop promoters, or investment newsletters, there is no shortage of opinions about what happens in the financial markets. The noise from the market can be overwhelming.

Are interest rates more important than earnings? What about inflation and other macro-economic factors? Do money policy and interest rates mean more than trade balances or unemployment?

These concerns are legitimate factors in shaping market direction; however, they all have one fatal flaw. While they may (or may not) accurately suggest a market direction, none of them give investors any reliable clues about how prices for individual securities are determined. A theory is of little use to traders if it does not produce a recognizable signal that can be translated into a buy or sell decision.

Heads Up

No one can predict what the market is going to do with any consistent degree of accuracy. However, technical analysis can help you spot price trends and capitalize on them.

What Moves It?

Market participants are commonly referred to as either "bulls" or "bears," depending on their attitude toward price at any particular time. Bulls are optimists. They expect prices to rise and thus are buyers of stocks. Bears, on the other hand, are pessimists. They expect prices to fall and thus are sellers of stocks. It is the relative balance between bulls and bears at any particular time that drives markets either upward or downward.

Here's a good way to avoid being confused between what bulls are and what bears are. As we all know, bulls fight with their horns. When bulls attack, they try to lift their prey with their horns, thus thrusting upward. Bears, on the other hand, fight with their claws. They will rise on their hind legs, raise their claws, and pull down their prey. So, figuratively speaking, bears want to pull markets down, while bulls want to push markets up.

On most days, the financial markets move either up or down. On fewer days, the markets remain virtually unchanged. While you may be able to identify factors that move the markets, you are, in most cases, looking back for a reason to describe what has already happened. Obvious knowledge is shared by all, so there is no one with information that no other trader has (at least, not legally). The two major camps of investing strategy, fundamental analysis and technical analysis, see the markets very differently, however.

Traditional (Fundamental) Views on Markets

The investor practicing fundamental analysis is not immediately concerned with the market price of a security. His first concern is identifying the intrinsic value of the security. The fundamental analyst determines the *intrinsic value* of a stock by deeply examining the company and its operations, markets, financial health, and management. Using financial ratios, the fundamental analyst calculates the intrinsic value of the company and its stock. Most fundamental analysts also apply a margin for error, which is a safety factor that covers any oversights or mistakes.

def•i•ni•tion

Intrinsic value is an analytical judgment of the "real value" of a company based on projected earnings and other perceived characteristics inherent in the investment—such as quality of management, brand name, and uniqueness of product—that are often difficult to calculate. Different fundamental analysts use different techniques to calculate intrinsic value.

For example, the fundamental analyst might look at Acme Widgets and determine that the intrinsic value of the company is $25 per share. However, to be on the safe side, the analyst factors in a margin for error of 20 percent, lowering the intrinsic value to $20 per share. With this target in mind, the investor looks at the market price to see how close or far it is from its theoretical intrinsic value.

If Acme Widgets is selling at $15 per share, the investor may decide that the market has undervalued Acme Widgets and may buy at that price. His strategy is that the market will soon recognize the stock as being underpriced, and that demand will ultimately cause the per-share price to rise.

While this strategy can work, it may take a long time (months or years) for the market to reach the so-called intrinsic value. During this period, many things can also happen to change the intrinsic value. Also, unless the stock pays a strong dividend, the investor has capital tied up in an investment that may be earning little or no return. There is also the possibility that the stock may never reach its intrinsic value, or it can produce a paper profit only to reverse and wipe out all profits.

When the vast majority of investors are overly optimistic, they invest heavily and exhibit greedy tendencies. Conversely, when investors are confronted by deep-seated fears, they become panicky and sell stocks on a broad scale. Excessive optimism (greed) is synonymous with market tops, while too much pessimism (fear) warns of an approaching market bottom. Informed investors should recognize such states of extreme emotion as opportunities for profits. The thing is, we need some timing-oriented tools to detect the presence of extreme investor sentiment in either direction. The foundation for these market timing tools rests in the discipline of technical analysis.

Technicians try to avoid subscribing to consensus viewpoints and majority opinions for stock market profits. Investment returns depend on our ability to make independent decisions while escaping the influence of ill-timed investment advice, public opinions, and generally accepted theories. In effect, we need to be contrarians. We should contest the popular view and make investment decisions on the basis of market realities rather than emotions.

Proper investment action requires timing, which in turn depends on identifying and understanding market cycles. Correctly timed investment decisions must correspond favorably to strategic points in market cycles.

How Technical Analysis Views the Markets

Practitioners of technical analysis are concerned with real prices being set by real buyers and real sellers. Supply and demand drives the price of securities, and it is the technician's task to understand how traders have shaped the price in the past and to what extent they are likely to follow those previous price patterns.

Technicians view the markets as a stream of prices that *trend*, *consolidate*, and *reverse* direction in response to supply and demand. The objective of technical analysis is to identify conditions that would allow a trade with a high probability of a profitable outcome combined with an acceptable risk level.

def•i•ni•tion

A **trend** is the tendency of a securities price to move relatively smoothly in an upward or downward direction.

To **consolidate** is the tendency of a securities price to remain in a horizontal channel for a period of time.

To **reverse** is the tendency of a securities price to change trend direction from an uptrend to a downtrend or from a downtrend to an uptrend.

To win in the business of trading and investing, as in most other businesses, you must have an edge. The edge you want to develop is the ability to recognize when a market trend is beginning so you can enter a position in the direction of the trend in the very early stages of the new trend and exit in the very late stages of the trend.

Just as a farmer needs to know the optimal time to plant and harvest a crop, the technician needs to be able to find the optimal time to buy and sell a position. Buying or selling too early or too late can result in, at worst, unacceptable losses or, at best, not maximizing the return from an existing position. A technician works to identify specific time and price target zones for possible trend change in any time frame.

Why Price Matters

Changes in price are driven by supply and demand. In turn, supply and demand are driven by the human emotions of fear and greed. When there is significant demand for a security, those seeking to get in on the action will buy in at ever-higher prices. For many, the urge to be a part of "the next big thing" drives investors to jump in at whatever price they must offer to possess the security.

At some price point, investors will decide it is time to sell—hopefully at a profit. However, what happens often is that demand for a stock evaporates and sellers must lower the price to find a buyer. As the price begins to drop, investors who got in late on the upswing are now afraid of a big loss, so they seek to sell, lowering the price even more. The result is that the price falls to the point where it is once again attractive to buyers, and the cycle starts over again.

It may appear that price movement is random and unpredictable. However, a closer study of the price history can reveal probabilities about future movements.

All price movements zigzag in all time frames, and those zigzags have characteristic shapes that are different when they are in an uptrend than in a downtrend. The zigzags are the result of the human emotions of fear and greed. They are also the result of unchangeable geometric relationships that occur when prices move up and down with time. The ability to recognize the shapes of those zigzags when one sees them gives the technical analyst a leg up on understanding whether the long-term trend is up or down or sideways.

In addition, past price history gives us an idea about the "personality" of the potential investment. Is it stable or highly volatile? Is it trending or moving sideways? If we are in a trend, is it accelerating or decelerating, giving us a clue regarding its future movements? Where did prices find *support* and *resistance* in the past? Are these levels where it may pause or reverse again?

def•i•ni•tion

> **Support** is a price level below the current price where prices have previously consolidated or reversed. Frequently prices in a downtrend will pause or reverse at earlier support levels.
>
> **Resistance** is a price level above the current price where prices have previously consolidated or reversed. Frequently prices in an uptrend will pause or reverse at earlier resistance levels.

Most investors have been taught that the only way to make money in the markets is to buy and hold for the long term. But we all know that stocks go down as well as up in a zigzag fashion. Statistics show that when prices do fall, stocks tend to drop twice as fast as they rise. When investors only go long, they are effectively throwing out half of their profit opportunities. Technicians point out that if a stock drops 50 percent, it must move up 100 percent just to get back to even. Why hold through a 50 percent drop if technical analysis can warn you of an impending drop and you can exit your long position to lock in your profits?

Selling Short

Many savvy traders not only close out long positions when their technical tools predict a drop, but to make additional profits when the market drops, they will sell short. *Selling short* is an important tool in the technician's arsenal.

What does selling short mean? Essentially, the investor is betting that the stock will go down. In other words, he enters a form of trade that will increase in value when the price goes down. "How can that be?" you may ask. "How can I avoid losing money when the price goes down?" The answer is simple. Traders make money when they buy a security at a given price and sell it at a higher price, right? Most of us think in terms of buying first and then selling later. However, what if we sold a security first, then bought it back later at a lower price? By selling first and then buying later, we can make money when the price goes down. This is what happens when you sell short.

def•i•ni•tion

Selling short, or "shorting" a stock, is the practice of selling securities the seller does not then own but has borrowed from a brokerage firm or bank in the hope of repurchasing them later at a lower price, thus making a profit if the price goes down or incurring a loss if the price goes up.

"How can you sell something you don't have?" you may ask. If you stop and think about it, it happens all the time in business. For example, suppose you go to your friendly auto dealer to buy a car. Unfortunately, he doesn't have in inventory the exact model and color with the accessories you have your heart set on. Nonetheless, the dealer promises to deliver the car of your dreams to you in a few days or weeks, and you and he agree on a price. The dealer then orders the exact car you wanted either from the manufacturer or perhaps from another dealer that has one in stock. When the car arrives, your dealer delivers it to you and collects his money. Assuming the dealer is a good businessman, he will have sold the car to you for more than he paid for it, therefore earning a profit. The important point here is that the seller sold a vehicle he didn't have at the time of the sale and then bought it at some later time at a lower price to earn a profit.

A short seller in the securities markets does essentially the same thing. In this case, he borrows the stock he wants to sell short from the broker and then sells it on the open market. Eventually, the short seller must return the borrowed stock by buying it back on the open market. If the stock has fallen in price, he is able to buy it back for less than he sold it, thus making a profit. On the other hand, if the stock has risen in price since he sold it, he must buy it back for more than he received for it, thus incurring a loss.

Although the process of selling short sounds complicated, it is usually very smooth and easy because brokerage firms are set up to routinely make such transactions. To make a short sale, a trader typically contacts his broker and tells him to sell short "X" shares of ABC stock, and the broker takes care of the details of the transaction in short order.

Let's illustrate the process with an example: XYZ stock is currently trading at $60 per share. Your technical analysis indicates that the stock appears ready to drop in price, so you enter an order with your broker to sell short 100 shares at $60 per share. Your broker will credit your account $6,000 less commissions, and you will then be "short" 100 shares of XYZ. Now, let's assume that some time after executing your short sale the price gradually drops to $40, for example, and your technical analysis studies suggest that the stock is bottoming out and may be ready to reverse back to the upside. Accordingly, you decide to take your profits and "cover" your short position. You do this by buying 100 shares of XYZ at $40 and returning them to the broker you borrowed them from.

So what you have done is earn $20 per share, or $2,000 minus commissions, by selling short 100 shares of XYZ stock at $60 and buying them back at $40. In the meantime, the broker has earned a commission and a small amount of interest on the $6,000 in good faith money you deposited with him to borrow the shares initially.

Learning to sell short in addition to buying long can increase your overall trading profitability considerably. Nonetheless, shorting stocks is not for the faint of heart, nor those who are not watching their investments on a daily basis. There are risks associated with shorting stocks that you don't get with buying shares.

For example: If, after you have sold the shares short, the stock goes up instead of going down as you had anticipated, you could theoretically lose an infinite amount of money. In reality, what is most likely to happen is that you would get your shares called back by your brokerage firm before your losses swallowed you alive, but by then you may already be in deep trouble.

Let's continue our previous example. Say XYZ goes from $60 to $120 and you are still short. If you then bought back your shares to "cover" your position, you would lose double your initial investment! It would cost you $12,000 to cover your position, while you only deposited $6,000 to start the short position in the first place. So you can see how your losses can keep accelerating as the price of the stock goes up instead of down.

On the other hand, your profit potential if the stock does go down is strictly finite. The most you can make from shorting a stock is 100 percent of your investment in the event the stock went to 0, or $6,000 in the case of your XYZ short sale.

When you short a stock, you must have what is called a "margin account," which means you must be preapproved by your broker to have a sort of revolving line of credit to buy more stocks than you have the money to buy. Think of this as money you have access to if you want to go above and beyond the cash in your account. If you take a short position and your stock goes up instead of down and your broker gets nervous, or if you trigger predetermined limits in your margin account, you will get a margin call. A margin call is a notification from your broker that you must either add more money to your account or buy back some of your shares to meet your margin requirement. If you don't do anything within the time limit set by your margin call, your broker will do it for you! So be sure you are sufficiently well capitalized before you sell short.

Charting Your Future

Most technical analysts use price charts to describe changes in price and direction. The charts tell an unedited story. The technician learns to recognize patterns and trends on the charts that help him establish a probability of future changes in price and direction. Technicians strongly believe that charts can help provide the answers we need to make timely and profitable buy and sell decisions. To a technician, the chart is the truth. With that certainty, we can ignore the noise of the market and make decisions based on established and unemotional foundations.

Understanding charts and how to use them is key to technical analysis. Because charts are so important to technical analysis, a brief history may help set the stage for the more in-depth discussion in future chapters.

The History of Charting and Technical Analysis

Where commerce has flourished in civilizations past, so have the traders who have paid close attention to prices and their movements. Some of the earliest known examples of technical analysis date back over 200 years to when Japanese nobility traded paper coupons against future rice harvests.

The rice coupons' prices often changed rapidly despite the fact that there was no change in the weather or any news about the size of the expected harvest. These changes in price were captured on charts, and the charts were studied very carefully. Obviously, something was going on that didn't have anything to do with the relatively unchanging fundamentals. The chartists began to realize that what was going on was constantly changing supply-demand patterns as buyers and sellers entered and exited the market. Consequently, traders began to look for characteristic price chart patterns to anticipate a change in price.

Tulip Mania

One of the early realizations of the effect of crowd emotions on price behavior was when Charles Mackay, in his 1841 book, *Extraordinary Popular Delusions and the Madness of Crowds*, detailed the Dutch tulip mania of 1637 and the 1720 meteoric rise in the stock prices of the Mississippi and South Seas Companies. In 1593, tulips were brought from Turkey and introduced to the Dutch. The novelty of the new flowers made them widely sought after and therefore fairly pricey. By the 1630s, a nonfatal virus known as "mosaic" struck the tulip industry. Fortunately, this virus didn't kill the tulip population but instead caused "flames" of color to appear on the petals. These exquisite color patterns came in a wide variety and increased the rarity of an already unique flower.

The increasing demand for these beautiful flowers, which were already selling at a premium, led to a rise in price based on their colorfulness and beauty. Rising prices attracted other profit-seeking buyers. Soon prices were rising so fast and so high that people were reputedly trading their land, life savings, and anything else they could liquidate to get more tulip bulbs that they expected to be able to resell at higher prices, thereby reaping enormous profits. At one point, the already-overpriced tulips enjoyed a twentyfold increase in value—in one month! Needless to say, the prices became an inaccurate reflection of the value of a tulip bulb.

As it happens in many speculative bubbles, some prudent people decided to sell and take their profits. A domino effect of progressively lower and lower prices took place as everyone tried to sell while not many were buying. The price began to dive, causing people to panic and sell regardless of losses.

The mania finally ended, according to Mackay, with individuals stuck with the bulbs they held at the end of the crash. It is said that at the peak of the market a person could trade a single tulip for an entire estate, and at the bottom one tulip was the price of a common onion. This was an example of market value far exceeding intrinsic value. Another speculative bubble, the South Seas bubble, initially began as a result of the fact that exclusive access to the South American trade and new world colonies had been given to a single company. The frenzy that resulted as both peasants and lords feverishly snapped up shares inevitably resulted in credit defaults, bankruptcies, and economic hardship—the same results that we have seen frequently since as "irrational exuberance" overrides common sense. History is littered with booms and busts—manias that led to unsustainable price levels based purely on our primal emotions of greed and fear, and an understanding of this phenomenon of fear and greed helps technical analysts make the right trading decisions at the right times.

The Dow Theory

Charles Dow was an early pioneer in price charting during the nineteenth century after he observed that by the time important corporate news entered the public domain, the share price had already moved, due not least to insider trading. Looking for clues to trending market action, he began observing the open outcry "curb market" in New York, writing down prices in a notebook. Finding a page of price changes confusing, not surprisingly, he decided to plot price action graphically in the form of a chart. This allowed him to see at a glance the formation of trends and consolidation periods.

Dow also began writing a series of articles known as "Dow Theory" for *The Wall Street Journal* in the latter years of the nineteenth century. This body of work formed the initial basis for what became known as technical analysis in the Western world. The most important concepts that Dow recognized were that prices reflect the current balance of supply and demand (in other words, the hopes and fears of investors) and, most importantly, that an imbalance of supply and demand causes prices to form recognizable trends, up and down.

 Info/Tips

The relationship between supply and demand and the price of securities is one of the most important market truths Charles Dow illuminated.

Recent History—Technical Advances

The concept of studying price action was fairly well established by the early twentieth century. By the 1940s to 1950s, additional pioneers of technical analysis—including William Jiler, Robert Edwards, John Magee, Alexander Wheelan, and Abe Cohen—were making steady progress not only in the types of charts used to depict trends but also in developing techniques for analyzing price action.

The introduction of mainframe computers in the 1960s dramatically changed the landscape for technical analysis. Charts that previously had to be meticulously drawn by hand and primitive analysis techniques that had been calculated with slide rules and adding machines could now be processed by computer. This made it possible to develop much more sophisticated analysis tools and for hypotheses and indicators to be calculated and back tested much faster and in much greater depth.

By the 1970s, the appearance of the personal computer moved the power of computerized analysis from the major players, brokerage houses, and investment firms with access to large mainframe computers to the common citizen. It also prompted the development of relatively inexpensive software for the creation of price charts and analysis tools.

Real-time price information began to be disseminated from the stock and futures exchanges to the public via the airwaves and later via the Internet. Now every person with an interest in technical analysis could create and analyze charts and obtain up-to-the-minute price information without having to place a phone call to his or her broker. Not only that, he could even place orders directly with the exchanges without relying on a broker intermediary to place the orders for him.

These days, more and more private individuals with money to invest are analyzing and trading the markets from their own personal computers, setting up home trading rooms, and either trading part-time before or after their regular day jobs or becoming full-time traders from home, placing trades at all hours of the day or night. (See Chapter 15 for more information on trading tools.) Today, no matter what time of day or night it is, there is a market open for trading, and anyone with a computer and a trading account can access and trade that market from anywhere in the world.

The Least You Need to Know

◆ Supply and demand drive market prices.

◆ Technical analysis is concerned with actual prices rather than theoretical pricing.

◆ Price history suggests patterns that may repeat.

◆ Technicians often sell short in a downtrend as well as buying into an uptrend to improve their profitability.

◆ The technique of charting has a long history in tracking and understanding how changes in supply and demand affect prices.

Chapter 3

Bringing Order to Market Chaos

In This Chapter

- ◆ Learn how charts show the truth
- ◆ Grasping information quickly with charts
- ◆ Finding patterns in charts
- ◆ Using charts to compare securities

A chart is the drawing board, literally, for the technical analysis of a trading symbol. It is the crystal ball that the technician looks into while trying to decipher the future. It is in the chart that we look to find our information for changes in the movement of the investment.

Saying that a stock is up or down 2 points today means nothing to the technician. He needs to see the big picture, the forest instead of just one tree. If you were to say that IBM is selling for $50, this lone number floating around out there means nothing to a technician. When one listens to the radio or television and hears a bunch of numbers "up a point, down a point, up from the close, up for the day," it is just an overwhelming and confusing flood of numbers. What does it all mean?

The Chart Is the Truth

A chart converts historical data into information that the technician can use to make an educated guess as to future price behavior. The technician wants to see prices in visual form on a graph to see their movement from past to present and to interpret patterns that those movements make. The technician relies on charts and the information they represent to express the truth of what is happening to prices. The chart is the truth to the technician. This is just an introduction here; more detail on important charts is covered later in the book. So let's take a look at our drawing board, the chart.

> **Info/Tips**
>
> Mastering charts is important to successfully learn technical analysis. Fortunately, many of the chart types are easily identified with practice.

Technology Is Your Friend

When I first began charting stock prices in the 1960s, I drew my charts by hand on graph paper purchased at the blueprint store. Every night, or maybe once a week, I would open *The Wall Street Journal* and look up the prices of the stocks I was following and plot the most recent prices. Then, like a doctor examining a cardiogram, I would step back and try to absorb the entire chart to give me an idea of its changing personality characteristics and to look for characteristic patterns that would give me a clue as to the health and future likely movement of the price.

In those days this was quite a tedious task, and experimentation involved a lot of work. With today's computers and advanced software, this is easily done with a keyboard stroke. Technology gives you the tools to trade in fast-moving markets with real-time price information. Technology also lets you take a longer-term approach and analyze a potential trade from several perspectives.

Basic Chart Types

The charts used in technical analysis range from the simple to the more complex. Charts are the language of technical analysis. You cannot understand technical analysis if you don't master charts. The charts used in technical analysis are your playbook. They tell you when to buy or to sell. They anticipate changes in price and direction. Readers new to technical analysis may fear becoming overwhelmed by the number and different types of charts.

While there are many different types of charts, most technicians stick with a set that provides the type of information they need to execute their trading plan. You will find that charts become easier to read with practice, and you'll soon be picking out the important information from most charts easily.

Charts can contain as much or as little information as you want. In most cases, you define what you want to look at, and your charting software draws the chart for you. In this chapter and in Chapter 4, we will go over the basic types of charts to give you an idea of what they can tell you. Putting the power of that information to work is covered in detail in later chapters. For now, get a feel for the major types of charts and how you can use them to trade more effectively.

The Line Chart

 The most elementary chart is a simple line chart (see Figure 3.1). A line chart is a snapshot of price readings (usually the closing price) over time connected by a line. Many stock market charts in the daily newspaper are line charts. This type of chart gives an overall idea of the direction and volatility of movement of the price.

Although the closing price is the most common number chosen, the line could easily connect any value of the technician's choosing, such as the opening price; the high; the low; the average of the high and low; the average of the open and close; and so on. The line chart is simple to understand but limited in the amount of information it displays. It doesn't suggest anything about what may come next.

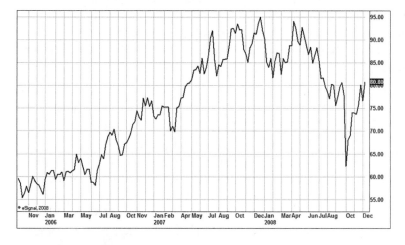

Figure 3.1

Here is a line chart showing the weekly closing price of Exxon Mobil stock from 2006 through 2008.

The Bar Chart

 The problem with a line chart is that it only displays a snapshot of what the price was doing at the end of the trading period (that is, daily, weekly, 10-minute). But during that period many trades were made at a range of different prices. This would be useful information for technicians, so they developed the concept of the bar chart, which is the most common form of market charting today (see Figure 3.2).

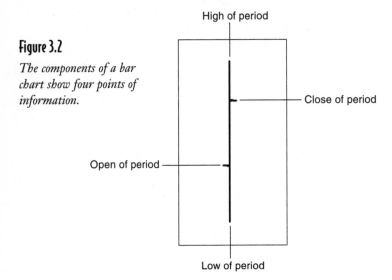

High of period

Figure 3.2

The components of a bar chart show four points of information.

Close of period

Open of period

Low of period

A bar chart consists of a set of vertical bars representing each time increment measured, such as a daily bar, a weekly bar, or a 10-minute bar. The bar extends downward from the highest price reached during that period to the lowest price reached during that period. In addition, the bar has a tick mark to the left at the height of the bar's opening price and a tick mark to the right at the height of the bar's closing price. Thus, it gives the user a more complete set of information about how the price behaved during the term of the bar than a line chart would.

Info/Tips

Charts let you digest vast amounts of information quickly. Human minds grasp pictures more quickly than numbers or even words. This is the secret power of technical analysis.

The bar chart in Figure 3.3 shows the same weekly chart of Exxon Mobil from 2006 to 2008 that we used in the previous line chart but plotted as a bar chart instead of a line chart. Note the added detail provided by the bar chart. It shows not only where the price closed at the end of the week but also how the price moved up and down within the week. This information gives you a clearer picture of what traders were doing with a security.

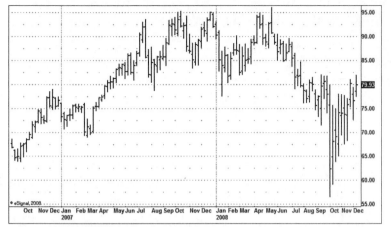

Figure 3.3

Weekly chart of Exxon Mobil from 2006 to 2008 plotted as a bar chart.

The Candlestick Chart

 A Japanese price charting technique known as candlestick charting dates back to the 1700s, long before bar charting had even been invented in the Western Hemisphere. Japanese traders, on the other hand, were already using the candlestick charting technique to trade their rice markets. This technique of charting was confined strictly to Japan until Americans learned the technique from Japanese traders who traded the U.S. financial markets in the 1980s.

Now, traders worldwide have enthusiastically embraced this form of charting because it provides a visually clearer image of price action during the duration of each bar.

A candlestick bar (see Figure 3.4) consists of a thin "wick" or "shadow" bar connecting the high and low reached during the period, just like a bar chart. However, instead of ticks to the right and left of the bar denoting the open and the close, a candlestick bar has a thicker "real body" whose height represents the distance between the open and the close of the bar.

If the close is greater than the open, the body of this up-bar is typically an open rectangle. This represents an up day or a strong day, a day where the bulls are victorious over the bears. On the other hand, if the close is less than the open, the body of this down-bar is typically a solid rectangle. This represents a down day or a weak day in which the bears are victorious. The length of the real body measures the strength or weakness of the move.

On colored charts, the body of the up-bar is usually colored green, and the body of the down-bar is usually colored red. Thus, the technician can get a lot of information about the price behavior from a single glance at a candlestick chart.

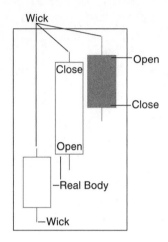

Figure 3.4

This is an example of candle-stick bar components.

The Power of Candlestick Charts

The psychology of the market participant, the supply and demand equation, and the relative strength of the buyers and sellers are all reflected in one candlestick or in a combination of candlesticks.

To interpret the psychology behind the single candle, there are four elements to look at: the size of the body, the relative length of the shadows, the location of the bar with respect to its neighbors, and its color. For example, a large-body candle with small shadows suggests tremendous strength and power behind the move. A large candle is also indicative of more volatile market conditions.

> **TA Intelligence**
>
> Candlestick charts reveal a multitude of patterns, each depicting specific points of information about price and movement.

The color of the candle is also important in determining whether the bulls or bears are in control. A green candle designating an up day indicates that the bulls are in control, while a red candle designating a down day indicates that the bears are in control.

Since the development and acceptance of the candlestick chart analysts have discovered dozens of multibar candlestick patterns with exotic names like "doji," "shooting star," "hammer," "hanging man," "dark cloud cover," and "three white soldiers" that have been found to be powerful predictors of future action.

Figure 3.5 illustrates some of the more significant candlestick bar patterns, as follows.

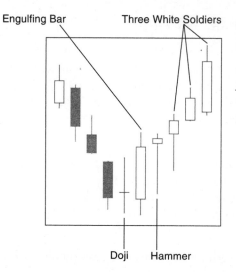

Engulfing Bar   Three White Soldiers

Doji   Hammer

Figure 3.5

This example of patterns found in candlestick bars identifies key information points.

The Doji

One of the most important and most easily recognizable candlestick shapes is the doji (see Figure 3.6). It is created when the opening and closing prices are nearly the same. Thus, it looks like a cross since it doesn't have much of a real body. The upper and lower shadows can be long or short.

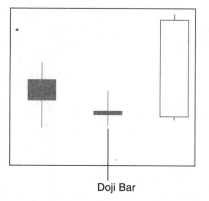

Doji Bar

Figure 3.6

Dojis are one of the most recognizable of all candlestick shapes.

A doji is classified as a neutral candle if it is found within a sideways market. It takes on significance when it is spotted at a high-price area (for example, after an uptrend) or at a low-price area (after a downtrend). In such a situation, the doji is likely to warn of a market reversal. It represents uncertainty about the upcoming market direction.

Hanging Man and Hammer Patterns

Two other popular candlestick patterns are the hanging man and the hammer. They comprise a narrow body accompanied by either a long upper shadow or a long lower shadow. The longer the shadow, the more significant the pattern. These two patterns represent potential price reversal points at price peaks and valleys. The hanging man pattern typically portends the end of an uptrend, while the hammer pattern typically portends the end of a downtrend.

What the hammer pattern is telling us, for example, is that prices opened near the high of the bar, at which point sellers came in and pushed the price down strongly. At a lower level, the buyers came in and caused the price to rise again sharply, and the bar ended at or near the high of the day. Trend reversals often begin with a hanging man or hammer pattern.

Figure 3.7 is a weekly candlestick chart of Exxon Mobil. Note the hollow candles when prices are going up and the solid candles when prices are going down.

Figure 3.7

Candlestick chart of Exxon Mobil.

It is often helpful to think of price movements as the results of battles between buyers and sellers. Candlestick patterns are nothing more than shorthand ways of describing how these battles turned out. As you use them more and more, you will notice yourself "processing" the pattern groups mentally in much the same way that a fast reader processes groups of words and phrases on a page instead of looking at individual words. In a subsequent chapter, we will explore in more detail some of the most significant candlestick patterns and their usage.

Heads Up

It takes some time and practice to master the different chart forms. Don't make hasty buy or sell decisions based on inexperience working with charts.

Popular Tools

There are five reasons why candlestick charts are so popular among technicians today.

1. **Leading indicator**—They have the ability to show reversal signals earlier than western charting techniques. As such, candlestick charts are a true leading indicator of market action. They regularly identify potential moves before they become apparent with western technical tools.

2. **Pictorial**—They are very pictorial and describe the state of traders' psychologies the moment they unfold, all of which can be utilized to make meaningful trading decisions. Terminology like the "hangman," "shooting star," "dark cloud cover," "hammer," and "abandoned baby" paint indelible word pictures that can assist the trader to remember the pattern through remembering its name. The candlestick pattern technique consists of hundreds of different pattern groups that accurately identify specific traits and tendencies of trader behavior.

3. **Versatile**—The candlestick technique better promotes the ability to recognize complex pattern groups and predict the next possible outcome based on them.

4. **Can be applied to any time dimension**—Candlestick charts can be applied to follow as many markets as desired—whether stocks, futures, currency, or commodity contracts—and on any time frame.

5. **Time tested, dependable, and useful**—The fact that candlestick analysis is still very much in use today after more than 300 years since its discovery is testimony to its usefulness.

Swing Charts

When we create a price chart, we often want to emphasize certain aspects and de-emphasize others. For example, bar charts and candlestick charts provide detailed information about price behavior on each and every successive bar. By observing bar and candlestick charts, we can really focus in on the details of the market action.

Swing charts, on the other hand, de-emphasize the bar-by-bar action by focusing our attention on the big picture … the significant thrusts and pullbacks in price behavior. Swing charts achieve this by drawing straight lines connecting successive swing lows with swing highs in a zigzag fashion (see Chapter 5 for more on swings). Figure 3.8 is an example of a swing chart. When we look at a swing chart, we can immediately see the thrusts and pullbacks of price action. This information helps the trader find potential future price and time targets. We can see the direction of the major trend and can spot the characteristic patterns that occur at major trend tops and bottoms.

Figure 3.8

Swing charts connect swing lows and highs with straight lines in a zigzag pattern.

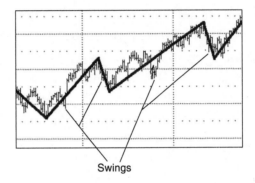

Swings

Swing charts are created by drawing a straight line connecting the most recent swing low to the highest high reached thus far in the current swing. Each time a new high is achieved, the line is extended to connect to the new high. This process continues until prices stop making new highs, reverse, and begin making new lows.

Defining Conditions

When we set up a swing chart, we have to define how many dollars or what percentage the price must reverse in direction before we can define the reversal as a newly confirmed swing in the opposite direction. This number of dollars or percentage is known as the switch parameter because it is a parameter that controls when we confirm that the price swings have switched direction. Depending on the stock price, we may choose to use a 1 percent reversal or a 3-point reversal, for example. Whatever the value of the switch parameter chosen by the technical analyst, the price must reverse direction by that amount to start a new swing in the opposite direction.

One of the things we do with a swing chart is to determine the longer-term trend that contains short-term swings. How do we define the direction of the longer-term trend, consisting of a series of upswings and downswings, using a swing chart? Well, if we want to know if we are in a long-term uptrend, we look at the recent pullback valleys of the shorter-term swings. So long as each successive pullback valley is higher than the previous one, we are still in a major uptrend (see Figure 3.9). Conversely, so long as each successive pullback peak is lower than the previous pullback peak, we are in a major downtrend (see Figure 3.10).

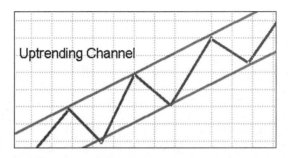

Figure 3.9

A sample swing chart in uptrend.

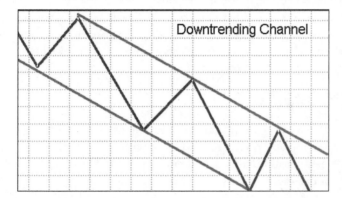

Figure 3.10

A sample swing chart in downtrend.

Transition Patterns

What is fascinating to see when looking at the zigzag patterns on a swing chart is how those patterns change as prices transition from an uptrend to a downtrend (see Figure 3.11). Think about it. In an uptrend, thrust swings up are longer than the pullback swings down. In a downtrend, thrust swings down are longer than the pullback swings up. This means that at a top where prices are rounding over we should see a thrust swing up followed by a thrust swing down. The upthrust and downthrust legs are likely to be approximately of similar length since the next pullback leg up in the downtrend must be shorter than the previous thrust leg down. So just by looking at the relative length of the thrust and pullback swings, we can see when the trend is transitioning from up to down or from down to up.

Figure 3.11

An example of uptrend transitioning to downtrend.

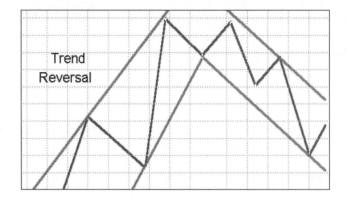

Trend
Reversal

A long-term downtrend reverses into an uptrend when the price is higher than the previous pullback peak for the first time. Conversely, an uptrend reverses into a downtrend when the price is lower than the previous pullback valley for the first time. This can only happen if the new uptrend thrust is at least as long as the previous downtrend thrust. This geometric phenomenon leads to repeatable, identifiable swing patterns such as double and triple tops and head-and-shoulders patterns (more about them in Chapter 11).

Point-and-Figure Charts

Now that we have seen the value of swing charts in filtering out the background noise and identifying trend direction and reversals, what if we removed time from the picture entirely, along with the daily or minute-by-minute price bars, and just focused our attention on the magnitude of the successive upswings and downswings?

Imagine, if you will, taking a swing chart, removing the price bars from it, and squeezing the horizontal axis until all you could see were the swing lines moving up and down in an almost vertical manner. What you would be looking at is the genesis of what is called a "point-and-figure" chart.

Point-and-figure charts were invented by traders on the floor of the exchanges as a shorthand way to keep track of significant price swings. After all, most of price activity on the exchange floor is noise created by prices moving back and forth in small increments in a sideways direction without establishing an easily identifiable direction up or down. Floor traders wanted a way of charting only significant, directional price moves and ignoring the noise and minor moves. If nothing of interest is happening, nothing is plotted. This is in contrast to a standard bar chart in which a bar is plotted for every fixed time period, whether it is a month, a week, a day, or an hour, regardless of whether or not a significant move occurred during that time period.

Out of this need evolved the point-and-figure charts. They look quite different from ordinary bar charts. Point-and-figure charts have no time axis. Time is completely ignored. The emphasis of point-and-figure charts is on moves up and down in price in excess of a specified minimum amount. The only scale on these charts is a price scale along the right side of the chart (see Figure 3.12).

Instead of a set of bars, a point-and-figure chart consists of consecutive columns of X's and O's. X columns designate rising prices and are comparable to upswings on a swing chart, while O columns reflect falling prices and are comparable to downswings on a swing chart.

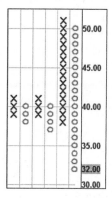

Figure 3.12

This point-and-figure chart shows the recognizable alternate X and O columns.

Each X or O represents a movement in price of a user-selected amount. The user can decide what price increment is significant to him or her. For example, on a $50 stock, a point-and-figure chartist may decide that each X or O should represent a $1 movement. This is called the *box size*. Too small a box size will give you a chart that is too cluttered. Too large a box size and you lose detail.

Let's say a stock has been rising and is currently trading at $50. During the day, prices move up and down: 50.10, 50.20, 50.30, 50.10, 50.00, 49.90, 50.00, 50.10, 49.90, etc. A point-and-figure chartist will ignore all of these minor price changes until the price rises by at least one point to 51.00. At that point he places an X on his chart in the rightmost column at the 51 level. He won't mark another X on his chart until and unless prices rise to 52. As long as prices are rising, he will continue to build a column of X's, with each X representing a $1 increase in the price.

def•i•ni•tion

Box size is the minimum price movement in a point-and-figure chart. It is the distance the price has to move to create a new X or O. The technician decides what minimum price change to use for the chart.

Now let's assume that the price reaches 52 and stops rising. In fact, the price begins to drop. The chartist stops drawing X's and waits. He waits until the price drops by at least three $1 increments: in this case, from 52 down to 49. If the price reaches 49, he starts a new column to the right, this time of O's signifying that the price is moving down. The O's are plotted beginning one box below the highest box of the previous column. The highest box of the previous column was at 52, so he will begin his new column of O's at 51 and then at 50 and 49. If the price drops to 48, another O will be plotted at the 48 level.

def•i•ni•tion

Reversal size is the number of boxes the price has to move in the opposite direction from the direction of the current column before a new column of X's or O's can begin. This gives the technician a signal that a change in trend direction is occurring.

The requirement that prices must move a *reversal size* of three boxes before starting a new column in the opposite direction is a flexible one. Some chartists may prefer a one-box reversal, while others may wait for a five-box reversal. The reversal size value is comparable to the switch parameter value used in swing charts. Most P&F chartists find a three-box reversal size to be the most useful.

As prices continue to drop, the column of O's continues downward until prices stop dropping and reverse upward by the number of boxes controlled by the reversal size selection. For example, a three-box reversal from 45 back up to 48. At that point, a new column of X's is begun, starting one box above the previous lowest O (46 in this example). This process continues with a new column beginning every time the price direction reverses by at least three boxes.

So when a new trading period has completed, we first look to see if the period high was at least one box greater than the value of the current box. In other words, if the highest $1 box in the column is at 54 and the highest price today was 54.60, we would not plot anything new. However, if the price today was 55.20, we could plot a new X in the 55 box. Before we can plot a new X in the 56 box, the price must go to 56 or above. Now, if the highest $1 box in the X column is at 54, the highest price of the day is 53.90, and the lowest price is 52.80, we would plot no new X's or O's. The price must increase to at least $55 to plot the next X. On the other hand, the price must decrease by at least $3 to 51 before we can plot a new O column. In that case, we would start the new downtrend column by plotting three O's: an O at 53 (1 below the highest X), an O at 52, and an O at 51.

To reiterate, if the trend does not continue, check for a discontinuation or price reversal. In a column of X's, you should look at today's high to see if an X can be added. If not, look at the low to see whether a reversal should be recorded. A movement of three boxes constitutes a price reversal in the opposite direction. In a column of O's, look to see if a new O can be added. If not, look at today's high to see whether a three-box up reversal should be recorded.

The point-and-figure reversal process leads to a chart that looks something like Figure 3.13.

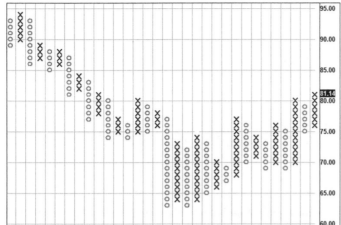

Figure 3.13

In this example of a point-and-figure chart, each X or O represents a $1 move, and a new column forms when prices reverse by $3.

Each column of X's represents an up move. Each column of O's represents a down move. You don't mix X's and O's in the same column. Thus, each significant directional move in price has its own column, regardless of time.

How do you determine what box size to use? This is an individual decision depending on your time horizon. If you are a day trader, you will select a much smaller box size than if you are a long-term trader only interested in major moves.

The beauty of point-and-figure charts is their simplicity. By eliminating extraneous noise, point-and-figure charts make it easy to spot trends and other characteristic price patterns. More detailed interpretation of point-and-figure charts will be covered in a subsequent chapter.

The Least You Need to Know

- ◆ Basic charts are the foundation of understanding technical analysis.
- ◆ Charts can show trends in price and volume.
- ◆ Charts are the playbook for technical analysis—they are the truth.
- ◆ Technicians use a variety of chart types to help them spot major changes in price direction.

Chapter 4

Charts Point the Way

In This Chapter

- ◆ More detailed charts
- ◆ Varying the results
- ◆ Price and volume matter
- ◆ Comparing one stock to another

Thanks to technology and a competitive market for providers of price data on securities, technicians have access to powerful tools for analyzing possible trades. Of course, the tools aren't helpful if you don't know which one to use or how to interpret the information. As you become comfortable with creating and reading charts, you will gain confidence in your trading decisions.

More sophisticated charts let you change variable information to produce charts that zero in on the information that is most important to you. Technicians have the ability to change parameters on many charts to produce a different picture of what is happening to the security. Price, volume (of trades), and time are the primary markers that technicians change to produce charts that match their trading needs.

Change Your View

More complex charts are not necessarily harder to understand, but they do deliver more information. Plus, many charts let you change variables so that the charts tell you a different story based on what you want to see.

With all of this power comes the need to understand how and when to use these charts. The task in this chapter is to introduce you to some of the more complex charts and show you how technicians can change variables to produce more comprehensive information.

Tick and Volume Charts

The advent of powerful personal computers has made it possible for technical analysts to develop new charting methods that would have been too cumbersome to plot by hand. Two examples of this are the closely related forms of charting known as "equal-tick bar charts" ("tick charts" for short) and "equal-volume bar charts." Like point-and-figure charts discussed in Chapter 3, neither of these charting forms is plotted on a time axis. Time is immaterial. All that matters when creating a tick chart is the passage of a given number of trading transactions, no matter how long it takes to achieve them. Each bar on a tick bar chart displays the highest and lowest price reached during the course of a specified number of trades, along with the opening and closing price of that bar. During a slow day it may take a considerable amount of time to accumulate enough trades to create one bar. On the other hand, during a busy day it will take much less time to accumulate enough trades to create one bar, and accordingly there will be more bars on the chart for a day's worth of trading.

For example, a 100-tick chart would create 1 bar (open, high, low, close) for every 100 trades, regardless of the size of each individual trade. If 100 trades came in an hour, we would get 1 bar in an hour. If 1,000 trades came in an hour, we would get 10 bars over an hour's time. Time is not the criterion. The amount of buying and selling is the focus.

Let's consider an example that illustrates how tick charts can enhance the quality of information being transmitted to the analyst.

Tick chart watchers feel that traders moving the price up and down with one or two trades may keep the flow of prices moving, but when "the crowd" comes in and begins moving the market with a large number of trades, that increasing amount of activity is what is important and more emphasis should be given to those trades.

Typically, traders on the trading floor of exchanges can actually sense a buildup in excitement and noise when "the crowd" enters the market in a big way, and this sense of the order flow gives them an advantage over the average trader off the floor. The user of a tick chart is attempting to calibrate his chart to reflect this buildup of trading activity in order to get a better "feel" for the order flow through the use of his computer. An active tick chart tells the trader that trader interest is high, which may lead to an attractive buy or sell situation.

Equal-volume bar charts are very similar in appearance to equal-tick charts, except that each bar on an equal-volume chart represents the price range of a fixed number of shares traded instead of a fixed number of actual trading transactions. When a major player in the market comes in and makes a multimillion-share purchase, the amount and direction that the price moves as a result of this transaction, as compared to how the price moves when individuals are bidding the price up one *lot* at a time, is useful information to the technical analyst when judging the strength of a price move.

> **TA Intelligence**
>
> Thanks to high-speed Internet connections and sophisticated software, individual traders have narrowed the information and performance gap between themselves and traders on the floors of the exchanges.

def•i•ni•tion

> A **lot** is a unit of 100 shares. So if a trader wants to move 2 lots, he is trying to sell 200 shares of stock.

For example, a 10,000-share volume bar chart would create one bar (open, high, low, close) for every 10,000 shares traded, no matter how much time it took for a total of 10,000 shares to cross the tape. If a total of 10,000 shares traded in an hour, we would get 1 bar in an hour. If a total of 100,000 shares traded in an hour, we would get 10 10,000-share bars over an hour's time. Time is not the criterion on a volume bar chart. The amount of buying and selling share volume is the focus.

Many technicians find equal-tick bar charts and equal-volume bar charts to be superior to simple charts that track price over a specific period because they incorporate transaction volume into the price analysis process and often produce smoother, less choppy charts than price-time charts. Activity during slow trading periods will generate fewer bars than activity during active trading periods, thus placing more emphasis on those periods when serious trading is taking place.

Percent Change Charts

Technical analysis generally consists of two parts: selection and timing. Selection is the process of deciding which stock, mutual fund, option, or futures contract, among the thousands available, to trade at any particular point in time. Timing, on the other hand, is the process of determining when to enter and exit a trade once you have selected a suitable stock or futures contract to trade.

There are numerous methods, both fundamental and technical, that can help in the selection process. One of the selection questions many traders ask is, "How has this stock performed relative to alternative choices recently, and which is likely to be the strongest in the upcoming time frame?" In order to answer this question, we must be able to provide a level playing field for comparing stocks whose various prices could range from a dollar to hundreds of dollars.

For example, let's say you are comparing a $10-per-share stock with a $100-per-share stock. Since the beginning of the quarter, both of these stocks have gone up exactly $10. If you plot these stocks on the same standard price chart with a linear price scale, the charts of the two stocks will show an identical increase for the quarter. In fact, the $10 stock has doubled in price, while the $100 stock has only increased by 10 percent.

What we really need is a "normalized" way to display the behavior of multiple securities on the same chart so that we can compare their percentage change behavior over a specific period. Most computerized charting programs today offer two alternative ways of displaying price scales: linear or logarithmic (also referred to as "semi-log").

> **Info/Tips** _____
>
> When you see a chart that you did not create, be careful that you understand exactly how the chart was built (linear or logarithmic). It makes a big difference.

The most common way of displaying price is to use a linear scale, in which price increments are displayed at equal intervals. That is, equal dollar price moves represent an equal amount of distance on the price scale. Thus, on a linear-scaled chart, a $10 move on a $10 stock (doubling) represents the same vertical distance as a $10 move on a $100 stock (a 10 percent move). On the other hand, when using a logarithmic-scaled chart, a $10 move on a $10 stock will be 10 times as large as a $10 move on a $100 stock.

Many computerized charting platforms now offer the option of creating charts that allow the user to compare percentage change moves of various symbols on the same chart. Such charts are called percent change charts. These charts give the user the ability to plot the change in price of many different symbols on the same chart, as a percentage of their price beginning at a specified starting date.

Using Anchors

All percent change charts require that you specify an anchor bar. This is the bar from which all percent change calculations are made. The anchor bar can be the first bar of the chart, the last bar of the chart, or any bar that you may select between the first and last bars. Once an anchor bar has been selected, a percent change value is calculated by the charting program for each bar on the chart by subtracting the average price of each bar from the closing price of the anchor bar and dividing this value by the closing price of the anchor bar.

For example, if the price of a stock at the anchor bar was 100 and the price 10 days ago was 90, then the relative price on the percent change chart for the bar 10 days before the anchor bar will be displayed as –10 percent. If the price 30 days after the anchor bar is 125, then the percent change chart will display +25 percent on that bar.

What to Look For

When you look at a collection of stocks on a percent change chart, most tend to move up and down more or less together, responding to overall market fluctuations. However, stocks with increasing strength will begin coming out of the pack, and you will see these stronger stocks crossing above the less-strong stocks. Conversely, weakening stocks will begin crossing below the lines of stronger stocks. This is one of the main characteristics we look for on a percent change chart. As buyers, we are looking for stocks coming up out of the pack. As sellers, we are looking for weakening stocks dropping down through the pack.

It's sort of like a horse race, with horses moving up and falling back within the pack as the race progresses. The difference between selecting a winning horse in a horse race and selecting a winning stock, however, is that you can't change your bet in the middle of a horse race. In the stock market there is no finish line, and you can switch from a struggling stock to a stronger stock as often as you want and at any time in the "race."

Working with Percent Change Charts

So how do we use percent change charts to identify fast-moving stocks? As an example, suppose we have chosen four different companies to follow:

- ◆ Amalgamated Aquanautics Corp.
- ◆ Better Biscuits, Inc.
- ◆ Cheerful Car Rental Corp.
- ◆ Destiny Drugs & Chemicals, Inc.

The first line chart (see Figure 4.1) shows each of these four companies plotted in the same window with the same linear price scale.

Figure 4.1

This standard line chart shows the four stocks with the same linear price scale.

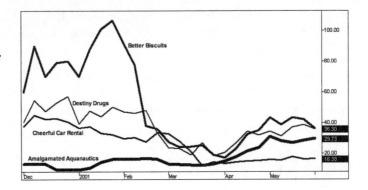

The percent change chart shown in Figure 4.2 shows these same four companies from December 2000 to June 2001. This chart has been created using January 1, 2001, as the anchor bar. We see from this chart that by June, stock A, Amalgamated Aquanautics, was up over 200 percent over the period. Stock B, Better Biscuits, was essentially flat for the year; stock C, Cheerful Car Rental, was down 36 percent; and stock D, Destiny Drugs, was down 56 percent.

Figure 4.2

Percent change chart with anchor bar on January 1.

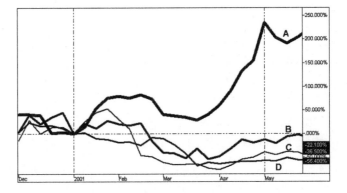

A conclusion we can reach from examining Figure 4.2 is that we would have achieved the greatest return between January and June 2001 had we bought Amalgamated Aquanautics on January 1. But the question we really want to answer is, "How would we have known to choose Amalgamated back in January?"

Info/Tips

The ability to compare several securities on one chart is a powerful tool in the selection process. The charts depict how each security reacted to the same market conditions, giving the technician a strong basis for comparison.

The answer is, "Choose the strongest stock on a percent change chart and go with it until it is surpassed by one of the others." The power of the percent change chart is its ability to display the relative change in prices of a number of stocks through a given time period.

For example, during the time shown in Figure 4.2, the stocks changed places a number of times in their relative rate of change. Although Amalgamated Aquanautics ended up having the greatest percentage increase in value since January, it had its biggest upward move between March and May. Examining the chart more closely, we see that Cheerful Car Rental initially was quite strong as well, but by mid-February it was dropping down through the pack.

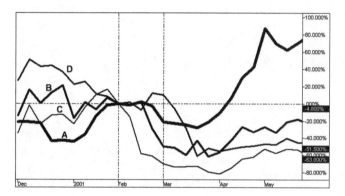

Figure 4.3

Percent change chart with a different anchor bar on February 1.

Let's follow the progress of our four stocks month by month during the six-month sample period, moving our anchor bar forward one month at a time so that we can see what the chart looked like to an observer at the end of each month.

The anchor bar is at February 1 in Figure 4.3. We see that between January 1 and February 1, Amalgamated Aquanautics has begun to move up sharply, Cheerful Car Rental has also moved up, Better Biscuits has remained relatively steady, and Destiny Drugs is weakening. Amalgamated Aquanautics is clearly the strongest stock at this point and should be our prime buying candidate.

In Figure 4.4, the anchor bar has been moved to March 1. During the month of February, Cheerful Car Rental has continued its downward trend, along with Better Biscuits. Destiny Drugs rose marginally, and Amalgamated Aquanautics experienced a pullback from its strong showing in January. At this point, no new leader has emerged from the pack that would encourage us to change our pick from Amalgamated.

Figure 4.4

Percent change chart with the anchor bar on March 1.

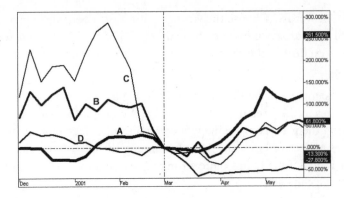

Figure 4.5

Percent change chart with the anchor bar on April 1.

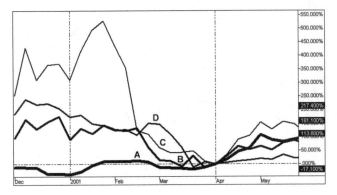

In Figure 4.5, the anchor bar has moved to April 1. During the month of March, Amalgamated is once more moving up from below, Destiny and Cheerful continue to weaken, and Better Biscuits is holding its own. Conclusion: stick with Amalgamated.

Figure 4.6

Percent change chart with the anchor bar on May 1.

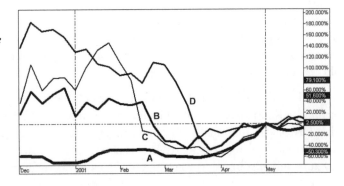

In Figure 4.6, the anchor bar has moved to May 1. During the month of April, all four of our stocks rose. Amalgamated continued to be the strongest. Cheerful made a dramatic reversal to the upside, more than Amalgamated. Better Biscuits improved significantly, and

Destiny moved up marginally. At this point we are beginning to see a change in leadership. With Cheerful coming up through the pack past Amalgamated, we should consider adding Cheerful to our portfolio.

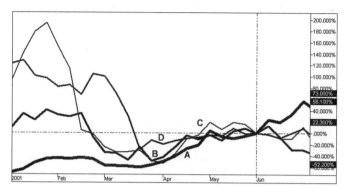

Figure 4.7

Percent change chart with the anchor bar on June 1.

Looking back at February 1 in Figure 4.3, Amalgamated Aquanautics turned out to have been an excellent pick in February, having grown by almost 200 percent between February and June.

Conclusion: percent change charts are a useful tool in providing a "level playing field" for comparing the performance of a group of stocks or commodities in order to select the most likely prospect for future growth.

Spread Charts

Spread charts are another way to observe the differences in behavior between two related stocks or indexes. Spread charts can display either the difference between the prices of two stocks or the ratio of the prices of the two stocks.

In either case, what traders are looking to see when they examine a spread chart is whether the spread is widening because the price of one item is moving away from the price of the other or whether the spread is narrowing because the prices are approaching one another. When the spread becomes wider than it normally has been in the past, savvy traders may buy the weaker item and sell the stronger item in anticipation that the spread will return to its normal relationship. This is what is called a "mean reversion" strategy because traders expect the spread to revert to the mean, or more normal, relationship.

Figure 4.8 is an example of a spread chart. In this example, we have plotted the prices of two closely related energy products: crude oil and natural gas. Since oil and natural gas often can be used interchangeably as a source of heat energy (as in electric power plants, for example), their prices usually move up and down more or less together. Sometimes, however, the spread between these two related products widens or narrows in response to relative supply-demand imbalances. In these cases, large energy consumers may switch from oil to gas or gas to oil, whichever is relatively cheaper at the time. To keep track of the difference in the prices of these two related commodities, technicians and traders create a spread chart.

Figure 4.8

A spread chart of crude oil and natural gas prices.

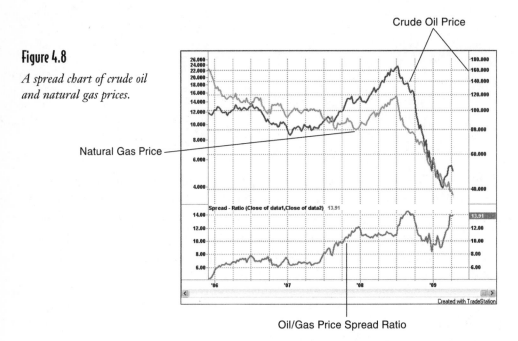

The upper portion of the chart in Figure 4.8 displays the price histories of both crude oil and natural gas over a three-year period beginning in 2006. The crude oil price scale is on the right side of the chart, and the natural gas price scale is on the left side of the chart. So that equal percentage changes in each of the two prices show up as equal distances on the chart, the price scales are displayed as logarithmic scales, as described earlier in this chapter.

When we examine the chart, we see that in early 2006 the price of crude oil (right scale) hovered in the neighborhood of $110 per barrel. During that same period, natural gas was selling in the neighborhood of $13 per thousand cubic feet (left scale). So the ratio of the price of oil to the price of gas (110/13) in 2006 was approximately 7 to 1. This ratio of the spread between the two prices is plotted on the spread ratio graph in the lower third of the chart example. As you can see, the spread ratio stayed relatively flat until around the middle of 2007, when it began to rise as the price of crude increased while the price of natural gas stayed relatively flat.

By the end of the second quarter of 2008, the price of crude oil had risen to $160, and the price of natural gas had risen to $15, for a spread ratio of about 11 (160/15). This widening of the spread from a value of 7 in 2006 to a value of 11 in 2008 meant that the price of crude oil had risen faster than the price of natural gas. Traders would expect that the natural tendency would be for these prices to eventually come back together.

In the third quarter of 2008, the spread ratio rose to as high as 14 as natural gas prices dropped more quickly than crude oil prices dropped. Smart traders, observing this widening spread, suspected that the spread between the prices was an aberration and that it would eventually narrow to more "normal" levels. So what did they do? They sold short crude while at the same time buying natural gas. This way, they would profit if the spread ratio between the two prices did indeed narrow.

By the beginning of 2009, the spread ratio had narrowed back to a value of 10, giving those traders who had sold crude and bought natural gas at a spread of 14 a very handsome profit.

As this book was written in the second quarter of 2009, another interesting spread relationship developed on the far right edge of the chart. While natural gas continued its precipitous descent to below $4, the price of crude rose to over $50, bringing the spread ratio back up to a very high value of almost 14. This gave spread traders a new opportunity to sell short crude and buy natural gas in anticipation of a future narrowing of the spread ratio to a more "normal" ratio of around 10 to 11. By the time you read this book, you should have the answer.

Pitfalls and Limitations of Charts

Chart reading is an art, not a science, and many a pitfall awaits the trader who forgets this. Let's review some of the limitations.

Bombshells

Dynamic unexpected events can reverse chart trends without warning. Such events as war scares, assassinations, terrorist attacks, or surprise action by the government can quickly affect overall market sentiment. Individual stock prices can experience sudden jolts as the result of merger news, new products, executive turnover, or scandals. A chart, in short, is not a Ouija board.

Indecision

Stocks often spend over half their time making up their minds what they are going to do next. Frequently the answer to "What does the chart say?" is "Nothing." However, while many stocks are giving no signal whatsoever much of the time, some stocks are always on the move, either up or down or getting ready to move. The technician with access to many charts will always be able to find plenty of promising trends or formations.

No Two Are Alike

Part of the attraction of the markets is that every situation is at least a little different from all the others. Since no two patterns form in exactly the same manner, their interpretation depends on the experience, judgment, and imagination of the technician. One famous chartist once compared chart reading to piano playing. Anyone can learn to follow the notes on the score, more or less, but what comes out is something else again.

Each stock has its own personality and often tends to repeat certain patterns. One stock may regularly form double tops or bottoms; another may prefer rounding bottoms, while others may turn on a dime. This individual personality of stocks may be listed as a pitfall, but for experienced technicians it can also be an opportunity to the extent that they may be able to call a turn with increased confidence if they are familiar with the long-term behavior of the stock.

As mentioned previously, the most clearly defined patterns of individual stocks can disintegrate without warning if the entire market experiences a wave of selling. Hence, a good technician is aware of the technical and economic condition of the overall market as well as that of individual stocks.

How Charts Can Help You

Charts can't guarantee a winner every time, but here are some of the things they can do:

- ◆ They can help determine when to buy and when to sell by indicating probable levels of support and resistance and by signaling trend reversals.

- ◆ They can call attention, by unusual volume or price behavior, to something happening in a stock that can be most rewarding.

- ◆ They can help to identify the current trend, whether up, down, or sideways, and whether the trend is slowing down or speeding up.

♦ They provide a life history of the stock at a glance and reveal whether it is rallying or reacting and whether the price is historically high or low.

♦ They offer a way to confirm or reject a decision to buy or sell based on fundamental data, stock tips, or hunches.

The Least You Need to Know

♦ More sophisticated computer-generated charts give the technician more options.

♦ Technological advances put powerful tools to work in technical analysis.

♦ Charts showing the relationship between price and volume changes provide important information.

♦ Percent change charts and spread charts provide a means of comparing relative percentage movement between securities over time.

5

Surfing the Waves and Swings

In This Chapter

- ◆ Market psychology leads to market waves
- ◆ The rhythm of the market swings
- ◆ How chart patterns evolve
- ◆ How geometry affects the shape of market swings and reversals

Technical analysts recognize that no market rises or falls like a straight rocket shot. Prices don't go straight to the moon; they follow a jagged path up and eventually come back down again. At times, markets and individual securities seem to be in random motion for no obvious reason, but you will find it difficult to make good buy and sell decisions if you can't make sense of price movement.

Technical analysis gives you tools to help you understand and anticipate probable future price movement. The up and down movement of prices creates opportunities for the trader who has an edge anticipating the direction of the next move.

It's important to realize that both psychological and geometric factors affect the markets' patterns. If you have a grasp of these factors, it will help you to more easily understand what technical analysis is all about and why it works.

How Does Supply and Demand Affect Price Swings?

 Market prices react to supply and demand. Supply and demand are driven by human emotions and cause prices to rise and fall.

The markets are made up of many different individual buyers and sellers, each with his or her own concept of where the market is going and each motivated by varying degrees of the basic human emotions of fear and greed. All of these individuals, each acting in his or her own best interest, are what create the swinging market patterns we see in every price chart.

An investor will typically resist paying more for a stock than the price other people have recently been paying for it, unless it continues moving up, which will give him some confidence or hope that it will keep going up. Conversely, an investor will resist selling a stock for less than the price other people have been getting for theirs, unless the price keeps declining and he fears it will continue to decline.

Let's begin our analysis of swing behavior by looking at a long-term swing chart of the market as a whole. Figure 5.1 is a price chart of the S&P 500 Index from 1997 through 2003. This particular time period was chosen because it illustrates the evolution of a complete market cycle from the beginning of a major uptrend, ending in a climax peak, followed by a sharp drop.

Figure 5.1

As you can see, prices zigzag up and then zigzag back down again.

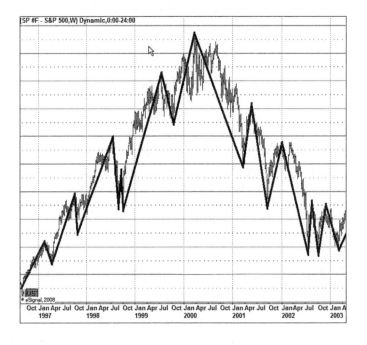

What Are Swings and Waves?

The sequence of price upswings and downswings that we call "market waves" is a manifestation of the market's "breathing in and out" as it moves in a meandering fashion along its path from point A to point B. Although these meanderings may appear to be random, there is, in fact, an underlying pattern and logic to their movement. If you want to be a successful trader, it's important that you understand these patterns, the reasons for them, and how best to exploit them.

The Attributes of a Successful Swing Trader

A swing trader tries to exploit the *swings* of the market with as little exposure to risk as possible. Trading the swings means looking for optimum times to jump in at the beginning of a new swing and exit at or near the end of that swing to await the development of a new swing trading opportunity in the same or opposite direction.

One of the most important attributes of any successful trader is patience. Exposure is risk, and an important characteristic of a successful trader is that he must always be aware of the balance between risk and reward and strive to maintain as large a ratio as possible of reward over risk. Clearly, the points at which the trend changes direction from up to down or from down to up represent the opportunities with the lowest risk of loss and the highest potential for profit, so that's why it is so important for technicians to understand how and why markets swing.

A successful swing trader is like a surfer, waiting offshore on his board for just the right wave to ride to the beach. He may let several *waves* go by because they don't "feel" quite right, or maybe he wasn't paying attention and missed catching the wave until it was too late, but he doesn't mind because there will always be another wave, and in the meantime he waits patiently.

def•i•ni•tion

Swings are the individual legs (the zigs and zags) of market waves. Market **waves** are the zigzag path up and down that prices follow on a chart based on changing human emotions.

Why Do Markets Swing?

Markets exist to facilitate trade. To facilitate trade, markets have to entice both buyers and sellers. To entice buyers and sellers, there must be both price movement and price uncertainty.

Buyers will buy if they expect prices to rise in anticipation of being able to sell later at a higher price. On the other hand, sellers will sell if they expect prices to drop. Sellers will hold back in anticipation of higher prices if they expect prices to rise. As supply catches up with demand and buying begins to dry up, the sellers lower their prices to attract more buying.

This constantly self-adjusting process between buyers and sellers is what causes markets to move not in a straight line from point A to point B, but in a more or less erratic, zigzag fashion consisting of *thrusts*, or price moves in the direction of the underlying trend, followed by pullbacks, or moves against the underlying trend (see Figure 5.2).

> ### TA Intelligence
>
> One of the main reasons technicians use swing charts is that they make it easier to spot trends and patterns. Traders and investors could arrive at the same conclusions by viewing a large number of prices in a list, but it would be more difficult to visualize and comprehend.

Figure 5.2

An example of a thrust and pullback.

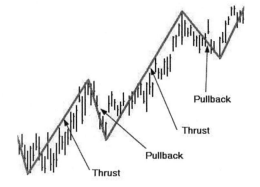

Pullback

Thrust

Pullback

Thrust

def•i•ni•tion

A **thrust** is a market move in price in the direction of the trend. Thrusts can be either up or down, depending on the overall trend direction.

It's like when I take my dog, Lucy, for a walk around the block. I will stay on the sidewalk, strolling from one street corner to the next. Lucy, however, having a curious nature, usually meanders from one side of the sidewalk to the other, sniffing a bush, investigating a squirrel, running, and then walking again. The result is that Lucy's path, while constantly moving forward, travels a much greater distance to reach the next street corner than I do.

Just like Lucy meandering along the sidewalk, in a relatively flat market there's an equal degree of uncertainty between the buyers and the sellers as to the future trend in prices. Consequently, prices meander back and forth within a well-defined, relatively narrow range. A narrow range of prices is known as a channel since prices bounce from high to low without breaking out in either direction. Channels can slope upward, downward, or sideways and display the range of prices the security is bouncing back and forth between.

When the channel is basically horizontal, it is referred to as a "consolidation" market phase. Upswings within the horizontal channel are generally the same length as downswings (see Figure 5.3). If consolidation is subsequently followed by a major uptrending move, it is referred to as "accumulation," as the smart money is accumulating a position in the stock before it moves higher. If consolidation is subsequently followed by a major downtrending move, it is referred to as "distribution," as the smart money is distributing its position in the stock while the price is high and before it moves lower.

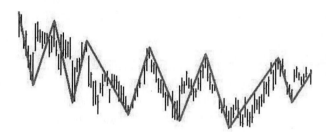

Figure 5.3

Upswings within the horizontal channel are generally the same length as downswings.

Swing Channels

Swing traders often draw channels to highlight the primary trend—for example, an upward trend (Figure 5.4) or downward trend (Figure 5.5).

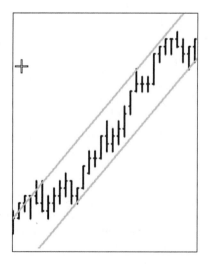

Figure 5.4

An upward trending channel.

Figure 5.5

A downward trending channel.

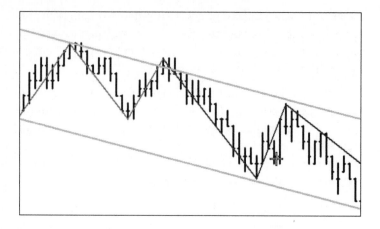

Just like our earlier "walking the dog" example, so long as prices remain confined by the channel, the primary trend is expected to continue. As prices approach the lower channel line, or support line, expect them to react back up to the upper channel line. As prices approach the upper channel line, or resistance line, expect them to react back down to the lower channel line.

When prices break out of a channel, it often signals the beginning of a powerful move in the new direction, and traders should look to take positions consistent with the new direction.

Technical analysts recognize that all market charts, whether they record monthly, weekly, daily, or five-minute time intervals, reflect this type of zigzag behavior of prices. That is why it is so vitally important to be able to understand and interpret this phenomenon.

A Typical Market Swing Cycle

A complete market cycle (see Figure 5.6), from neutral to an uptrend to a reversal at the top, and finally, to a downtrend, typically follows a pattern consisting of the following seven steps:

Step 1: Accumulation—The market is in neutral territory, meaning it is basically trading up and down within a rather narrow horizontal range of prices. This is typically the time when the smart money is quietly accumulating shares, so this sideways period is called the "accumulation" period.

Step 2: Initial thrust—This is where an increase in the number of buyers begins to push prices up. As the awareness of the interest of buyers grows, more and more discerning buyers jump on the bullish bandwagon. Rising prices attract more buyers and a significant price move upward, an initial thrust, occurs.

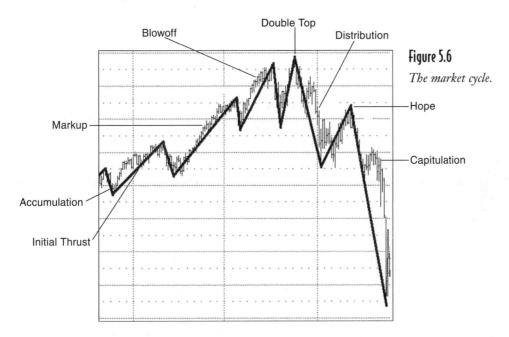

Figure 5.6

The market cycle.

At some point in the upward thrust, the initial flurry of buying slows down. Short-term buyers begin selling to lock in their profits, and serious long-term buyers back away as the upward trend weakens. This situation leads to a pullback in the uptrending channel.

Pullbacks are usually steeper and shorter in duration than thrust moves. Pullbacks in strong trends may retrace or retreat 35 to 40 percent of the upthrust swing. Pullbacks in weaker trends may retrace 50 to 60 percent of the upthrust swing. If the pullback exceeds 65 percent of the upthrust swing, it's a sign of overall weakness, and the major upthrust in all likelihood is over.

Step 3: Markup—After the initial pullback in which the market catches its breath and regains its energy, a new upthrust begins, usually with greater force and duration than the initial thrust. By this time the uptrend has become well known by the public, and buyers are eager to climb on board this accelerating train. This upward phase of the market cycle is often referred to as the "markup" phase because the earlier buyers from the accumulation phase are now marking up the price as they sell to new buyers arriving later in the uptrend.

At some point, selling pressure begins to increase as buyers who bought near the beginning of the trend begin selling to take their profits. At the same time, traders believing the market now to be overpriced begin selling short, even though the trend may still appear to be rising. This generally leads to a steep selloff as sellers begin flooding the market and reluctant buyers back away.

Step 4: Blowoff—Eventually the selling is offset by another urgent wave of buying by bargain hunters who missed out on the earlier rise of this obviously strong stock and who sense an opportunity to buy at prices lower than the recent highs. This behavior often leads into the final, or blowoff, phase in which extreme optimism drives a strong and rapid upward movement of prices. Eager late buyers, fearing that they will once again be left behind, clamor to get back on board. Professional traders accommodate them by selling their earlier purchases at increasingly higher prices.

Step 5: Distribution—Once sellers outnumber buyers, prices begin to collapse. This is called the distribution phase. Prices usually move down faster than they moved up as sellers rush to the exits and buyers back away, anticipating lower prices.

Step 6: Hope—At some point following a strong down move, the market usually pauses to take a breath with a sharp pullback move back to the upside. Such a move gives encouragement to the optimists who now buy the stock at "bargain prices."

Step 7: Capitulation—Prices collapse again and make new lows. At this point panic sets in and sellers cave in to sell out their holdings at any price. "Just get me out!" they cry to their brokers. This is known as the "capitulation" phase. After the crash there's usually a period of dormancy, eventually followed by quiet Step 1 accumulation as the cycle begins again.

Types of Swing Patterns

A characteristic five-swing market pattern consistent with a longer-term uptrend consists of an initial upthrust, an initial pullback, a main upthrust, a secondary pullback, and finally a blowoff upthrust followed by a three-swing reversal pattern downwards. This classic trading pattern, referred to as an Elliott wave pattern (see Figure 5.7), was popularized by trader R. N. Elliott and is widely used by technical analysts.

Think of swinging market prices as a child on a swing. We know from physics that the swing will go up and then stop and come swinging back down. You can approximate when these changes will occur by observation. While the market doesn't respond with the same predictability as a child's swing, the technician can anticipate when there is a high probability that the price direction is going to change. This is the geometry of price movement, and it goes to the heart of technical analysis—sensing through charts when the momentum of a price direction is going to change.

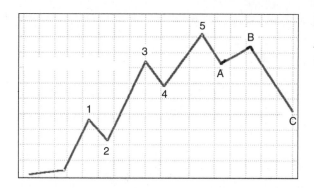

Figure 5.7

An example of an Elliott wave pattern.

The psychological factor driving market swings can be explained with the same analogy. Children will push the swing higher and higher because they enjoy the sensation; however, they reach a point at which it becomes uncomfortable and even frightening. At that point, they will slow down, and the swing will not reach its previous high point. As long as children find pushing the swing higher fun, they will continue because they enjoy the sensation. When they go too high, they become fearful of a fall and slow down.

Technicians use terms such as "double top," "head-and-shoulders," "cup-with-handle," and "flag" patterns that may sound quite arcane to the casual listener. However, being the clever souls they are, chartists just name them for what they look like. A flag pattern looks like a flag on a flagpole. A double top has two peaks at approximately the same price close together in time. Jargon is everywhere in technical analysis, but it need not muddy the waters of understanding.

The budding chartist will do just fine with "up," "down," and "sideways" to describe how prices are moving over time. Strip away the names and whiz-bang concepts and that is all that really matters. Buy it when it is going up. Sell it when it is going down.

Reversal Patterns

The process of changing trend direction from up to down or down to up almost always leads to one of the classic transition patterns, usually a double or triple top or a head-and-shoulders pattern. Very rarely do we see a single V-shaped top or bottom. Most of the time there is at least one retest or return of prices to the previous peak/valley to test its validity.

Double Tops and Double Bottoms

Sometimes referred to as "M's" or "W's," double tops often form at the end of uptrends, and double bottoms often form at the end of downtrends (see Figure 5.8). Double tops consist of a pair of price peaks of approximately the same height. Similarly, double bottoms consist of a pair of price valleys of approximately the same depth.

Figure 5.8

An example of the double tops pattern.

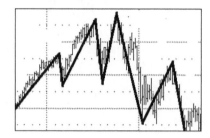

Frequently the second top in a double top formation is slightly higher than the first. Similarly, the second bottom in a double bottom formation is frequently slightly lower than the first (see Figure 5.9). There is a reason for this. In the case of a double bottom, for example, after the first bottom is formed and prices begin a new uptrend rally in what will become a double bottom, many traders will believe that the previous downtrend has run its course and will be buying in anticipation of a strong uptrending move. After buying into the expected uptrend, many of these traders will place protective orders to close out their purchase in case they guessed wrong. Typically, they will place their orders to sell just below the low price of the first bottom.

Figure 5.9

An example of the double bottoms pattern.

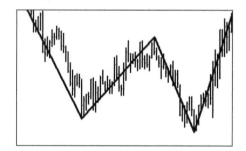

Savvy traders, anticipating the existence of a substantial quantity of contingent sell orders below the low of the previous bottom, will wait until the initial thrust runs out of steam and pauses to take a breath. These savvy traders will then issue sell orders of sufficient strength to force prices back down to levels lower than the previous bottom to encourage the previous buyers to sell out at a loss. The savvy traders will buy these shares at a bargain price from the unwitting sellers, thus pushing prices back up, and eventually will take their own profits at higher prices. Thus, in telltale fashion, the second bottom in a double bottom pattern will usually be lower than the first bottom, thanks to the extra push down from the savvy traders.

A similar situation occurs with double tops in which investors, after the occurrence of the first peak, will place standing buy orders if prices rise above that previous peak. Savvy traders again anticipate the existence of these standing buy orders above the previous peak and, on the first pullback after a down thrust, will force prices back up above the previous peak to trigger contingent buy orders and will sell to the unwitting buyers before driving prices back down sharply. Thus, in the same tell-tale fashion, the second peak in a double top will usually be higher than the first peak.

It's similar to the example of pushing the child in the swing, where the second push is harder than the first so that the child swings higher the second time.

This constant buying and selling activity by the smart money and the dumb money, the motivated buyers and the motivated sellers, drives prices up and down and creates the characteristic zigzag patterns we see on a price chart. Buyers want in at the lowest price possible, and sellers want out at the highest price possible.

The actual trading process is somewhat more complicated, but for now think of buyers and sellers as two teams in a tug of war match. Each team wants to maximize profits while minimizing risk. The mix of smart traders, amateur traders, and professional traders results in many different ideas about when to buy or sell and at what price. This interaction, coupled with the imbalances in supply and demand created by buyers and sellers, leads to the sometimes-erratic movement of market prices and accounts for all of the patterns you will observe in technical analysis.

Info/Tips

As time moves on, a double top or double bottom can easily evolve into triple top or bottom, a head-and-shoulders pattern, or an inverse head-and-shoulders pattern. As you become familiar with technical analysis, you will see how patterns evolve as trading activity responds to market pressures.

Head-and-Shoulders Patterns and Triple Tops

One of the most common and most reliable reversal patterns is the head-and-shoulders pattern (see Figure 5.10). This price pattern consists of three peaks. The first peak (the left shoulder) is lower than the second peak (the head)—remember the double top example previously discussed—and the third peak (the right shoulder) is also lower than the second peak and completes the head-and-shoulders reversal pattern.

Similarly, inverse head-and-shoulders patterns (see Figure 5.11), where the second bottom is lower than the first and third bottom, frequently occur at major trend reversals and signal the beginning of a significant uptrend after an extended downtrend.

Figure 5.10

A sample head-and-shoulders pattern.

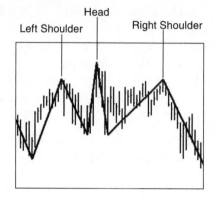

Figure 5.11

A sample inverse head-and-shoulders pattern.

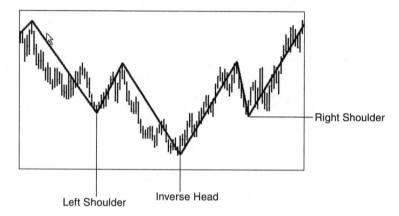

After the formation of a head-and-shoulders top pattern, if the price crosses below a line connecting the two intervening pullback lows (called a neckline), the crossing of the neckline signals the beginning of a new major downtrend (see Figure 5.12). The vertical distance between the top of the head and the neckline can be used to project the distance to an approximate target for the downward move.

Sometimes the head is approximately the same height as the two shoulders. In this event, the pattern is referred to as a triple top (see Figure 5.13). Its interpretation is the same as for the head-and-shoulders pattern.

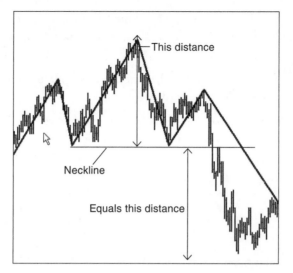

Figure 5.12

Neckline and downside price projection for head-and-shoulders pattern.

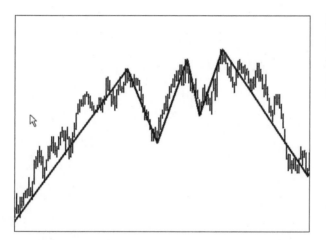

Figure 5.13

When the head is approximately the same height as the two shoulders, it's called a triple top pattern.

The Least You Need to Know

◆ Interactions between buyers and sellers create characteristic patterns on price charts.

◆ Reversal patterns—such as double or triple tops/bottoms and head-and-shoulders patterns—foretell reversals in trend direction.

◆ Trading channels define the direction of the prevailing trend. The skillful trader should know how to recognize and exploit market waves and patterns.

♦ Markets breathe in and out with thrusts and pullbacks, both uptrending and down-trending, driven by investor emotions. Pullbacks are generally shorter and steeper than thrusts.

♦ Market trend reversals are frequently characterized by double and triple tops and bottoms or head-and-shoulders patterns.

♦ Swing tops and bottoms, where market direction reverses, represent the lowest-risk entry points and the highest profit potential for a trader.

Chapter 6

Bridging the Gaps and Waving the Flags

In This Chapter

◆ Typical wave patterns

◆ Reversal patterns

◆ Continuation patterns

◆ Consolidation patterns

◆ Breakout patterns

One of the strengths of technical analysis is the ability to spot change and graphically display it in such a manner that the technician can spot the opportunity. Change is opportunity to the technician, and patterns of price behavior tip him off to profit opportunities (or preventing a large loss). The technician is always on the lookout for a signal that a stock's price direction is about to change. The clever technician uses charts and patterns to spot price direction changes before they happen.

When Prices Gap—Irrational Exuberance?

 A gap pattern (see Figure 6.1) occurs in a price chart when the current bar's low is higher than the previous bar's high in an uptrend or when the current bar's high is lower than the previous bar's low in a downtrend. In both cases, some type of exuberance is driving the stock to create a gap between the extremes of the previous bar and the current bar. For example, a company might announce some important news (good or bad) after the market has closed. The next trading day's opening price may differ significantly from the previous trading day's close. There can also be economic news or some other stimulus that accounts for the exuberance.

Figure 6.1

Examples of different types of gaps.

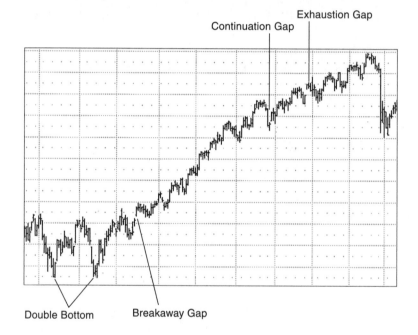

Breakaway Gaps

Breakaway gaps (see Figure 6.2) usually occur after the breakout from a *consolidation* region. They generally identify the start of a strong trend. High volume typically follows the occurrence of a gap, continuing for several days. The strong trend usually continues long enough for several new highs or lows to occur after the gap.

def•i•ni•tion

Consolidation is a period of trading in which a balance exists between buyers and sellers, leading to a sideways trend in prices. When an imbalance between buyers and sellers once more occurs, prices will break out of the consolidation zone and begin to trend in the direction of the imbalance.

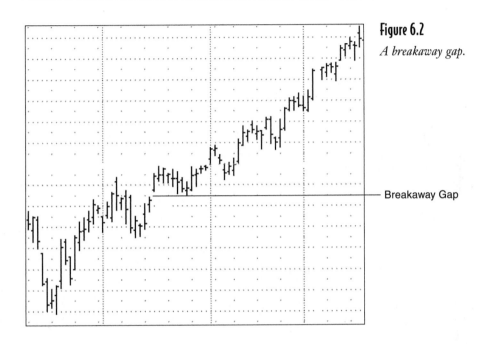

Figure 6.2

A breakaway gap.

Breakaway Gap

Continuation Gaps

Continuation or runaway gaps occur in the middle of a strong trend (see Figure 6.3). After a continuation gap, prices continue making new highs or lows without pulling back to close the gap. Such gaps are also referred to as measuring gaps because they often appear about halfway through the move, thus giving the trader an approximate indication as to how much of the move is left. Volume after the occurrence of the gap is usually high, propelling prices strongly in the direction of the trend.

Info/Tips

Gaps are considered to have been closed when prices reverse and fill the space previously created by the gap.

Continuation Gap

Figure 6.3

A continuation gap.

Exhaustion Gaps

Exhaustion gaps are excessively wide gaps that occur at the end of a trend (see Figure 6.4). Most exhaustion gaps occur on high volume. They are like the last gasp before the end of the trend.

Figure 6.4

An exhaustion gap.

Exhaustion Gap

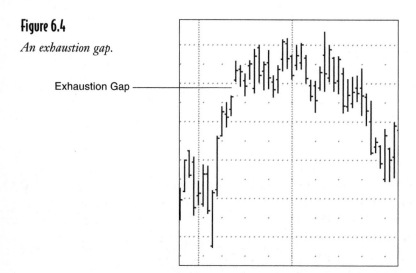

Exhaustion gaps are generally not followed by many new highs. After the gap, prices frequently enter a consolidation region, and the gap closes fairly quickly, usually within five bars or so.

Info/Tips _____

Sometimes a breakaway gap in the opposite direction follows an exhaustion gap, leaving what's called an island reversal pattern isolated by the two gaps. This pattern usually signals an important market turn.

When the market drops, it often pauses at the level of previous runaway and continuation gaps. To trade gaps successfully, you have to be quick, and you have to be ready to close out a trade at a moment's notice.

Consolidation Patterns

What does a market do when it pauses to take a breath? It consolidates, as traders gather their forces for the next assault up or down. During this process, the price charts generate consolidation patterns that provide a clue to the direction of the next market move. Consolidation patterns can be followed by either a continuation of the existing trend or a reversal of the existing trend.

Trend Continuation Patterns

Continuation patterns are consolidation patterns that suggest that the next move will be a continuation of the previous trend direction. They usually consist of a strong trending move followed by a brisk pullback move against the prevailing trend direction that shakes out the weak *trend-followers*. Typical continuation patterns are flag and pennant patterns.

def•i•ni•tion _____

Trend-followers are traders who always trade with the prevailing trend. Countertrend traders usually take positions against the prevailing trend in anticipation of a trend direction reversal.

Flags and Pennants

Flag patterns often resemble the rectangular shape of a drooping flag (see Figure 6.5). In an uptrend, an upward thrust line would represent the flagpole, while the subsequent pullback swing would be the flag. This is called a bull flag. In a downtrend, a downward thrust line would represent the flagpole, while the subsequent upward pullback would be the flag. This is called a bear flag.

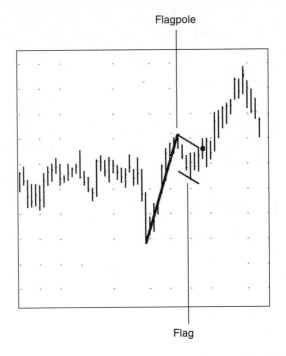

Figure 6.5

An example of a flag pattern.

Sometimes the flag is more triangle shaped, each bar shorter than and contained by the previous bar (see Figure 6.6). This is called a pennant and can be traded in a similar fashion as a flag.

Figure 6.6

An example of a pennant pattern.

In a primary uptrend, flags and pennants mark a consolidation before the previous move resumes. As a result, the upper portion of the flagpole typically is characterized by higher-than-usual volume, while the flag or pennant pattern itself occurs on dramatically diminishing volume.

Once you have identified a flag or pennant pattern on your chart, a breakout through the top of the flag or pennant on high volume signals a continuation of the uptrend (see Figure 6.7).

 You can project a price target for the trend continuation move after a flag or pennant pattern by measuring the length of the flagpole. In a bull flag pattern, if you add that length to the bottom right corner of the flag or pennant, you can usually predict where the next price swing is likely to end, and you can use that as a profit target to sell. Conversely, in a bear flag pattern, you can subtract the flagpole length from the upper right corner of the flag or pennant to predict how far down the downtrend is likely to extend.

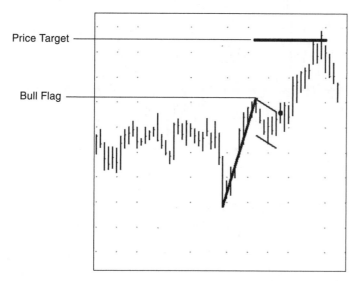

Figure 6.7

You can project a price target for the trend continuation move after a flag or pennant pattern by measuring the length of the flagpole.

If you were to sit down and study a number of charts today, with 20/20 hindsight you would be able to see quite a number of flags and pennants. The key is to be able to spot the formation of the patterns as they are developing.

Imagine a dramatic price move that produces a long straight-line price bar, or series of bars, that resembles a flagpole. In order for the market to catch up to this bold move, the next few days of trading will form a flag or a pennant as the investors settle in to this new price range. If the next few price bars witness the price trading in a narrow range with the highs and lows dropping in the opposite direction of the prevailing trend, then a flag or pennant is formed. A key to the recognition of this pattern is that the volume will diminish significantly during the creation of the flag or pennant.

 Bear flags and pennants also appear (upside-down) in downtrending markets (see Figure 6.8). Generally, the time it takes to develop bear flags and pennants will be dramatically shorter than that for bull flags, as investors tend to panic sell. Just take a look at the downtrends of the dot.com markets of the 2000–2003 period or the 2008–2009 market crash.

Figure 6.8

An example of the bear flag pattern.

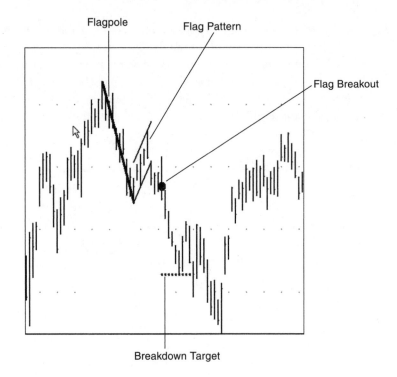

Triangle Patterns

As their name implies, triangle patterns are created in a consolidation period when each new bar is slightly shorter than and inside the bar preceding it. Triangle patterns represent a degree of uncertainty on the part of investors about the future direction of the trend. Like the coiling of a spring, they are gathering energy characterized by successively lower highs and higher lows. When prices break out of a triangle pattern, they contain a large amount of stored-up power that can generate a strong extended move in the direction of the breakout. The problem is that symmetrical triangles don't usually give you a clue as to the direction of the breakout (see Figure 6.9). You just have to be ready to follow the move in whichever direction it goes.

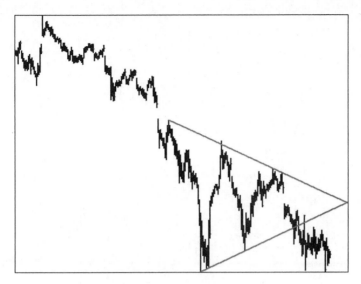

Figure 6.9

Triangle patterns represent a degree of investor uncertainty concerning the direction of the trend's future.

Ascending triangles display a relatively horizontal top while the bottom slopes upward (see Figure 6.10). They are important because they form less frequently than descending or symmetrical triangles. Ascending triangles generally signal the beginning of a strong uptrend. As a result of more aggressive buying than selling, the lows get progressively higher while the highs make it to about the same level each time before prices finally breakout to the upside.

Info/Tips

Generally speaking, triangle continuation patterns, in which the breakout continues the previous trend, are much shorter than triangle reversal patterns, in which the breakout reverses the previous trend. In other words, the longer the triangle, the greater the probability that the trend will reverse rather than continue.

Descending triangles, on the other hand, slope downward toward a relatively horizontal bottom (see Figure 6.11). They often signal the reversal of an uptrend. They are formed when a run-up in price levels is followed by a series of lower highs and relatively equal lows. Volume is typically higher at the beginning and then decreases as the triangle forms, followed by a volume surge during the breakdown.

Figure 6.10

An ascending triangle.

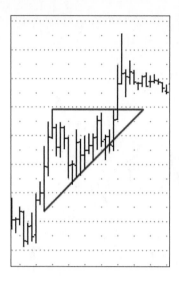

Figure 6.11

A descending triangle.

A breakout of a triangle pattern should occur prior to the completion of the triangle when the two converging lines meet. Generally, prices should break out in the direction of the prior trend somewhere between two thirds and three quarters of the length of the triangle. If the prices remain within the triangle beyond the three-quarters point, the triangle begins to lose its potency, and prices in all likelihood will continue to drift.

Heads Up

Watch out for prices retracing back toward the triangle after breaking out of the triangle. Usually they will reverse back again into the original direction of the breakout. On the other hand, if they move significantly back into the triangle pattern, the breakout has failed, and you should exit your position and wait for the next signal.

Triangles and flags work well on strong stocks in well-defined uptrends. As long as these continuation patterns keep showing up, the overall health of the market can be expected to be strong.

Cup-With-Handle Pattern

One of the most reliable patterns that precede a major uptrend is the cup-with-handle formation (see Figure 6.12). It is a favorite with stock traders, particularly with those who read *Investor's Business Daily*. This pattern often signals the start or continuation of a strong uptrend. The inverse can occur at tops as well.

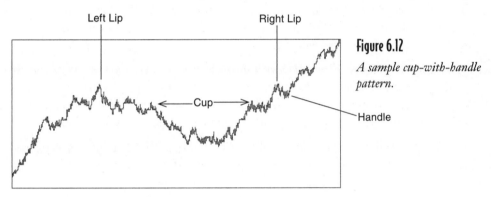

Figure 6.12

A sample cup-with-handle pattern.

The cup-with-handle is a long, bowl-shaped continuation pattern that develops after a previous price advance has stalled and is selling off. After the selloff, the price will basically trade flat for an extended period of time with no clear trend.

The next part of the cup-with-handle pattern represents the right side of the cup. This is a gradual bowl-shaped upward move back toward the peak of the previous selloff. The handle pattern then follows to the right as a short, brisk pullback move. Sometimes the handle resembles a flag or pennant that slopes downward; other times it is just a short price pullback. The handle represents the final consolidation/pullback that often leads to a big breakout to the upside.

The handle of a cup-with-handle pattern should retrace no more than one third of the height of the right side of the cup. The smaller the retracement, the more bullish the formation and the more significant the breakout.

The cup-with-handle pattern usually takes much longer to evolve and complete than triangle patterns.

Heads Up _____

> The development of the cup needs to be slow and gradual. If the shape of the cup is too sharp or too quick, it's not a good consolidation within the longer-term uptrend from which to take the potential buy signal.

On a daily stock chart the cup can extend from one to six months, sometimes longer on a weekly chart. The handle can be from one week to many weeks long, but ideally it should complete within about one to four weeks. There should be a substantial increase in volume on the breakout above the top of the handle.

The projected price target after the breakout above the handle can be estimated by measuring the distance from the right peak of the cup to the bottom of the cup and adding that distance to the bottom of the handle.

According to *Investor's Business Daily*, "One of biggest mistakes that amateur traders make is being quick to jump to the conclusion that just because a pattern they found is rounded, that it is a cup-with-handle. The cup-with-handle pattern has a lot of criteria and should not be confused with several other patterns out there that look similar to it."

Let's run through the very important criteria to make a pattern a true cup-with-handle. If the pattern fails to meet any one of these criteria, it should not be considered a cup-with-handle:

- The stock price rise leading up to the left cup lip is at least 30 percent.

- The cup duration is between 7 and 65 weeks. Skilled traders prefer to see a cup that is at least five months in length, with six months being ideal.

- The cup depth ranges from 15 percent to 35 percent of the price at the lip.

- The handle duration is between one to two weeks, with a one-week minimum.

- The handle carries a downward volume trend.

- The handle forms in the upper half of the cup on the right side.

- The buy signal on the cup-with-handle pattern comes when the price closes above the right cup rim on significant volume breakout.

- Handles that are shorter than 23 days show better performance after the breakout than those that are longer.

- The volume should also be a U-shaped pattern.

The Least You Need to Know

- ◆ Depending on where they are located, gaps in the price trend can portend the beginning, halfway point, or end of the trend.

- ◆ Flag, pennant, and triangle patterns designate pauses in the prevailing trend and can be used to project the length of the next leg of the trend.

- ◆ The cup-with-handle pattern is one of the most reliable patterns that often precede a major uptrend.

Part 2

Tools for Technical Analysis

Technical analysis offers you a set of tools to help anticipate future price direction. They will help you answer questions such as: Is the stock currently trending, consolidating, or oscillating? Where have prices found support or resistance in the recent past? Are prices making new highs or new lows? How are prices behaving relative to their moving average? Are key oscillators in overbought or oversold territory? Are oscillators diverging from price? Answers to these questions can alert you in advance as to when prices are likely to change direction and thus provide you with powerful information that can significantly improve your trading profits.

Chapter 7

Trendlines and Trend Channels—Connecting the Dots

In This Chapter

◆ Spotting trends

◆ Drawing trendlines

◆ Trend channels

◆ Channel definition tools

As we have learned, fear and greed drive price movements and create the tendencies for prices to trend. The reason for this is simple. A trader doesn't like to pay more for a stock than others have recently paid for it unless it is continually moving upward, giving him some confidence that it may continue to move up. On the other hand, a trader will resist selling a stock for less than the price other people have been getting for theirs, unless the price keeps declining and he fears it will continue to decline.

A cursory look at any set of price charts will show that prices often have a prevailing tendency to trend or move in a specific direction—up, down, or sideways—for a considerable amount of time. In Figure 7.1, I have drawn a set of arrows illustrating how the general trend direction and slope of a price chart varies with time. This happens to be a daily bar chart of McDonalds Corp. for the year 2007.

Figure 7.1

How the general trend direction and slope of a price chart varies with time.

Trendlines Show the Way

Traders seek to identify signs of the beginnings of a trend and then to ride that trend for all it is worth. The ability to spot a trend early can give a trader a significant advantage in determining his or her market tactics. Accordingly, traders often draw an upsloping trendline below an uptrend in prices and a downsloping trendline above a downtrend in prices to provide a guide as to where the boundaries of the trend are likely to lie.

When price movement is flat, or congesting, horizontal trendlines are drawn both above the highs and below the lows of the trading channel to define its boundaries. These are referred to as support and resistance lines. Trendlines gain more validity every time price bounces off the trendline. When prices break through a significant trendline, it is usually a sign that a change in the trend is taking place. The slope of the trendline shows the amount of change in price over time—the steeper the slope, the greater the rate of change (see Figure 7.2).

TA Intelligence
Beginning technicians should be aware that the highest price reached and the lowest price reached during a single trading bar are often more important pieces of information than the closing price because they reveal the maximum amount of energy or interest in the stock during that period. That's why trendlines are drawn connecting significant price lows in an uptrend and significant price highs in a downtrend.

Figure 7.2

Trendlines show the way.

Trendlines keep you honest. If the trendline is broken to a significant extent, so is the trend. The reality of price says that when the trend changes, you will lose money unless you go with the new trend.

How to Draw a Trendline

 As prices make their zigzag way across a chart, as few as two points, each marking successive tops or bottoms of a zigzag wave, may suggest the presence of a trend; more points may be needed to confirm it. The problem is that different traders looking at the same data for the same period may subjectively pick different points through which to draw trendlines. Not only that, the same person will sometimes draw totally different trendlines through the same data at different times, depending on his or her inclination at that time based on the additional data available.

In an effort to formalize the correct way to draw a trendline, technical analyst Thomas R. DeMark set forth a set of rules in the 1980s for drawing consistent uptrend lines and downtrend lines, which he refers to as "demand lines" and "supply lines," respectively.

According to DeMark, "Success in using trendlines requires both an attention to detail and a pattern of consistency."

DeMark's first rule is never to draw the trendline from left to right. A trendline should always be drawn from right to left since recent price activity is more important than past historical movement (see Figure 7.3).

The first step to drawing an uptrend line, according to DeMark, is to select the most recent price bar whose low is lower than the price lows on both sides of it. This will be point 1 of the trendline. The next step is to look to the left until you find the next low bar that is lower than point 1 and lower than the price lows on both sides of it. This will be point 2. Then draw an upsloping trendline connecting points 2 and 1 and extend the line to the right. This will be your uptrend line. The more lows on either side that are higher than the lows of points 1 and 2, the stronger and more reliable is the uptrend line.

Figure 7.3

An example of DeMark's uptrend line.

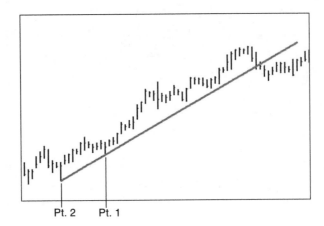

Similarly, the first step to drawing a downtrend line is to select the most recent swing high that is higher than the price highs on either side of it (see Figure 7.4). This will be point 1 of the trendline. The next step is to look to the left until you find the next swing high that is higher than point 1 and higher than the price highs on either side of it. This will be point 2. Then draw a trendline connecting points 2 and 1 and extend the line to the right.

Figure 7.4

An example of DeMark's downtrend line.

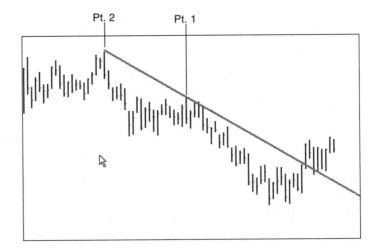

Note that an uptrend line is always drawn by connecting the lower points of a stock movement. A downtrend line is always drawn by connecting the higher points of a stock movement.

Trend Channels

Analysts often draw a parallel trendline on the opposite side of the main trendline to define a channel, or trading zone, through which prices move as they zigzag along the trendline to the conclusion of the trend (see Figure 7.5). The channel defines the major trend within which the minor trend swings occur. Once prices break out decisively from the major trend channel, a reversal of trend direction occurs.

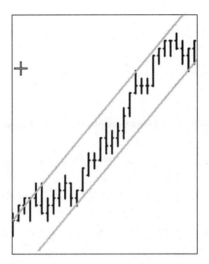

Figure 7.5

Trend channel lines with swing lines.

Note that trendlines are different from the swing lines that were described in Chapter 3. Trendlines define an ongoing trend by connecting successively higher lows in an uptrend and successively lower highs in a downtrend. Trendlines can change as time evolves and as new data is acquired either confirming the slope of an existing trend or revising that slope. Swing lines, on the other hand, connect the extreme low of a trending series of prices with the extreme high of that series and are usually not drawn until after the trend has reversed direction (see Figure 7.6). Swing lines are used in swing charts to help highlight the characteristic zigzag patterns occurring in the stream of market prices.

Trading in a direction consistent with the trend direction is usually a much safer strategy than trading against the trend. Nonetheless, it is important to give that trend the benefit of the doubt and not be shaken out too easily. If you are trading the trend, it usually pays to hang on for as long as the trend continues.

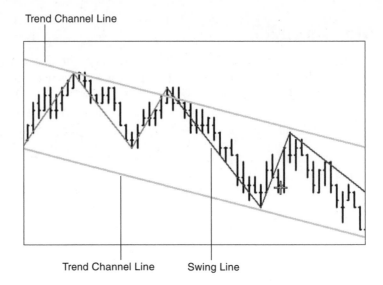

Figure 7.6

An example of an uptrend channel.

When prices break away from an established trendline and signal a true change in direction, they often have a tendency to return once more to the old trendline before proceeding in the new direction. An excellent example of this phenomenon is shown in Figure 7.7.
After the stock price, which had been in a strong uptrend, broke down through its uptrend
line, the price nonetheless pulled back up to test the uptrend line one more time before
resuming its new downtrend.

This magnetic attraction is common to trendlines and can be observed after the beginning
of many major trend reversals. An awareness of this tendency of prices to return to their
former trendline can help a technician with the timing of his entry into the new trend.

Figure 7.7

Trendline as a price pullback magnet.

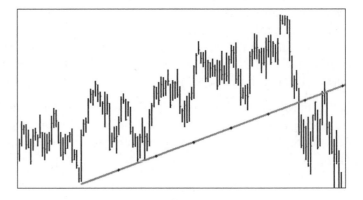

Although it is relatively easy to spot a trend after it has occurred in the middle of a price chart, as traders we are always dealing with the unknown future, where it is difficult to know how much longer an existing trend will continue or a new trend will begin. One of my favorite sayings is, "You don't know you're in a trend until you are in a trend!" In other words, by the time you identify the existence of a new trend, a significant chunk of it may already be gone, and you may lose money trying to trade as if the trend still has a long way to go.

 Info/Tips _____

When prices are found to be following a given trendline, they are more likely to continue moving along that line than not to.

Most trend traders look at more than one time frame to ensure that they are trading in a direction consistent with the longer-term trend. This means that if you are trading on the basis of a trendline or channel on, for example, a daily chart, it behooves you also to look at a weekly chart and a monthly chart of the same symbol to see if the trend direction in these longer time frames confirms the shorter-term trend. Similarly, if you are working with a five-minute price chart, for example, your odds of success in entering a trend consistent with the short-term trend would be improved considerably if the trend direction on your five-minute chart were the same as the trend direction on an hourly chart and a daily chart of the same symbol.

Trading Trendline Pullbacks

When planning your trade, it is to your advantage to find price levels at which to enter your trade where the risk of loss is low and the potential profit amount is high. A popular traders' saying is, "Cut your losses short and let your profits run." In other words, before entering a new position, weigh your possible profit against your possible loss and make sure the potential gain exceeds the potential risk.

One of the best risk-to-profit ratios occurs if you buy when prices are in a longer-term uptrend but have temporarily retreated to a level at which they almost touch the longer-term uptrend line.

If you buy at or near the uptrend line (see Figure 7.8), you are entering in a direction consistent with the longer-term trend and have the odds in your favor that prices will stop retreating at or near the uptrend line and will briskly and profitably move back up to the upper boundary of the uptrend channel. Nonetheless, if your judgment is incorrect and prices continue to decline and break decisively below the uptrend line, you should quickly sell out your long position to minimize your losses.

Figure 7.8

Buy pullbacks near an uptrend line.

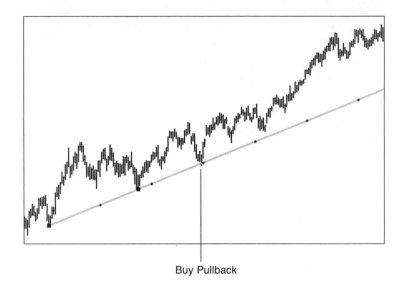

Buy Pullback

Traders always have to make their trading decisions based on probabilities in an atmosphere of uncertainty. In later chapters, we'll discuss other technical analysis tools that will help you make these difficult trading decisions.

Tools That Generate Trendline Channels

Tools that generate trendline channels serve to define a highway for prices to follow. The direction of the channel shows the overall trend, and prices tend to meander within the limits of the channel. There are three price channel definition tools that technical analysts can use to visualize where the price swings are occurring within the perspective of the larger-scale trend: Andrews' Pitchfork tool, the linear regression channel tool, and the Donchian channel tool.

Andrews' Pitchfork

In the late 1930s, Dr. Alan Andrews developed a linear price channel technique based on what he called his "median line" theory. This technique later evolved into a price pattern known as Andrews' Pitchfork because it resembles the shape of a pitchfork.

Let's look at how the pitchfork is drawn to create an uptrend channel in Figure 7.9.

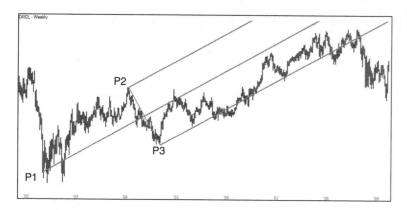

Figure 7.9

Drawing Andrews' Pitchfork.

We begin with a swing low. Let's call that point P1. P1 is followed by a swing high. Let's call that swing high point P2. Then we get another swing low that is higher than P1. So now we have three points: P1, P2, and P3. Now draw a line connecting points P2 and P3.

Next draw a trendline connecting point P1 to the midpoint of line P1-P2 and extend it to the right to the end of the chart. This line is referred to as the median line, and it serves as the handle of the pitchfork pattern. Price movement often tends to pause at this median line.

Now we need to draw the upper and lower fingers of the pitchfork. One finger begins at point P2, the other finger begins at point P3, and both are drawn parallel to the median line, extending to the right to the end of the chart. This gives the pattern the appearance of a pitchfork.

Typically, Andrews' Pitchfork defines an ongoing trend channel. Often, as prices approach the median line, the market will reverse direction when it reaches that line (see Figure 7.10). If prices do not reverse at the median line but instead trade on through, they will generally head all the way to the opposite channel boundary and then reverse. Note how in the preceding example the lower finger and the median lines serve as a channel boundary for price movement until price finally breaks out of the channel and starts to reverse direction.

Figure 7.10

Andrews' Pitchfork goes in a new direction.

A breakout beyond the limits of the Andrews' Pitchfork channel usually indicates the beginning of a new swing direction, and we can draw a new pitchfork to define the projected limits of the new price trend channel, as illustrated in Figure 7.10. Here we have identified points P4, P5, and P6 as the reference points to draw a new downtrending pitchfork after prices broke down decisively below the uptrending pitchfork.

Linear Regression Channel

Another method that technicians use to draw a trendline channel midline is to have the computer calculate and plot a linear regression line through the interval covering a given price swing. Linear regression analysis is a statistical concept sometimes referred to as the "least squares method" or "best fit line." Linear regression analysis calculates the best-fitting straight line through a series of data points.

The trend channel boundaries are then drawn parallel to the median line and spaced apart at a distance controlled by one of several possible mathematical techniques, the most common of which is to space the channel boundaries a given number of standard deviations (a statistical term) on either side of the center line. Again, don't worry about the math, because most charting programs include a linear regression channel drawing tool that you can use to draw your channel with a flick of the cursor. Figure 7.11 shows a linear regression channel spaced two standard deviations on either side of the mathematically derived centerline. The centerline acts as a magnet to pull the prices back to it when they start wandering too close to the channel boundaries.

Figure 7.11

An example of a linear regression channel.

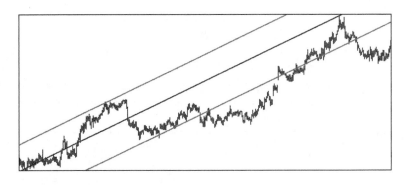

Andrews' Pitchforks and linear regression channels can be very useful tools to a trader since they provide several important pieces of information simultaneously:

- ◆ They indicate the direction of the immediate trend.

- ◆ The width of the channel is an indication of the level of price volatility within the immediate trend.

- The length of the channel is an indication of trend persistence.

- The channel boundaries and centerline are excellent trending support/resistance lines.

- A solid break of the channel boundaries signals a probable change in trend direction.

Donchian Channels

 Named after its developer, Richard Donchian, the Donchian channel is a price channel pattern based on the highest high price and the lowest low price over a specific number of time periods, typically 20 bars (see Figure 7.12). The upper line of the channel represents the highest high price over the last 20 bars, and the lower line of the channel represents the lowest low price over the last 20 bars.

If the current price action breaks above the high of the Donchian channel with vigor, it is a signal to buy into the beginning of a possible new uptrend. Conversely, if the current price action breaks below the low of the Donchian channel with vigor, it is a signal to sell or sell short into the beginning of a new downtrend. However, if prices break outside of the channel by only a small amount and then begin to pull back, it is usually a sign that the trend is in the process of reversing direction at that point.

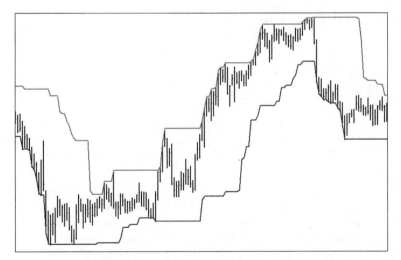

Figure 7.12

An example of a Donchian channel.

The Donchian channel is a useful indicator of how volatile the market price behavior is at any point in time. Since Donchian channels adjust immediately when new 20-bar highs or lows are achieved, prices will not stay outside the channel; instead, they will change the channel boundaries in a stair step fashion. If price movement is relatively stable, the Donchian channel will be fairly narrow. If the price begins fluctuating a lot, the Donchian channel will widen, indicating higher volatility.

Donchian channels are available on most computer charting programs and can be profitably applied by both novice and expert traders.

Putting It All Together

Now that we've examined trading opportunities using channel-based technical indicators, it's time to take a detailed look at two more examples and to explain how to capture such profit windfalls.

As an example, let's put a 20-bar Donchian channel indicator to work in Figure 7.13 on a daily chart of SkyWest Airlines, symbol SKYW, and go through the process step by step.

Figure 7.13

A trading example of a Donchian channel.

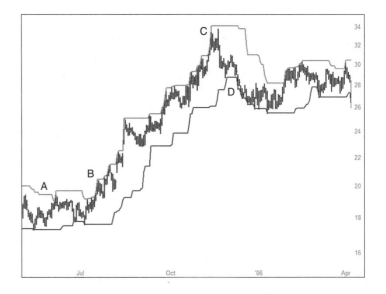

The upper Donchian channel line on this price chart reflects the highest price reached over the last 20 trading days, while the lower channel line reflects the lowest price reached over the last 20 trading days. In the zone marked "A," we see that price has been meandering in a sideways congestion channel between 17 and 19 for several months. In the zone marked "B," prices have broken above the congestion zone to 20, causing the upper Donchian channel line to begin rising. This is a signal alerting you to the possible beginning of an uptrend.

Point B would be a good point to buy the stock. So long as the price stays above the lower band of the channel, you would want to stay with your position. If the price breaks below the lower band, it would be time to sell and look for another opportunity.

From point B up to point C, prices never touch the lower Donchian channel, thus keeping you in the trade. Your potential exit point, the lower channel line, continues to rise at a comfortable distance below the price, thus locking in your growing profits.

At point D, the price breaks through the lower Donchian channel, indicating that it is time to exit your trade and take your profits. In this example, having bought at 20 and sold around 28, you would have made an $8 per share profit on a $20 per share investment, or a 40 percent profit over a five-month period.

To sum up, the steps to follow when trading with a Donchian channel are as follows:

♦ Apply the Donchian channel study to your price chart. With the indicator on your chart, the opportunities should show up clearly. You are looking for an opportunity where the price action breaks above or below the Donchian bands.

♦ Wait for the close of the session that is potentially above or below the band. It's necessary for the price to close outside the band to signal a valid entry. If the price penetrates the band but closes inside, chances are it could be a false breakout, so it is better to wait for the price to break out decisively. Once momentum has taken over, the directional bias should push the price past the close.

♦ Stay with the trade until the price closes below the lower band. Let the lower band define the amount of risk you should take to avoid being frightened out of your position by minor pullbacks in the price.

The Least You Need to Know

♦ Price movement has a tendency to trend.

♦ Uptrend lines connect prominent price bottoms.

♦ Downtrend lines connect prominent price tops.

♦ Parallel trendlines generate price channels that define the trend and often define a highway for future price movements.

♦ Prices often stop and reverse at trendlines and channel boundaries.

♦ Three forms of automatic price channels are Andrews' Pitchforks, linear regression channels, and Donchian channels.

8

Clarifying Raw Data with Moving Averages

In This Chapter

- ◆ What are moving averages?
- ◆ Types of moving averages
- ◆ Buy and sell signals
- ◆ Confirming trends

We technicians live by our charts. Our dependence on charts is not rooted in a particular love for lines and symbols, but we recognize the power charts have to digest and give meaning to large quantities of price information. If you go to any of several public websites that provide historic price information (such as Yahoo! Finance) and ask for the daily closing price of a stock for the past six months, you will get a spread sheet with around 130 prices. That many numbers is unwieldy at best and incomprehensible if you are trying to detect a pattern. However, if you apply some math to the problem and plot the results on a chart, patterns become clear. The math and the chart reveal what has happened over time to prices. More importantly, this information is a valuable tool that can help you make more profitable trades.

Smoothing the Bumps

Most price charts are "noisy." By "noisy," I mean that although prices have a tendency to trend, the underlying trend is often overlaid with many small, random moves that don't particularly support the trend but represent individual movements created by traders jockeying for position. Traders who trade the trend look to identify the trending moves and filter out the meaningless noise.

The previous chapter covered the subject of drawing straight trendlines connecting prominent peaks or valleys as a way of identifying the direction of the trend. The main problem with this method is the fact that you don't know you are in a trend until you are in a trend. In other words, the trend reveals itself when it has moved far enough and created enough small peaks and valleys to facilitate the drawing of a reasonable trendline. Often, by this time, much of the trend has already occurred, and the trader is left with the option of only trading the tail end of the trend.

> **Info/Tips** _____
>
> One of the most difficult jobs for any trader is sifting through the tremendous amount of data available to find those nuggets of information that will help him execute a successful trade. Moving averages are one of the tools that help the trader see what is important and filter out what is not so important.

One of the most common ways of filtering out the noise and identifying the direction of the trend is the use of a moving average line. A point on a moving average line is simply the average of a series of past prices, usually the closing price, of a selected number of price periods. The moving average line itself is made up of a string of these average prices.

How Moving Averages Work

To plot a 10-bar simple moving average—for example, on a price chart containing 200 bars—we begin by calculating the average of the closing prices of bars 1 through 10 and then plotting that value as a dot on the tenth bar of the price chart. Next we calculate the average of the closing prices of bars 2 through 11 and plot that value on the eleventh bar, connecting the two average value points with a line. The next average calculation is performed on bars 3 through 12 and so forth, connecting each new average point to its predecessor until we reach the end of the chart. This creates a moving average line that represents the average price of the most recent 10 bars as time marches forward. Over time, your chart will reveal a relatively smooth price trend of the average price of the last 10 bars.

You keep a moving average from historic prices up to the current price. As previously described, each day you add in the new price and drop the oldest out of the calculation. By connecting the calculated averages, your chart will reveal a price trend over time.

Here's another way of looking at moving averages:

First point: Add the closing prices of days 1, 2, 3, 4, 5, 6, 7, 8, 9, and 10; divide by 10; and plot the result on a chart.

Second point: Add the closing prices of days 2, 3, 4, 5, 6, 7, 8, 9, 10, and 11; divide by 10; and plot the result on a chart.

Third point: Add the closing prices of days 3, 4, 5, 6, 7, 8, 9, 10, 11, and 12; divide by 10; and plot the result on a chart.

Do this for 100 days and you will have a chart that tracks the average of the closing prices for those 100 days. Your chart will have 90 points connected by a line. This is called a moving average.

Moving averages can be used for any time segment you find helpful. You can use daily closing prices, or if you are trading in a short time frame, you can use prices on the hour, every half hour, every 15 minutes, and so on. Most technicians refer to the moving average time interval by the number of bars it covers. For example, a 10-bar moving average could cover 10 daily bars, but it could also cover 10 15-minute bars during a single day of trading if you are following a shorter time frame.

> **TA Intelligence**
>
> Fortunately for traders who are math challenged, modern charting software that is readily available and affordable does the entire heavy math lifting for you when creating moving average lines or other technical analysis tools. However, it is important for you to understand what you are seeing, even if you don't do all the calculations.

Types of Moving Averages

Three basic types of moving averages are used by most technicians: simple, exponential, and adaptive. The sections that follow describe how each of them work.

Simple Moving Average

A very common type of simple moving average is the 200-bar moving average (see Figure 8.1). Each point on this moving average line represents the average of the closing prices of the previous 200 bars. As each new bar is created, the moving average calculation is repeated for the closing value of each of the previous 200 bars. In this way, the moving average line smoothes out the otherwise noisy price action and gives the trader a better idea of the underlying directional movement of the price.

One problem with a simple moving average is that it responds relatively slowly to rapid changes in the overall price direction. Another problem is that a simple moving average changes twice in response to each piece of data. A new piece of data initially affects the average when it is the most recent point in the moving average calculation. This is good. We want our moving average to respond to each new piece of information that arrives.

Figure 8.1

This example shows a 50-bar simple moving average and a 200-bar simple moving average on a daily chart of Apple Computer. Since it is averaging over a longer time period, the 200-bar average is slower to respond and is smoother than the 50-bar one.

However, since a simple average only covers a finite number of points equal to the length of the average, at some point that piece of information is dropped from the tail end of the calculation. The removal of this piece of information thus again has an effect on the moving average value. But in this case it really has nothing to do with current events. It is old information whose removal affects how the current value of the moving average behaves. This is bad.

Exponential Moving Average (EMA)

To address this problem, technicians developed the exponential moving average. Whereas a simple moving average treats all the entries equally, an exponential moving average (EMA) places more emphasis on the recent price activity than on earlier price activity. Consequently, an EMA is more responsive to rapid changes in the overall price direction. Most technicians nowadays rely more on exponential moving averages than on simple moving averages because they feel that the more recent price action is more important and should carry more weight than the price changes that occurred 50 or 200 bars ago. See a comparison in Figure 8.2.

Calculating an EMA is different from calculating a simple moving average. Only two numbers are required in the calculation: the current bar's price and the previous bar's EMA value. To calculate a new point on an EMA line, you first take the difference between the current bar's price and the previous bar's EMA. You then multiply that difference by a fractional smoothing constant and add it to the previous bar's EMA to come up with a new EMA for the current bar.

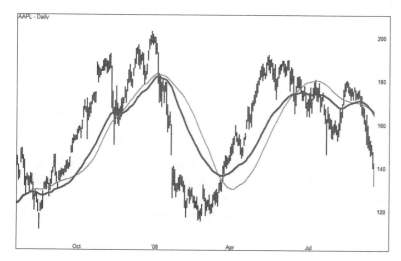

Figure 8.2

This chart shows the comparison of a 50-bar exponential moving average (thick line) with a 50-bar simple moving average (thin line) on a daily chart of Apple Computer.

The smoothing constant value is determined by the smoothness you want the EMA to display. If you want to look at long-term trends, the smoothing constant value will be quite small, for example .00995 for an EMA comparable to a 200-bar simple moving average. On the other hand, a smoothing constant value of .392 will create a more sensitive EMA, comparable to a 50-bar simple moving average. The rule of thumb is the shorter the average, the larger the smoothing constant.

Info/Tips

Moving averages are valuable in and of themselves. However, as you will see in later chapters, moving averages are also used as part of other popular indicators.

Mathematically, the "smoothing constant" for an exponential moving average is calculated as follows: a) add 1 to the number of days you want to include in the average calculation; b) divide 2 by the number you calculated in a. So for a 50-bar exponential moving average, for example, the smoothing factor would be 2/51, or 0.392. Every charting software program has the capability to calculate the EMA for you if you tell it what length value you want to use, so don't worry about the math.

The great advantage of using an EMA over a simple moving average is that it gives greater weight to the most recent data and responds to changes in price faster than a simple moving average. So, for example, for a 50-bar EMA, the most recent bar represents 39.2 percent of the total value of the average, while the fiftieth bar back will represent less than

1 percent of the average. In contrast, with a simple moving average, each bar is equally weighted at 2 percent (1/50). With a 50-bar EMA, the average does not drop the value of the fifty-first bar; its value simply slowly fades away to insignificance with the passage of time.

Adaptive Moving Average (AMA)

The continuing increase in personal computer power has led some developers—for example, Alan Hull, Perry Kaufman, Cynthia Kase, Mark Jurik, and Tushar Chande—to use more sophisticated mathematical algorithms to create a new class of moving average, the adaptive moving average (see Figure 8.3). Each developer uses a slightly different mathematical approach, but his or her objective is the same: to create a moving average that smoothes prices more effectively than exponential moving averages while providing a quick response time to changing price conditions and minimizing the adverse effect of unusual noise. Adaptive moving averages are being adopted more and more by smart traders and are becoming available for most popular computerized charting platforms.

> **Heads Up**
>
> Each type of moving average has its own strengths and weaknesses. Like any tool, you need to understand which one is appropriate for your trading decision. This comes through study and practice.

Figure 8.3

This chart demonstrates the difference between an adaptive moving average (thickest line) and the simple and exponential moving averages used in the previous example. Note that the adaptive moving average is much more responsive to changes in trend direction.

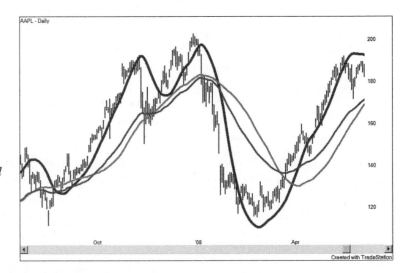

Deciding on a Time Period

Many chartists draw multiple moving average lines on their charts representing shorter and longer time periods. The time period of the moving averages used is a matter of personal taste. However, a simple rule of thumb is to match your moving average length to the length of the trend you are trying to catch. The longer the trend you are trying to catch, the longer the moving average you should be using.

Long-term investors often use a 200-day moving average to identify the major trend direction and its strength. For intermediate-term trends, a 50-day moving average is a popular length. For short-term trading, traders often utilize exponential moving averages ranging in length from 10 to 20 bars. A short-term moving average, since it covers a shorter time period, will also be more sensitive to minor moves while reacting more quickly to changes in market direction. This leads to more whipsawlike movements. A whipsaw is a quick reversal in the direction of the moving average line. A longer-term moving average will be more in tune with the longer-term trend and will lead to fewer whipsaws. However, the downside is that longer-term moving averages miss turning points by a wider margin.

The Basic Purpose of the Moving Averages

Moving averages are the most common, and one of the oldest, technical analysis tools used by the technician. The basic purpose of the moving average is to clarify the direction of the trend. An important point to remember is that moving averages will always lag price movement. However, one of the main values of moving averages is that they add context and significance to the current price. Is the current price continuing the direction of the moving average line, or is it indicating a change in direction, either up or down?

What many traders are really interested in is how the price is moving relative to its moving average (see Figure 8.4). Is it above a rising moving average and coming down? This would be a bearish sign. The crossing of price below an uptrending moving average is considered to be a sign of impending weakness.

Is the price below a falling moving average and going up? This would be a bullish sign. The crossing of price above a downtrending moving average is considered to be a sign of impending strength. As the moving average itself flattens out and begins to change direction, it will often confirm that a shift in the basic trend direction is occurring. Think of moving averages as a measuring tool to illuminate how the price is behaving currently compared to its overall trend.

Info/Tips

Moving averages are an important part of the technician's toolkit. They are useful in confirming other indicators and can give a trader confidence to move on a trend.

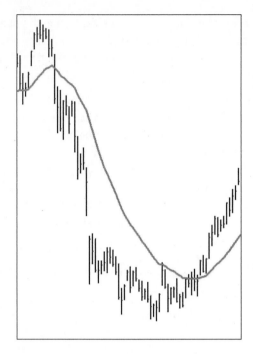

Multiple Moving Averages Add Confirmation

 The use of multiple moving averages on the same chart allows us to compare the short-term trend direction and magnitude with those of the longer-term trend. Traders generally look for agreement between the short- and long-term trend directions before taking a trading position.

One excellent rule of thumb that many traders use is that if the 20-bar moving average crosses the 40-bar moving average and then the two begin moving parallel to one another, we are in a strong trend and should only take a position consistent with the direction of that trend (see Figure 8.5). A favorite saying among traders is, "The trend is your friend. Don't fight the trend."

When the short-term trend direction is consistent with both the medium-term trend direction and the long-term trend direction, it significantly increases the odds of success for a trader who takes a position in the direction of those trends. Many trading systems utilize three moving averages of different lengths. They buy when the rising price first clears all three moving averages and take profits when the price first crosses below the nearest moving average.

Figure 8.5

An example of 20- and 40-bar moving averages crossing and then moving in parallel, signifying strong trending moves.

What Moving Averages Tell You

It can be said that a moving average is really a mathematical form of a trendline. Just as a trendline is drawn along price highs and lows, a moving average of price highs combined with a moving average of price lows can be used to form a channel enclosing the price trend. A moving average channel can meander like a river, however, while a trendline channel will always be straight. Moving average channels are often used by traders to identify levels where the probability is high that the short-term trend will reverse its direction and go the other way.

A rising moving average of the lows tends to follow below prices and serves as a floor below which uptrending prices should not fall. A falling moving average of the highs tends to follow above prices and serves as a ceiling above which downtrending prices should not rise. A skilled trader seeks to buy near a rising moving average at the bottom of the channel and sell near a falling moving average at the top of the channel.

Some traders lag the moving average plot behind price by one half of its length in order to center the average over its price interval. So a 50-bar simple moving average will be plotted with a 25-bar lag. Exponential moving averages are more heavily weighted on the right side, so a 50-bar exponential moving average will be shifted to about the thirty-fifth bar (see Figure 8.6). Making this shift often helps the channel to better fit the price trend. Most trading software gives you the option of shifting the plotting of the moving averages to the left or right.

Heads Up

Be careful to not fall into the trap of making the charts fit your idea of what should be happening with a stock's price. The chart is the truth.

Figure 8.6

A shifted moving average channel highs and lows on a daily chart of Apple Computer.

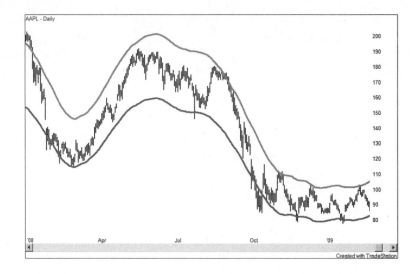

Using Moving Averages to Protect a Profitable Position

Because moving average channels provide an ongoing frame of reference with respect to price, they can be an effective way to protect a winning position and keep you from selling too soon. If you have bought a stock and are riding an uptrend, use a moving average line of the lows as a level where you would sell out your position if the price dropped to that point. Hold your position as long as the price does not break down through that line. If the price starts to round over and reverse direction, it would quickly catch the protective moving average line and get you out before you were in serious trouble. You would also avoid being whipsawed out of a good position because of small technical reactions and the temptation to sell out too early.

Trading with Moving Averages

Moving averages, like the other major tools of technical analysis, can give traders an edge in making profitable buy and sell decisions. They are guides to determining the long-term and short-term trend directions. Use moving averages to identify the direction of the trend and then trade in that direction.

One of the most important features of any moving average is its slope. Not only should you be looking at the actual slope of the moving average at any point in time, but also at the amount and direction of change in the slope. An upward-pointing moving average whose slope is getting steeper signals an increase in buying intensity and the likelihood of further strength. An upward-pointing moving average whose slope is decreasing, on the other hand, signals a reduction in buying interest and the likelihood of further weakness. If a moving average has not reached a new high or a new low in over a dozen bars, then the market is in a trading range.

When to Buy

Here are signs from your moving average charts that it is time to buy:

◆ The moving average has been declining and then levels off or advances, and the price breaks above the moving average.

◆ The moving average is rising, and the price has risen above the moving average, then drops down, touches the moving average, and reverses back to the upside.

◆ The moving average is declining, and the price falls too rapidly below the declining moving average. There's likely to be a snapback toward the moving average, so the stock can be bought for a quick technical profit.

When to Sell

Here are signs from your moving average charts that it is time to sell:

◆ The moving average has been rising and flattens out or begins dropping, and the price drops through the moving average.

◆ The moving average is dropping, and the price has been dropping below the moving average, then rises, touches the moving average, and reverses back to the downside.

◆ The moving average is dropping, and the price rises too fast and crosses sharply above the moving average. A second thrust back down to test the previous low is highly likely.

The Least You Need to Know

◆ Moving averages clarify trend direction by filtering out and smoothing price changes that are not significant to the trend.

◆ Simple moving averages are often slower to respond to changes in trend direction than exponential and adaptive moving averages.

◆ Technicians often use two or more moving averages of different lengths to identify and compare short-term and long-term trend direction.

◆ When prices cross their moving average, it often signals a possible change in trend direction.

Chapter 9

Understanding Oscillators

In This Chapter

♦ How oscillators are created

♦ Trading with oscillators

♦ The importance of price momentum

Technicians work hard at spotting trends and reversals. Tools that help a trader enter a profitable trade earlier or exit a losing situation sooner are the cornerstones of technical analysis. Oscillators help technicians see price changes before they happen. The various oscillators used by traders can help spot when prices are likely to reverse direction or continue on. This lead time helps traders make better and quicker decisions.

What Is an Oscillator?

Technical analysts use various tools that consider historical price and volume data of a stock to measure factors such as price trends, volatility, and momentum. Oscillators are important to traders because they often lead price by changing direction before the price changes direction. These factors are important to traders and help frame buy and sell decisions.

Oscillators are a type of technical analysis tool that is usually displayed in a separate subgraph below a price chart.

They are called oscillators because they oscillate up and down within a fixed range over and under a central line. That is, they don't follow a stock's price up and down a price chart like a trendline or a moving average; instead, they oscillate up and down from an upper overbought zone to a lower oversold zone. An oscillator chart can be compared to a football field, with the "red zone," the portion of the field between the 15-yard line and the end zone, being represented by the overbought and oversold zones on an oscillator chart.

Most oscillators are set up to operate over a range of 0 to 100, with overbought levels at 80 or 90 and oversold levels at 10 or 20. When the oscillator crosses above the overbought zone, it can be compared to an automobile exceeding the speed limit. If the oscillator crosses below the oversold zone, it's like an automobile going too slow for the prevailing traffic flow.

Types of Oscillators

In order to demonstrate and compare the various types of oscillator tools available to the technical analyst, throughout this chapter we will use as our example a daily chart of Netflix (NFLX) stock, covering a period beginning in late 2008 and extending through the end of the first quarter of 2009. This chart was selected because it displays a variety of price moves: a horizontal channel, a downtrend, and an uptrend.

The Momentum Oscillator

Technical traders can choose from many different oscillator tools. Let's begin with one of the simplest, the momentum oscillator. A momentum oscillator measures the speed, or rate of change, of price movement up and down. You can think of a momentum oscillator as a record of the speed displayed by the speedometer of your car over time. It doesn't tell you where you've been or where you're going; instead, it tells you how fast you were moving at any particular time. Truckers have a device called a "tattletale" that keeps a record of their speed history, which can be reviewed later by supervisors.

A momentum oscillator creates a similar type of record, noting the speed of prices over time. When the momentum oscillator rises to a new peak, it shows that crowd optimism is growing, and prices are likely to continue to rise. When the momentum oscillator drops to a new low, it shows that crowd pessimism is growing, and lower prices are likely ahead. When prices are rising but momentum begins to fall, it warns you that the price may be about to reverse course, and you'd better be thinking about taking your profit. When prices are falling but momentum begins to rise, it warns you that this may be a good time to buy.

The Value of Oscillators

 The great value of a momentum oscillator is that it is a leading indicator. That is, a reversal in momentum direction will occur before a reversal in price direction will occur. To understand why momentum can be of value in predicting market movement, let's use a simple example of momentum and price movement in a different context.

Imagine you are throwing a basketball up into the air and watching it come down again. You throw it straight up, watch it rise, slow down, come to a stop, and then reverse direction—at first slowly and then faster and faster until it hits the ground. Now think of the path of the basketball as price action on a chart. While the ball is in your hands and you are heaving it, it receives a force that accelerates it upward, increasing its velocity from zero to its maximum value at the point in time when the ball leaves your hands. At that point, gravity begins exerting a pull that gradually slows the ball until it stops moving upward and begins to reverse direction.

Now here's the interesting part. If we were to record and plot the change in the speed (momentum) of the ball versus time, we would see the momentum line initially rising as the ball accelerates until it leaves our hands. However, at the moment the ball leaves our hands and begins to slow down because of the pull of gravity, the momentum line will begin rolling over. The momentum line will gradually return all the way back to zero as the ball's upward velocity slows down and stops at the peak of the ball's arc. At the peak of its trajectory, as the ball starts to drop back down, the momentum line will cross below zero because the velocity is now negative.

What is important about this example is that if you track the movement of the ball (price), its momentum line actually predicts how it is going to move before it moves in that direction. That's because the momentum line begins to drop before the price itself actually stops going up and reverses its direction downward. In this way, momentum is a leading indicator and gives us an insight into the future movement of the ball or, in our case, the likely future movement of price. So if the price is going up and slowing in its upward trajectory, the momentum line will be turning down and will cross below zero when the price has reached its peak. This is why a momentum oscillator can be useful to the technician.

In the sample NFLX chart shown in Figure 9.1, a momentum oscillator is displayed below the price chart. It is measuring the speed and direction of price change. During the month of October, the price is dropping steadily, and the momentum line reflects this by the fact that it is in negative territory, below the zero line. However, by the end of October, the downward momentum of price has stopped, and the momentum line begins to reverse back toward the zero line.

The momentum line crosses above the zero line in mid-November, signaling an impending change in price direction at just about the time that price achieves a double bottom.

This is a signal to buy, and you can see from the price chart that price started to rise shortly afterward. Consequently, the momentum line stayed above the midline for the remainder of time of the example, confirming a continuation of the uptrend.

Figure 9.1

An example of a momentum oscillator.

You don't necessarily have to wait for the momentum oscillator to cross above its zero line before you get a reversal signal. For example, you could draw a downtrend line above a pair of oscillator highs during the September–October period. When the momentum oscillator eventually broke up through that line, it would have been an early sign that prices are beginning to turn up and that it might be a good time to buy this stock.

A New Technical Analysis Tool

In the previous chapter, we discussed the effectiveness of using the combination of a slow- and a fast-moving average (such as a 200-bar slow-moving average and a 50-bar fast-moving average) on a price chart. The fast average crossing above the slow average reflects the fact that price is accelerating upward and that it might be a good time to buy. If the fast average crosses below the slow average, it is an indication that prices are turning down and that it might be a good time to sell.

Now suppose we were to measure the distance between the two moving averages at each point in time and then display that distance value as an oscillator on a chart. When the two averages are crossing, the distance between them is zero, so the oscillator would be displayed as a point on the zero line of this new oscillator.

As the fast average begins to move upward away from the slow average because price is accelerating upward, the oscillator showing the difference between the values of the two averages begins to move upward also. The faster the two averages diverge, the higher the value of the oscillator based on the differences will be.

So with this oscillator we have designed, we are measuring the speed (momentum) and direction of price movement. The faster price moves, the steeper the slope of the oscillator line will be. Similarly, a downward price move would be reflected in the oscillator moving below the zero line at a level proportional to the downward momentum of price. This is similar to what a momentum oscillator would do, but now we are dealing with smoothed data, so the oscillator will not be as choppy as the raw momentum line.

The MACD Oscillator

This useful oscillator is referred to by technical analysts as the Moving Average Convergence/Divergence (MACD) oscillator since it is measuring the convergence or divergence between a short and a long moving average. To make it even more useful, many analysts add a moving average of the MACD line, referred to as the signal line, to smooth the MACD oscillator. A cross of the MACD line over or under (known as a *crossover*) its signal line usually means that the trend direction is reversing.

The response of the MACD line can be compared to a driver pressing down or letting off on his accelerator to change the speed of his vehicle. If the speed, or momentum, is constant, the MACD line will be relatively level. If momentum is accelerating, the MACD line will move upward. If momentum is decelerating, the MACD line will move downward.

def•i•ni•tion

A **crossover** occurs when an indicator moves through an important level or a moving average of itself. It is used to signal a change in trend or momentum.

Using the Signal Line

Figure 9.2 shows a MACD oscillator, along with its signal line, on the NFLX chart used earlier. In this case the oscillator is displayed as a solid line, while its signal line is displayed in the form of a histogram in order to more easily distinguish the two values from one another. A histogram displays information by using vertical bars extending upward and downward from the zero line at a length equal to the value of the signal line. The reason for this is simply one of visual clarity. For many traders, it is easier to visualize changes in the signal line value by viewing it as a histogram rather than as a line.

When the MACD line first crossed below the zero line in September, it hinted at upcoming weakness. The price weakness was confirmed by a second crossing below the zero line in early October and was further confirmed by a crossing below the oversold line at -1.

 However, in late October, the MACD line crossed above its signal line histogram and then above the oversold line. This was a clear signal of accumulating strength and was further confirmed shortly afterward by a crossing above the zero line in December. As the price continued to rise, the MACD lines confirmed the ongoing strength of the uptrend by remaining above the overbought line at +1.

Figure 9.2

The MACD oscillator cross-ing above the oversold line and the resulting price move upward.

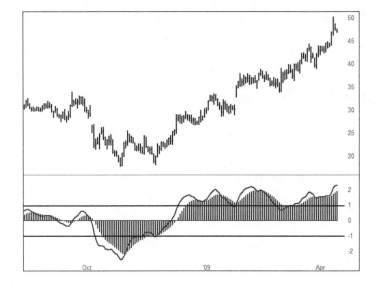

Using the MACD Oscillator

The MACD concept was first introduced in the 1970s by renowned trader Gerald Appel and has become one of the most popular technical analysis tools used by traders and investors in all markets. It is a featured indicator on almost every computer-based technical analysis charting platform.

According to Appel, "MACD is an indicator for all seasons. If monthly data is maintained, MACD can be used in the analysis of longer-term trends. It can be applied … in the analysis of intermediate and shorter-term market trends and on an intraday basis for time frames as short as hours or minutes. The indicator is frequently capable of producing precise entry and exit signals."

One of the strongest features of the MACD is its ability to detect the ends of trends and to identify favorable market entry points after a significant decline or favorable market exit points after a significant upward move.

Technical analysts like to watch for MACD values to climb above the overbought level and then to reverse below that level. This is a tip-off that the uptrend is slowing down and may be about to reverse, so traders should be considering selling. Conversely, if MACD values drop below the oversold level and then reverse back above it, traders consider that a propitious time to buy in anticipation of an acceleration move upward in price. An even stronger signal occurs when, after crossing the overbought/oversold lines, the MACD crosses its signal line.

Info/Tips

On multivalue oscillators, such as those comprising a fast line and a slow line, often the slow line will be drawn as a line and the fast line will be drawn as a histogram, as a way to distinguish them from one another.

Choosing MACD Average Lengths

What length moving averages should be used in the MACD calculation? There are no hard and fast rules. Anyone who tells you there is such an answer is full of beans and, I suspect, has a very high-priced trading course or system to sell you. Nonetheless, just remember that the long-term moving average length should be two or three times the length of the shorter-term average. The shorter the shorter-term average, the more sensitive the MACD indicator will be to small market fluctuations. A common length combination used by many technical traders is 12 bars for the short moving average and 26 bars for the long moving average.

What is the best way to decide which settings to use? It's very simple. Test a few settings on recent data and see which best meets your criteria for a useful indicator.

TA Intelligence

Price trends and momentum are key indicators for technicians. Oscillators give you an advantage in trading by signaling the probability of change in advance of an actual price change.

Advantages of the MACD Oscillator

The MACD oscillator offers the trader a number of advantages in simplicity and its advanced look. Since the indicator leads price changes, it is very helpful to traders. Here are some of the reasons they like it.

◆ MACD measures both price trend and momentum, where momentum can be thought of as the strength of the trend.

◆ If MACD is greater than zero, it suggests that prices are trending upward. Similarly, if MACD is less than zero, it suggests that prices are trending downward.

◆ The steeper the slope of the MACD plot, the more strongly the price is moving and, therefore, the stronger the momentum.

The important point to remember is that MACD signals usually are more timely and predictive of potential price direction changes than moving averages are by themselves. This is what makes the MACD oscillator so powerful and such a useful tool for traders in all time frames.

The Williams %R Oscillator

 In 1973, trader and author Larry Williams introduced an oscillator he called the Williams %R (pronounced "percent R"). It has been found to be particularly useful for identifying pullback buy points in an uptrend and pullback sell points in a downtrend.

The %R oscillator measures where today's closing price fits within the total range of the last 10 days. What do I mean by the total range of the last 10 days? The total range is the difference between the highest price reached in the past 10 days and the lowest price reached in the past 10 days.

Let's say we have a stock that traded as low as $50 over the last 10 days and as high as $60. Thus, the total range for the last 10 days is $60 minus $50, or $10.

Here's how that looks:

Day	High	Low
1	57	56
2	58	55
3	54	52
4	52	50
5	53	50
6	54	52
7	58	55
8	60	58

Day	High	Low
9	59	57
10	59	56

The highest high occurred on Day 8 at $60. The lowest low was on Day 4 at $50. The difference ($60 – $50 = $10) is the total range for this 10-day period.

Next we calculate how far today's closing price is below the high of the total range. Today's closing price is $59. In terms of percentage, the $59 price is $1, or 10 percent, below the top of the total range during the last 10 days ($60 – $59 = $1). If the stock had closed at $60, the retracement percent of the total 10-day range, the "%R," would have been 0 percent. If it had closed at $50, the retracement %R would have been -100 percent because the distance from $60 to $50 represents a 100 percent retracement of the distance from the top of the total range of $60 to the bottom of the total range of $50.

So to summarize, a value of -100 represents the fact that the close today was at the lowest low of the past 10 days, and a value of 0 represents the fact that the close today was at the highest high of the past 10 days. In an uptrend, %R values below -75 to -80 are generally considered to represent an oversold condition, while in a downtrend, values above -20 to -25 generally represent an overbought condition. Figure 9.3 shows how the %R oscillator anticipates price direction changes when it reaches the extremes of its range.

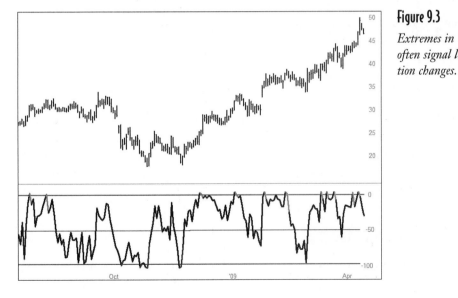

Figure 9.3

Extremes in %R readings often signal likely price direction changes.

How to Use the %R

In an uptrend, the rules for buying an oversold condition (a pullback) with the %R indicator are as follows:

♦ The longer-term trend is up, as shown by an upsloping moving average or high MACD reading.

♦ Price pulls back and %R reaches an oversold value of -100.

♦ Wait at least 5 bars since a value of -100 was last reached.

♦ During or after those 5 bars, %R must have crossed above and again below -90.

♦ When %R once more crosses above -90, buy.

In a downtrend, the rules for selling an overbought condition (a pullback) with the %R indicator are just the opposite:

♦ The longer-term trend is already down, as shown by a downsloping moving average or low MACD reading.

♦ %R reaches the high value of 0.

♦ Wait 5 bars since a value of 0 was last reached.

♦ During or after those 5 bars, %R must cross below and again above -10.

♦ When %R once more drops below -10, sell.

You can modify the 10-bar lookback number of the oscillator for either more sensitivity or smoother results. The more sensitive you make it, though, the more false signals you will get.

The fact that the %R oscillator is plotted on a negative scale, from 0 (highest) down to -100 (lowest) is a bit strange and confusing. Sometimes you will find a charting platform that changes the scale by adding 100, so don't be befuddled if you run into a %R chart displaying a scale of 100 at the top and 0 at the bottom. Just go with the flow. The %R lines will look the same in either case.

The Stochastics Oscillator

Another very popular oscillator among technical analysts is the Stochastics oscillator. The name is somewhat misleading, however. Webster's definition of a Stochastic process is "proceeding by guesswork." In reality, the Stochastics oscillator is based on a rigorous mathematical formula that would be tedious to calculate by hand but is a simple process for a computer to perform. Thus, it really didn't come into extensive popular usage until the advent of the personal computer in the 1970s.

Nowadays the Stochastics oscillator is a widely used technical analysis indicator available on almost every computerized charting platform. The theory behind this indicator is that, in an upward-trending market, prices tend to close near their high, and during a downward-trending market, prices tend to close near their low. Like many oscillators it consists of two lines, a fast line and a slow line, and we look for crossings of the fast line over or under the slow line to signal a change in trend direction.

In the Stochastics oscillator, the fast and slow lines are called %K and %D. The reason for these particular names is a mystery, as they don't tie at all into the characteristics or derivation of the two lines. In fact, the line called %K in the Stochastics oscillator is actually the same as the Williams %R line previously described, except that the scaling has been reversed (100 at the top, 0 at the bottom).

A 14-period %K, for example, performs its calculation by looking at where today's price closed with respect to the highest high over the last 14 periods and the lowest low over the last 14 periods. But in contrast to the Williams %R, it measures the distance of the close from the 14-period low instead of the 14-period high. (The number of periods, referred to as the lookback period, can be varied by the technician according to the sensitivity of the signals he wants to create, but 14 is a popular number that many technicians use.) The slow line, called %D, is usually a three-day simple moving average of %K. It acts as a signal or trigger line when crossed by %K.

Info/Tips _____

It is important to remember that technical analysis tools can be used on charts based on any time period. For example, you can use weekly or daily bars or, for the very short-term trader, hourly bars or five-minute bars. When technicians talk about "periods," they are referring to the time increment that one price bar encompasses, regardless of whether it is a day, an hour, or a minute.

Important Characteristics of the Stochastics Oscillator

What is unique about the Stochastics oscillator? First of all, it is a very fast oscillator. The Stochastics oscillator uses overbought and oversold zones (see Figure 9.4), plus a fast and slow line, just like the MACD does, but it functions in a different manner.

The characteristic of the Stochastics oscillator that stands out the most is its tendency to hang in the overbought zone in a strong uptrend and stay there while the trend is underway. When there is a strong downtrend, the Stochastics oscillator line will generally hang in the oversold zone while the trend is underway.

Another important characteristic of the Stochastics oscillator that you should be aware of is that the Stochastics oscillator generally does not reach the oversold zone on pullbacks in an uptrend or the overbought zone on pullbacks in a downtrend. Consequently, when the Stochastics oscillator hangs near the middle of the chart, the previous trend direction when it was oversold or overbought is still in effect.

Figure 9.4

Stochastics oscillator remains in overbought/oversold zones during strong trends.

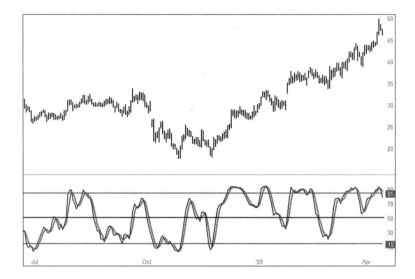

Stochastics Momentum Reversals

 When the fast line crosses the slow line, we call it a momentum reversal. It warns that prices are slowing down, which often leads to a subsequent change in price direction. If the %K crosses above the %D, it's called a momentum bullish reversal. If the %K crosses below the %D line, it is called a momentum bearish reversal.

In Figure 9.5, arrows point to the Stochastics momentum reversals; corresponding arrows on the chart indicate where the signals would have applied to the price.

Although the Stochastics oscillator was originated by a trader named Ralph Dystant in the late 1960s, it was popularized and promoted in the 1970s and 1980s by financial analyst George Lane, who later became known as the father of the Stochastics oscillator. A centerpiece of his teaching was the power of the divergence and convergence of trendlines drawn on Stochastics oscillators compared to trendlines drawn on price cycles to predict price tops and bottoms.

Figure 9.5

Bullish and bearish reversals in Stochastics momentum predict price direction changes.

Stochastics Divergences

 Technicians also watch for divergence between the direction of the Stochastics %D line (the slow line) and the corresponding direction of the price (see Figure 9.6). If the %D line is moving in an upward direction and the price is moving in a downward direction, it signals to technical traders that buying pressure is increasing, and the downtrend may be coming to an end. Conversely, divergence can also be used to signal a reversal in an uptrend when the %D line is moving downward while price is moving upward, signaling increasing selling pressure in the uptrend.

We will discuss divergence analysis in more depth in Chapter 10.

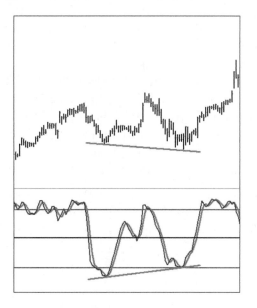

Figure 9.6

An example of divergence between Stochastics and price.

Wilder's Relative Strength Index (RSI)

No single tool is going to produce the right answers 100 percent of the time. A successful trader utilizes several different kinds of input in his or her decisions. Often the problem is in narrowing this input down to two or three things that work best for the trader.

While the MACD and Stochastics can help traders judge the strength of a trend and also identify when a new trend is beginning, another oscillator called the RSI is often used to help with timing when to get in and when to get out of a trade. The RSI can be a valuable input into this part of the decision-making process (see Figure 9.7).

Figure 9.7

Characteristic behavior of the RSI oscillator on the same price chart as that of the Stochastics oscillator in Figure 9.4.

The RSI oscillator is a type of momentum tool that determines overbought and oversold conditions on a price chart. It does this by comparing the size of recent upmoves in price to the size of recent downmoves in price over a given number of price bars. It then converts that information into a number value ranging from 0 at the bottom to 100 at the top. The RSI reveals whether a stock has seen more buying or more selling pressure over the selected time period. The most common RSI formula uses 14 bars as the basis for the calculation, but this can be adjusted to meet the needs of the user. As with other oscillators, if the number of bars used in the calculation is lowered, then the RSI will be made more volatile.

Because of its simplicity, the RSI is one indicator that is easy to understand intuitively. The calculation is simply based on the ratio of the average number of bars that closed above the previous bar's close to the average number of bars that closed below the previous bar's close over the selected time period.

The RSI was developed by J. Welles Wilder and was introduced in his 1978 book, *New Concepts in Technical Trading Systems* (Trend Research). The RSI's full name, Relative Strength Index, is actually rather unfortunate because it is easily confused with other forms of relative strength analysis such as John Murphy's relative strength charts and *Investor's Business Daily*'s relative strength rankings. Most other kinds of relative strength tools involve comparing one stock to an index or to another stock. However, the Wilder RSI only needs one set of price values to be computed: the close. And the comparison is between the relative number of up closes to down closes. In order to avoid confusion, however, many people avoid using the RSI's full name and just call it "the RSI."

How the RSI Is Used

There are two basic ways in which the RSI oscillator can be used to generate signals: crossovers and divergence. Crossovers of the overbought, oversold, and centerlines are used to generate buy and sell signals. In the RSI, the overbought line is typically set at 70, and when the RSI is above this level, the price is considered to be overbought.

The price is seen as oversold when the RSI is below 30. These values can be adjusted to either increase or decrease the number of signals that are generated by the RSI.

A buy signal occurs when the RSI crosses the oversold line from below the line to above the line. A sell signal is formed when the RSI crosses the overbought line from above the line to below the line. Using the football analogy again, think of a football player tied to a long bungee cord anchored at the 50-yard line. The closer he gets to the end zone, the greater the pull on the bungee cord is to force him back in the other direction. Similarly, the closer the RSI gets to extreme values of 100 or 0, the stronger the pull on prices is to move back in the opposite direction.

Another technique used by some technicians is to use a crossing of the RSI midline to confirm the direction of the trend. A downtrend is confirmed when the RSI crosses from above 50 to below 50. An uptrend is confirmed when the RSI crosses from below 50 to above 50.

Recent research by trading expert Larry Connors has shown the value of using an RSI period as short as two bars. This research shows that stocks that were overbought with a 2-bar RSI greater than 98 went down significantly within five trading days. Similarly, stocks that were oversold with a 2-bar RSI value of less than 2 rose significantly within five trading days. Figure 9.8 shows an example of the 2-bar RSI in action.

Figure 9.8

The arrows on the RSI oscillator point to where the 2-bar RSI touched the overbought and oversold lines, and the arrows on the price chart show the corresponding buy and sell signals.

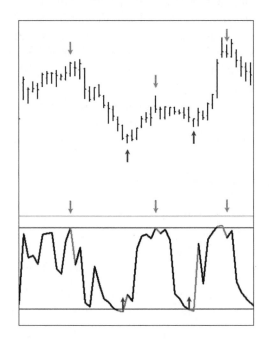

The Least You Need to Know

♦ Oscillators are technical analysis tools that oscillate up and down within a fixed range over and under a central zero line as a function of price volatility and direction.

♦ Oscillators can help traders understand the momentum driving price movement. Changes in momentum can signal a potential change in price direction—either up or down. They can also tell you whether or not the current trend is likely to continue.

♦ The value of oscillators to the technician is that they generally lead price in pointing the way to a change in trend direction. Oscillator signals can be generated in several different ways, but the two most popular methods are by looking for overbought-oversold zone crossovers or for divergence with price trends.

◆ The %R oscillator looks for overbought and oversold setups based on the relationship between the current bar's close and the distance between the highest high and the lowest low of a user-selected number of bars back.

◆ The Moving Average Convergence/Divergence (MACD) indicator is one of the most popular oscillators to analyze price momentum and trend. The Relative Strength Index (RSI) is a useful oscillator for timing entries and exits.

◆ The Stochastics oscillator is a fast-responding oscillator that hangs in the overbought and oversold areas during a strong trend and is often also used in divergence analysis.

Chapter 10

When Oscillators and Price Diverge

In This Chapter

- ◆ Divergence as a powerful technical analysis tool
- ◆ Comparing oscillators and price movements
- ◆ Understanding pivot and trend divergence
- ◆ Spotting trend reversal points

Timing is everything, and that is certainly true about trading. Knowing when or if price trends are going to change gives traders an edge. Technical analysis is a way to help you identify potential changes in the direction of the trend. This chapter has a very practical focus, with many tips and tools to improve your trading skills by identifying potential changes in price trends.

Using Oscillators

In the preceding chapter, we discussed the fact that there are at least three ways to utilize oscillators in the technical analysis process.

- ◆ Look for crossovers of the slow line by the fast line.

- ◆ Look for the oscillator to cross out of overbought or oversold territory.

- ◆ Look for divergences between the movement of the oscillator and the movement of the price.

 When an oscillator moves in the opposite direction from the price, we have what technicians refer to as a "divergence." Divergences occur when oscillator highs diverge from price highs or when oscillator lows diverge from price lows.

For example, consider the chart in Figure 10.1 of price and an oscillator such as the Stochastics oscillator. On the left of the price chart we see two price peaks, or "bumps," in a strong uptrend. Observe that the more recent bump is higher than the preceding bump. Now look at the two oscillator bumps occurring at the same time as the price bumps: notice that the most recent oscillator bump is lower than the oscillator bump corresponding to the earlier price high bump. If a trendline is drawn from one price bump to the next price bump and another trendline is drawn between the two corresponding oscillator bumps, the two lines can be seen to diverge away from one another. This is referred to as "divergence" and is usually a sign that the uptrend in price is losing steam and energy and that we may be approaching the end of the uptrend.

Figure 10.1

An example of bearish and bullish divergences.

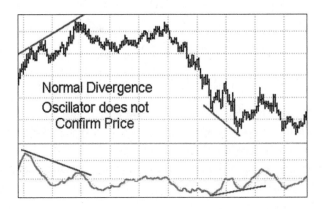

Normal Divergence
Oscillator does not
Confirm Price

Now let's look at the right side of the chart where prices have reversed and gone into a downtrend. This time the "bumps" are price valleys as prices pull back up from a price downthrust. A downtrend line has been drawn connecting two adjacent valleys in the price. Notice that the rightmost price valley is lower than the previous price valley, while at the same time the corresponding rightmost oscillator valley is higher than the previous oscillator valley.

Now let's draw a trendline from one price valley to the next price valley and another trendline between the two corresponding oscillator valleys. What do we see? We see that the two lines are pointing in opposite directions, converging toward one another. This is a sign that the downtrend in price is losing steam and energy and that we should be looking for an opportunity to buy instead of to sell.

Confusingly, most traders use the term "divergence" to refer to both of the conditions just described, even though the trendlines converge in downtrends and diverge in uptrends. Nonetheless, to conform to popular usage, we will be using the term "divergence" for the rest of the chapter to refer to both divergence in uptrends and convergence in downtrends.

Pivot Divergence

The two divergence examples illustrated in Figure 10.1 are referred to as "pivot divergence" or "normal divergence" patterns. Both names mean the same thing, and the patterns suggest an impending reversal in the direction of the major trend. Later in this chapter we'll discuss another type of divergence, "trend divergence," but for now let's focus on how traders use normal divergence.

Normal or Pivot Divergence

Price makes higher highs	Oscillator makes lower highs
Price makes lower lows	Oscillator makes higher lows

Figure 10.2 is a diagram to help you remember the definition of pivot divergence.

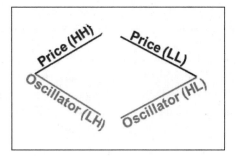

Figure 10.2

A pivot divergence diagram.

Remember, we look for bumps in the oscillator first and then look at price to see if they are diverging. In uptrends, we are looking for divergent oscillator highs. In downtrends, we are looking for divergent oscillator lows.

The most common oscillators used to look for divergence from price action are the Stochastics, RSI, and MACD oscillators, described in previous chapters. Like most technical traders who mix and match various indicators to find the perfect stew to unlock the pot of gold hidden in the markets, aficionados of the divergence concept combine divergence analysis with other indicators or theories to find reliable trade signals.

Deep Dip Double Divergence

One problem with divergence analysis is this: Changes in trend direction come in many sizes, from very brief to very deep, so the trader has to decide what kind of divergence pattern is most reliable for putting on a winning trade. When the price bars are in a strong uptrend and the oscillator hangs in the overbought zone, you will often see a lot of small divergences caused by "sloppiness" in the price wiggles. These false signals can cause a lot of frustration for the divergence trader, so we must use a set of rules that allow us to identify only significant divergence patterns that are likely to anticipate a major trend reversal.

For example, the diagram in Figure 10.3 is an oscillator divergence. The first major bump contains minor wiggles that should be ignored. We call that pattern a "prong." Once the oscillator crosses below the midline and back above it, we get a second bump that we call a "smoothie" because it is relatively smooth.

Figure 10.3

"Prong" and "smoothie" oscillator bumps.

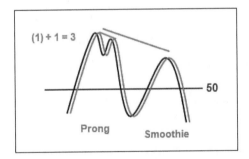

One of the most reliable ways to make sure your divergence signal is valid is to look for what is known as a "deep dip double" divergence pattern. The concept of the deep dip double was first introduced by trader and divergence expert Jay Dorger in the 1990s. The concept is to require that the oscillator must cross the midline between bumps to ensure that the divergence is big enough to be taken seriously.

Heads Up

Like many patterns, there is a danger that the technician will read into a chart what he or she has already decided the chart should say, which is to confirm the technician's idea. One of the key values technical analysis brings to trading is an objective look at prices. That value is lost if the trader only looks for confirmation of his or her thoughts. Remember, the chart doesn't lie.

A pure deep dip double looks something like Figure 10.4.

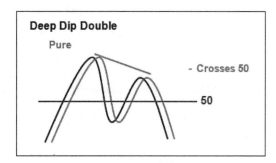

Figure 10.4

Example of a pure deep dip double.

Let's assume we are in an uptrend and are watching for a divergence pattern to signal the end of the uptrend and the beginning of a new downtrend. The first step is to look for a hill to form in the oscillator while it is above the midline. The oscillator should then move down and cross below the midline. Before reaching the oversold zone, the oscillator should reverse back up above the midline, forming a valley below the midline and above the oversold zone.

The oscillator should then create a second, lower, hill-shaped bump above the midline. When it again crosses below the midline while the price continues to reach new high levels, we have a strong sell signal.

Although the oscillator must display a pair of distinct successively lower peaks interspersed by a distinct valley below the centerline for an uptrend reversal signal, the prices, on the other hand, don't necessarily have to display recognizable peaks and valleys over that interval.

For a valid divergence in an uptrend to occur, the price corresponding to the most recent (lower) oscillator peak must simply be higher than the price corresponding to the previous (higher) oscillator peak.

For a buy signal in a downtrend, we must wait for an up-divergence to develop in the oscillator valleys below their midline. The first valley will have to break back above the midline before returning to create a second valley. After the divergence forms between the oscillator valleys and a downtrending series of prices, the next break above the midline confirms the divergence, and we have a strong buy signal.

Figure 10.5 is an example of a real price chart displaying both a deep dip double sell divergence at the end of the first uptrend and a deep dip buy divergence at the beginning of the next uptrend. The oscillator below the price is a Stochastics oscillator. The point on the price chart at which the divergence pattern on the oscillator was confirmed by a divergence recognition tool developed by Jan Arps' Traders' Toolbox is marked with a dot and a "DDD" symbol at the end of an automatically drawn trendline.

Figure 10.5

Deep dip double divergence confirms trend reversal points.

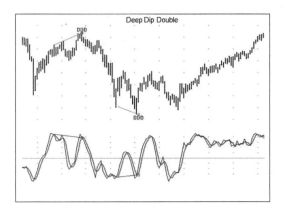

As you can see, divergence can be a very powerful tool in the hands of a skilled technical analyst to identify major reversal points in the price trends.

How to Look for Divergences

It sometimes takes a trained eye to quickly spot divergences between the price and an oscillator. Here's a reminder: always look for significant bumps in the oscillator first. Then look at price to see if these bumps are diverging from the price trend direction. In the oscillator, look for rising bottoms and falling tops. Then look for falling bottoms and rising tops in the price.

 You want to be quick in identifying oscillator bumps. If you wait until an oscillator bump is fully formed, known as a roundover, you may have lost the opportunity to get into a trade near the beginning of the trend. Many divergence traders don't wait for the roundover to look for significant oscillator bumps. Instead they look for crossings, where a fast line crosses the slow line near the top of the bump. If the developing bump is part of a pair that is diverging from price and meets our other qualifications, we have a strong and timely indication that prices are about to reverse direction when the fast line crosses the slow line.

Info/Tips

Mastering technical analysis takes time and practice. Identifying key indicators as they are forming comes with experience. The more you practice and study, the quicker technical analysis will become second nature to you.

In Figure 10.6, we see the fast oscillator line crossing below the slow oscillator line before the slow oscillator line actually rounds over. Consequently, the oscillator crossing signal occurs approximately three bars before the actual price peak. This gives the technical analyst enough time to set up for a trade when the next price bar makes a lower high.

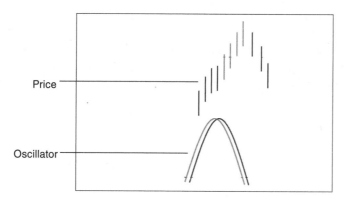

Price

Oscillator

Figure 10.6

Fast oscillator line crossing slow oscillator line sets up a divergence trade.

Triple-Bump Divergences

Double-bump divergences work well in oscillating markets, meaning markets where prices are moving sideways or gently trending. However, in strongly trending markets, double-bump divergence signals sometimes go astray and give signals before the end of the trend. One way to deal with this problem is to wait for a triple-bump divergence to confirm the end of the trend. Triple-bump divergences are just what the name implies: three bumps in the oscillator forming a diverging pattern with respect to the price trend, instead of just two bumps.

Figure 10.7 shows three different forms of a triple-bump divergence, depending on where the middle bump falls between its brothers on either side. When we work with triple-bump divergences, it's the first and third oscillator bumps that are significant. The middle bump can be either taller than the bumps on either side ("head-and-shoulders"), smaller than the first bump but bigger than the third bump ("straight three"), or smaller than both bumps on either side ("hunchback"). The important thing is that the first and third bumps must diverge from price. The position of the second bump is ignored.

Figure 10.7

With triple-bump divergences, ignore the middle bump.

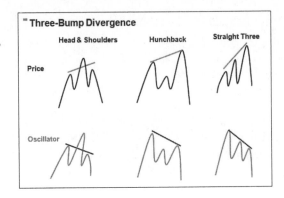

Triple-bump divergences are more likely to occur at the end of significant trends and less likely to occur in the middle of a trend. Figure 10.8 is an example of a price chart with the Stochastics oscillator displaying a deep dip triple buy divergence pattern near the bottom and a deep dip triple sell divergence pattern near the top.

Figure 10.8

Example of deep dip triple divergence patterns occurring at major tops and bottoms.

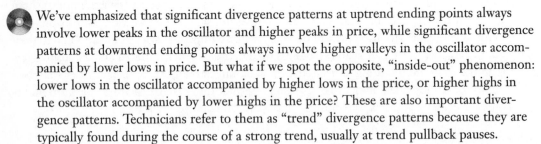

Trend Divergence

We've emphasized that significant divergence patterns at uptrend ending points always involve lower peaks in the oscillator and higher peaks in price, while significant divergence patterns at downtrend ending points always involve higher valleys in the oscillator accompanied by lower lows in price. But what if we spot the opposite, "inside-out" phenomenon: lower lows in the oscillator accompanied by higher lows in the price, or higher highs in the oscillator accompanied by lower highs in the price? These are also important divergence patterns. Technicians refer to them as "trend" divergence patterns because they are typically found during the course of a strong trend, usually at trend pullback pauses.

The trend divergence diagram (see Figure 10.9) shows the characteristics of a trend divergence pattern:

♦ A "trend" divergence pattern suggests the continuation of a trend

♦ Price makes lower highs (LH); Oscillator makes higher highs (HH)

♦ Price makes higher lows (HL); Oscillator makes lower lows (LL)

Some people call this pattern an inside-out divergence pattern, and a glance at Figure 10.10 shows you why.

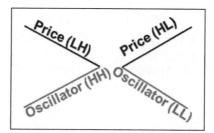

Figure 10.9

The trend divergence table.

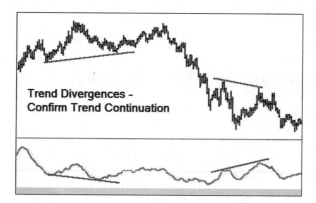

Figure 10.10

A trend divergence example.

Trend divergence patterns are telling us that the prevailing trend is still in effect and that it's not yet time to abandon your position, if you have one, consistent with the prevailing trend. Trend divergence patterns also highlight excellent places to enter a position consistent with the longer-term trend. Thus, by turning standard divergence analysis inside out and looking for trend divergence patterns, we achieve a powerful additional ability to trade divergences in the middle of a strong trend as well as at the end of a trend.

Here's a chart to help you keep track of the two types of divergence—pivot divergence and trend divergence:

Divergence Type	Price	Oscillator
Pivot divergence up	Lower lows	Higher lows
Pivot divergence down	Higher highs	Lower highs
Trend divergence up	Higher lows	Lower lows
Trend divergence down	Lower highs	Higher highs

Automatic tools for identifying divergence patterns are generally not available on most technical analysis platforms, but add-in divergence pattern recognition tools are available from several trading software providers, including the Arps AutoDiv program from Jan Arps' Traders' Toolbox (www.janarps.com).

Info/Tips

Spotting divergent price movement of correlated securities or indexes gives traders insight that something may be amiss. It is a useful strategy that may lead the technician to unsuspected trends.

Intermarket Divergence as a New Field of Technical Analysis

Divergence doesn't always involve oscillators. We can gain useful information by looking for divergence between two sets of prices. Maybe the Dow is diverging from the NASDAQ, or Exxon's price is diverging from British Petroleum. Based on linkages between related financial markets, the study of these kinds of divergences is called intermarket analysis and represents an area of growing interest for technical analysts who are looking for new and more sophisticated ways to trade the markets using computers and so-called neural networks. A leader in the field of intermarket analysis is Louis B. Mendelsohn at www.traderplanet.com.

The Least You Need to Know

◆ Divergence is a powerful tool to identify potential reversals in price direction. Waiting for a divergence signal can greatly help the trader with his timing.

◆ Look for divergent peaks and valleys in the oscillator first and then correlate them with corresponding points in the price.

◆ Divergences don't have to occur just between two adjacent bumps. Triple-bump divergences work well to identify the beginnings and endings of trends.

◆ Pivot divergence suggests potential trend reversal. Price makes higher highs, oscillator makes lower highs. Price makes lower lows, oscillator makes higher lows.

◆ Trend divergence suggests continuation of a trend. Price makes lower highs, oscillator makes higher highs. Price makes higher lows, oscillator makes lower lows.

◆ Looking for trend divergence is one way of confirming the continuation of an existing trend and overcoming the problem of fighting the trend with pivot divergence signals.

Trading with Point-and-Figure Charts

In This Chapter

- ◆ Ease of use
- ◆ Understanding patterns
- ◆ Price targets
- ◆ Price warnings

Technical analysis can be overwhelming to the novice. There are many charts and patterns to learn and apply. However, if you take one bite of the apple at a time, you'll find becoming a technician is easier than it may appear at times. One of the ways you can keep your enthusiasm up is to begin with simple tools and work up to the more complicated ones. In this context, point-and-figure (P&F) charts are just what the doctor ordered. These charts are easy to create and, more importantly, easy to master. P&F charts focus on price and make it easy to visualize a lot of information quickly. This is a great tool for beginners to gain confidence and, at the same time, have a powerful tool to help with trades—and that's the point.

A Simple and Powerful Form of Charting

P&F charts can be an extremely effective market analysis tool. They reveal an interesting context to the market. The philosophy of their construction isolates and emphasizes the price action that propels the market to new highs or lows and also those price levels that stopped the market in its tracks. P&F charts are also very useful in identifying likely price target levels.

The nice thing about P&F charts is that they are relatively simple to use and interpret. Particularly for someone just beginning in technical analysis, a P&F chart simplifies the visualization of the market swings. The subjectivity inherent in other techniques, such as vertical bar charts, disappears. Basic P&F chart patterns are easy to spot and interpret. Price movements above a previous top generate a buy signal, while falling prices that penetrate an earlier bottom generate a sell signal.

P&F trendlines are always drawn at 45-degree angles, and traders usually look for trendline breakouts and multiple top and bottom patterns for trading signals. Simple buy and sell patterns such as double and triple tops and bottoms, symmetrical triangles, low poles and high poles, and others are easy to spot. They either appear on the charts or they do not. Little is left to the imagination, so problems of interpretation are minimized.

The construction of a P&F chart was reviewed in Chapter 3. You may recall from that discussion that time is not a consideration in a P&F chart. An up bar consists of a column of X's. The space occupied by each X or O is called a box (see Figure 11.1). As long as the price is rising, we continue to add an additional X to the top of the most recent column of X's every time the price increases by a given amount, say $1.

Figure 11.1

An example of a typical P&F chart.

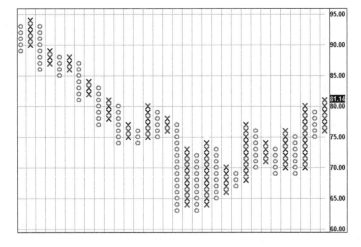

A new bar begins when the price reverses direction by at least three X's, say $3. If we were in an uptrend, signified by a column of X's, and prices reverse into a downtrend by at least $3, a new downtrend column is begun, signified by a declining column of O's. The first O box of a new down column is always plotted one box below the highest X box in the previous column. Similarly, the first X box of a new up column is always plotted one box above the lowest O box in the previous down column.

If you are drawing a P&F chart and the last column is a column of X's, it is telling us that the current trend is up. The alternating columns of X's and O's reflect the interplay of supply and demand. As sideways price movements continue with additional columns of X's and O's, an overall state of equilibrium exists between supply and demand. Buy and sell signals from P&F chart patterns reflect a change in the balance between supply and demand.

Info/Tips

P&F charts are unusual in that they don't consider a time element. The focus is on price and changes in direction, which emphasizes the importance of price to new technicians.

Upside and Downside Breakout Patterns

The simplest P&F pattern is the double top or double bottom. The logic is straightforward. The highest X in a series of columns represents a potential trouble spot for future price advances. This level is usually referred to as a resistance level. Any move that exceeds a top or series of tops can be called an upside breakout because it penetrates previous resistance areas where selling was anticipated (see Figure 11.2).

Conversely, the lowest O in a series of columns represents a potential stopping point for future price declines. This level is usually referred to as a support level. Any move that breaks below series of O's can be called a downside breakout because it penetrates previous support areas where buying was anticipated.

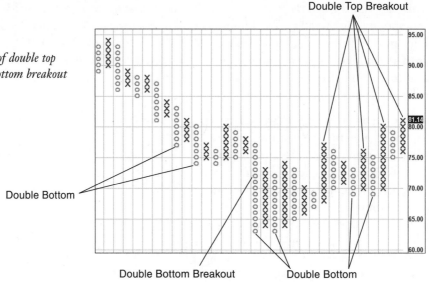

Figure 11.2

An example of double top and double bottom breakout patterns.

Double Top and Bottom Reversal Patterns

Double top and double bottom reversal patterns occur when an existing trend consolidates and then reverses direction. For example, in Figure 11.3, the price has been in a consolidation range between 69 and 76. A double bottom was formed at 69, followed by a sharp reversal to the upside. A buy signal occurs at 77 when the price breaks above the highest X of the previous up-column.

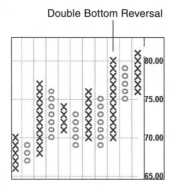

Figure 11.3

An example of a double bottom reversal.

Heads Up

P&F charts are one of the easiest to read and understand, but make sure you are letting the chart tell you what is happening and avoid spinning conclusions to fit how you think the price should act.

Determining the Box Size

You determine what amount of price movement constitutes one box on a P&F chart by considering the price and volatility of the stock you are trading. For example, for a $50 stock that moves up or down $5 in a month's time, we may choose $1 for our box size. On the other hand, for a $10 stock that moves up or down $1 in a month's time, we may choose a smaller box size (for example, 25¢) in order to display enough "action" to create a meaningful chart.

Typically, each box below $5 carries a value of 25¢. Boxes between $5 and $20 carry a value of 50¢, while boxes between $20 and $100 carry a value of $1. Above $100, most analysts use a box size of $2 or $5.

To illustrate the box size concept, Figure 11.4 shows a P&F chart of Apple, Inc. (AAPL). This stock was trading around $100 a share in early 2009 when the chart was created. Using a $5 box size gives us a good view of the stock's action over the past six months without cluttering the chart with too much extraneous detail.

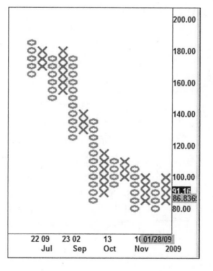

Figure 11.4

A sample P&F chart using a $5 box size.

The chart is clearly in a downtrend and shows a series of three double bottom breakout signals at 160, 145, and 120. Another double bottom breakout at 90 led to double bottom support at 80. The last four columns show that the stock is in a consolidation zone with a double bottom at 80 and a double top at 100. A breakout to one box above 100, or 105, would be a buy signal, and a breakout to one box below 80, or 75, would be a sell signal.

In contrast, the AAPL P&F chart in Figure 11.5, based on a $1 box size and covering approximately the same time period, is much more difficult to interpret with its greater volatility and numerous whipsaw moves, so it's important to select a workable box size.

Figure 11.5

A sample P&F chart using a $1 box size.

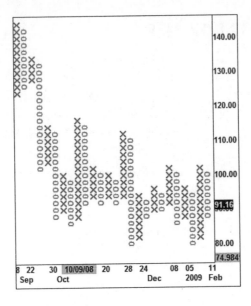

Since P&F charts are time independent, you may wonder why there are dates along the bottom of these charts. Notice, however, that the dates on these charts are not evenly spaced. They are there simply as a point of reference to give the user an idea as to when a particular column was completed and a reversal to the next column was initiated.

Stocks that are not so volatile may require a much wider consolidation pattern (more short columns) before reversing into a trend in the opposite direction. Triple, quadruple, and more tops or bottoms may form before a breakout occurs. Many times in a triple or quadruple top consolidation you will see higher or rising bottoms, further reinforcing the transition from bearishness to bullishness.

> **TA Intelligence**
>
> How do you determine the best box size? One way is to try different values and see if the resulting chart drawn by your trading software is meaningful. Trading or charting software makes this type of experimenting easy.

Support Levels

Support levels are price levels at which buyers have entered the market in the past and have stopped the price drops. Double bottoms represent a simple support level. Triple, quadruple, and greater multiple bottom formations indicate stronger and stronger buying at the support level. Based on this past support of the price at the support level, traders expect more buyers to enter the market the next time price again drops to the support level. Support levels are easily identified on P&F charts by multiple columns of O's bottoming out at the same level (see Figure 11.6).

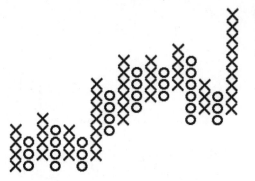

Figure 11.6

P&F support levels are easily identified.

Resistance Levels

Resistance levels are price levels at which sellers have entered the market in the past and have stopped price rises. Based on this past resistance to higher prices at the resistance level, traders expect more sellers to enter the market the next time price again rises to the resistance level. Resistance levels are easily identified on P&F charts by multiple columns of X's topping out at the same level (see Figure 11.7).

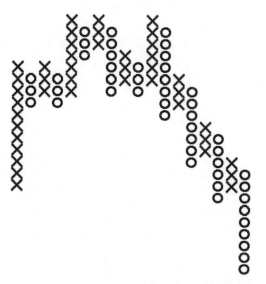

Figure 11.7

When penetrated, resistance levels often become future support levels.

If a strong support level does get penetrated by several boxes, any pullback move back up usually stops, or at least pauses, at that old support level. When support levels often become levels where subsequent rising prices will find resistance, we call these resistance levels (see Figure 11.8).

Figure 11.8

When P&F resistance levels become support levels.

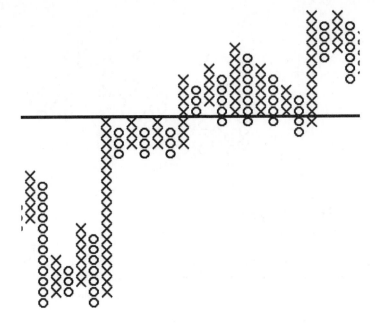

Breakouts

Any time prices break through a resistance level, it's a bullish signal, and prices are likely to continue to move higher (see Figure 11.9). Conversely, any time prices break through a support level, it's a bearish signal, and prices are likely to continue to move lower (see Figure 11.10).

Figure 11.9

A breakout above a resistance level is a bullish signal.

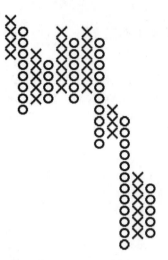

Figure 11.10

Penetration below a support level is generally bearish.

Bullish and Bearish Signs

When you encounter penetration of a support or resistance level, examine the preceding columns to look for supporting evidence to confirm the validity of the breakout. What should you look for? If you see a pattern of rising columns of O's preceding a bullish breakout, that is further confirmation that the breakout is probably the beginning of a strong move upward (see Figure 11.11). Conversely, if you see a pattern of declining columns of X's preceding a bearish breakdown, that is a further confirmation that the breakout is probably the beginning of a strong move downward.

 Info/Tips _____

Technicians are very concerned about patterns that indicate a change and then present other confirming signs. These confirmations don't guarantee an action, but they do signal that the odds have increased that the change is coming.

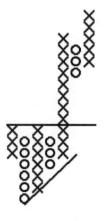

Figure 11.11

Rising columns of O's give strength to a bullish breakout.

Trendlines on P&F Charts

Trendlines are very helpful and powerful tools on a P&F chart. They identify the direction of the current overall trend. P&F trendlines are always drawn at 45-degree angles, extending to the right from significant price peaks and valleys. The basic rule with P&F trendlines is always to trade in the direction of the trendline. A trendline penetration is a strong signal to trade in the direction of the penetration.

The specific rule for drawing a new P&F trendline is this: To draw a downtrend line from a P&F high, wait until you spot a double top breakout followed in the next column by a double bottom breakout. In other words, look for a column of X's that exceeds the high of the previous column of X's (a double top breakout). If the next column of O's breaks below the previous column of O's (a double bottom breakout immediately after a double top breakout), draw a 45-degree trendline starting at the upper-right corner of the column of X's and passing through the upper-right corner of the top of the column of O's to its right, extending downward to the right.

Similarly, an upward-pointing trendline can be drawn any time we see a double bottom breakout followed immediately by a double top breakout, as illustrated by the arrows in Figure 11.12. The upward trendline should be drawn starting at the lower-right corner of the column of O's and passing through the lower-right corner of the column of X's to its right, extending upward to the right.

Figure 11.12

An example of 45-degree P&F uptrend and downtrend lines.

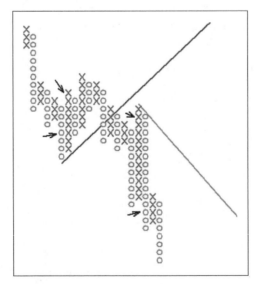

Figure 11.12 illustrates the construction of a pair of P&F trendlines. In the case of the uptrend line, the arrows to the left point to a double bottom breakout followed by a double top breakout. Thus, a new uptrend line can be drawn connecting the bottoms of the lowest column of O's and the next column of X's.

An uptrend line will always be first penetrated by a column of O's and a downtrend line by a column of X's. Thus, a sell signal would have been generated at the first double bottom breakout after the column of O's crossed below the uptrend line.

In the case of the downtrend line in the example, the arrows on the right point to a double top breakout followed by a double bottom breakout. Consequently, a new downtrend line can be drawn connecting the tops of the highest column of X's and the next column of O's. So long as prices stay below the downtrend line, the trend should continue to stay down.

All trendlines should extend across the entire page because they serve as a reference point for future areas of support and resistance. Beware if a double top breakout occurs within one or two boxes below a downtrend line. There is a high probability that prices will reverse back down as they approach the trendline. Similarly, if a double bottom breakout occurs within one or two boxes above an uptrend line, watch out! There is a high probability that prices will reverse back up.

Heads Up

Traders should pay close attention to the P&F chart rules that indicate a high probability of change. These are profit opportunities (or signals to avoid or reduce a potential loss).

As long as a P&F trendline remains intact and is not penetrated, long-term traders should only trade in the direction of the trendline. On the other hand, if a double bottom breakout occurs below an uptrend line, be ready for a major further move down. If a double top breakout occurs above a downtrend line, look for a major move up.

Triangle Patterns

Another important P&F pattern is the symmetrical triangle. A triangle on a P&F chart, like a triangle on a bar chart, is like a coiled spring gathering energy for a breakout. For a valid triangle to occur, there must be at least two retracement columns counter to the prevailing trend: two columns of O's in an uptrend or two columns of X's in a downtrend.

To trade a triangle, follow the breakout. When price breaks out of a triangle formation, it usually does so with great force and momentum. Figure 11.13 is an example of a P&F triangle formation with a breakout to the upside.

Figure 11.13

A P&F triangle formation with a breakout to the upside.

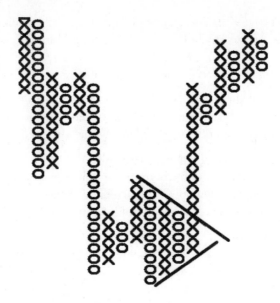

High and Low Pole Formations

A P&F high pole formation is a price spike with a sharp reversal. It occurs when a column of X's rises above a previous high by three or more boxes and then reverses to give back at least 50 percent of the rise. The price reversal to the downside implies the demand that was making the prices rise has given way to supply pressure. A high pole formation is a warning that lower prices could be seen in the future (see Figure 11.14). The more extended the upthrust move, the stronger the downside reaction is likely to be.

A low pole formation occurs when a column of O's drops below a previous low by three or more boxes but then reverses back up by at least 50 percent of the drop (see Figure 11.15). The reversal implies that the excess supply that was making the prices drop has given way to demand pressure. The pattern is a warning that higher prices could be seen in the future. High poles and low poles are also referred to by some analysts as "catapult" formations since prices pull back after the pole is completed and consolidate before being catapulted in the opposite direction from the pole formation.

If you are new to technical analysis and are intimidated by oscillators and other sophisticated technical analysis tools, you may well want to consider beginning your voyage into technical analysis by studying and working with simple P&F charts.

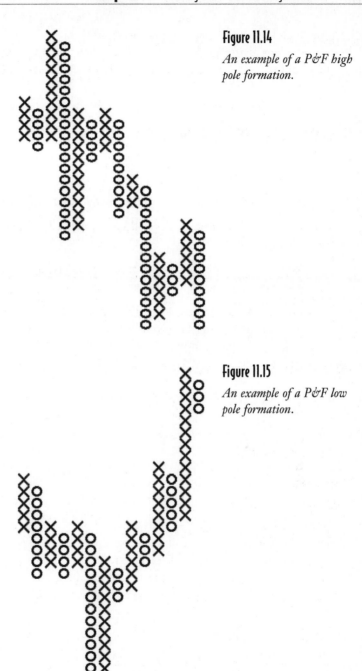

Figure 11.14

An example of a P&F high pole formation.

Figure 11.15

An example of a P&F low pole formation.

Not all computerized charting platforms offer the option of creating P&F charts, but two excellent platforms that do are eSignal (www.esignal.com) and TradeStation (www. tradestation.com). P&F pattern recognition tools for TradeStation are available from www. janarps.com.

The Least You Need to Know

- P&F charts represent one of the simplest methods of charting and interpreting stock price behavior.

- Buy and sell signals are created by penetrations of previous tops and bottoms.

- Levels at which price highs and lows previously stopped are known as resistance and support levels.

- Movements above tops and bottoms are called breakouts because they eliminate previous areas of support or resistance.

- P&F charts contain two major trendlines—bullish support lines (uptrend) and bearish resistance lines (downtrend). Valid trendline penetrations warn of impending significant trend direction reversals.

Chapter 12

Price and Volume as Key Indicators

In This Chapter

◆ Greedy bulls and fearful bears

◆ The importance of volume in technical analysis

◆ Volume patterns

◆ Tools to measure volume-price behavior

Thus far in this book, we have focused our attention on ways to look at and interpret price behavior. After all, traders and investors ultimately are looking for ways to profit from price changes, so it's natural to look at price behavior first. However, the number of shares traded during a specific period can have a meaningful effect on current and future prices. Technical analysts believe that the number of shares trading hands during a given time period can be as important in figuring out which direction price is headed as the examination of price trends and patterns.

How Volume Information Helps Traders

Think of volume as the fuel behind a market move. Is the gas tank full and providing powerful momentum for that Corvette speeding down the interstate? Or is the gas tank nearing empty, making the engine sputter and slow down and the car limp toward the shoulder of the road? For a trader who is looking to put on a stock trade, having an idea how much gas is likely left in the tank is an important consideration.

 Volume information is plotted on a chart as a series of vertical bars whose height reflects the volume associated with the corresponding price bar (see Figure 12.1). This form of chart, referred to as a volume histogram, is usually displayed directly below the main price graph.

Figure 12.1

A price chart of the S&P 500 index showing volume bars in the lower subgraph.

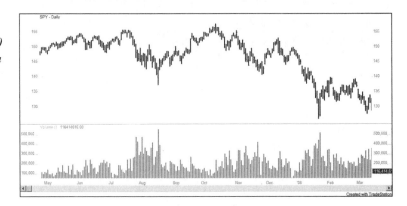

Info/Tips _____

The New York Stock Exchange (NYSE) and the NASDAQ measure volume differently. For every buyer there is a seller, so for every purchased share there is a sold share. The NYSE counts the buy and the sell together as one trade with one share of volume. The NASDAQ, on the other hand, counts this transaction as two shares of volume, one each for the bought and the sold shares. So much for consistency in the marketplace!

What Volume Analysis Can Tell Us

Since volume movements reflect the activity of buyers and sellers, volume information helps traders study market liquidity and puts price movements into context. Changes in volume reveal how traders react to price swings and provide clues as to whether trends are likely to continue or to reverse. An imbalance between sellers and buyers creates the supply and demand for shares that leads to the movements up and down of price as the balance shifts in one direction or the other.

Bulls, Bears, and Volume Behavior in Trending Markets

 In the trading world, participants are often considered to be either bulls or bears. Bulls are buyers. They buy because they expect prices to go up. Bears are sellers. They sell because they expect prices to go down. But within each of these two categories there are two more subcategories that characterize their motivations for buying and selling: greedy and fearful. We have greedy bulls, fearful bulls, greedy bears, and fearful bears, and each has different reasons for buying and selling.

When prices are rising, greedy bulls are buying in hopes of making a profit by selling the shares they purchase today at higher prices later. On the other hand, when prices are falling, the motivating force for the fearful bulls is to sell their holdings in order to avoid, or at least minimize, a loss if prices continue to fall. Greedy bulls anticipate a profit when prices rise and fear a loss if prices fall.

Greedy bears, on the other hand, expect to profit by selling at a high price before prices begin to fall and then buying the shares back later at lower prices. Those greedy bears will become fearful bears if it appears that they are going to lose money because prices rise instead of falling as they expected.

If prices do rise, many fearful bears will rush to buy shares to cover their short positions. This creates further demand, thereby flushing out more fearful bears, and the process feeds on itself. At the same time, greedy bulls, sensing an opportunity to profit from rising prices, join the feeding frenzy of buying, driving prices ever higher and further increasing the volume of shares traded.

At some point in the uptrend, most of the fearful bears will have given up on their short positions and run for cover, and some of the buying enthusiasm of the greedy bulls will have tapered off. As a result, volume begins to decline. That is usually a sign that the end of the trend is near and a reversal is about to occur.

A similar process drives volume up when a downtrend begins. Greedy bears and fearful bulls both feel that prices are too high and begin selling. Fearful bulls bail out of their long positions, while greedy bears are selling short. This usually leads to increasing volume as the price decline accelerates.

Greedy bulls buy from fearful bears; fearful bulls sell to greedy bears. So there is always the yin and yang of fear and greed driving every trade transaction.

As a rule of thumb, a trend that moves on steady volume or increasing volume is likely to continue. At some point, though, as a trend reversal is about to occur, a decrease in volume often signals the approaching end of the trend.

Figure 12.2 illustrates the daily price and volume behavior of Google stock over a seven-month period from September 2008 through April 2009. The histogram bars display each day's volume, while the line on the volume chart represents the 21-day moving average of volume.

Figure 12.2

The daily price and volume behavior of Google stock over a seven-month period from September 2008 through April 2009.

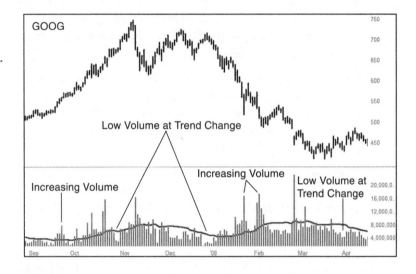

From September through November 2008, prices are in a strong uptrend, and volume continually increases as buyers rush in. However, just before the sharp drop in November volume declines dramatically, foretelling a possible change in trend direction.

As the price of Google begins to drop sharply in early 2009, volume again increases as the downtrend gains strength and sellers rush for the exits. By April, several low-volume days signal a possible end to the downtrend.

TA Intelligence

Do you find terms with multiple direction words confusing—for example, "rising volume in a downtrend"? The more you work with technical analysis, the easier the language becomes.

Volume Behavior in Sideways Markets

So far we have addressed volume behavior in uptrending and downtrending markets. But markets are not always rising or falling. They often spend much of their time moving sideways. Usually in sideways markets volume is lower than in trending markets because investors tend to avoid trading stocks that are in the doldrums.

If the price should break out above a sideways channel on steady or lower volume, chances are that the move won't go very far. Normally, in a valid price breakout, you would expect the losers to run for the exits, thus increasing the volume of shares traded. A breakout on low volume shows a lack of commitment to the new trend and increases the odds that prices will soon return to their original trading channel.

If the first breakout of the channel is accompanied by a large increase in trading volume, however, it may indicate the possible beginning of a new trend. But be careful. Many times it proves to be a "fakeout breakout," and the price will reverse and break out of the other side of the channel instead. How can we tell which one it will be? Well, we need to wait to see if within a bar or two the breakout falters and price pulls back into the sideways channel. This does not necessarily mean that the breakout has failed. If the pullback is soon followed by another breakout in the same direction as the previous breakout, then in all likelihood we are seeing the beginning of a valid new trend.

Figure 12.3 is an example of a stock trading within a horizontal channel. You might be tempted to buy this stock at the support level of 16, but it would not be advisable for two reasons:

♦ The stock could continue to trade in the 16–19 range for a long time while your money is tied up.

♦ The stock price could break downward, putting you into a potential losing situation.

In mid-March, the price knocks at the door of the resistance level of 19. It knocks four times before finally breaking through the resistance on relatively low volume. The next bar confirms the breakout on higher volume, and the resistance level of 19 now becomes a support level, thereby confirming the breakout.

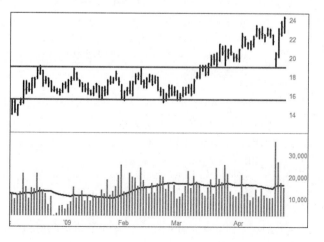

Figure 12.3

Stock trading within a horizontal channel.

Climaxes and Blowoffs

 Now for the exciting stuff: blowoffs and climaxes. No, this doesn't refer to some kind of exotic mating ritual. Blowoff volume patterns tend to occur near major market peaks, while climax volume patterns occur near market bottoms. These terms refer to large price moves accompanied by significantly greater-than-average volume. They usually occur near the end of a major market move and are followed by an abrupt price reversal.

One of the important things to recognize is that blowoff tops and climax bottoms do not necessarily signal the absolute end of a trend. Volume has a strong tendency to peak out ahead of price in both uptrends and downtrends. Trend highs and lows are almost always retested on lower volume, leading to a double bottom or double top pattern. A *retest* of a blowoff top, for example, consists of a high-volume peak, a moderate-volume pullback, and then another upward surge but on much lower volume. More often than not this second, and final, surge will slightly exceed the earlier blowoff top.

def•i•ni•tion

A **retest** occurs when the price encounters resistance, pulls back, and then again tries to cross through the resistance level. If price is unable to break through the resistance level, it is referred to as a failed retest. If price does break through the resistance zone, it is referred to as a successful retest.

Info/Tips

In the majority of past bull markets, the volume high did not occur at the price peak but some months before.

Conversely, if the market falls to a new low and the volume reaches a new high, that price bottom is likely to be retested before a true trend reversal takes place. Such a climax bottom is almost always retested on low volume, offering an excellent buying opportunity.

In Figure 12.4, we see a buying volume blowoff in early July prior to the final surge in late July towards a peak. Conversely, in early August we see a selling volume climax occurring prior to the trend low, which occurs in mid-August on lower volume. In Figure 12.5, a daily chart of Broadcomm, notice that the large volume bar does not occur at the lowest bar in the trend but several bars before it.

Trading Volume Breakouts

Volume breakouts often occur when an unexpected news event spawns a dramatically greater amount of buying and selling in a particular stock. The best way to identify volume breakouts is to compare the current bar's volume against its moving average. For example, some traders define a volume breakout as any circumstance when volume exceeds its five-day moving average by more than 50 percent. One of the basic rules of thumb for traditional volume analysis is that a healthy uptrend will see expanding volume on up days and contracting volume on down days. Declining volume during an uptrend is a warning flag.

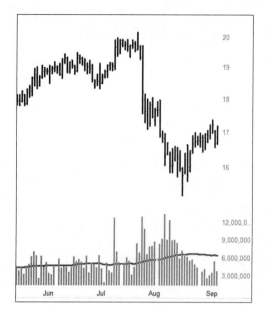

Figure 12.4

A price chart with a buying climax.

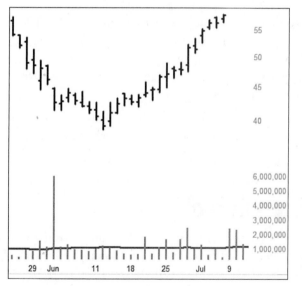

Figure 12.5

A price chart with a selling climax.

Heavy volume in an uptrend without a corresponding move in price can signify a possible change in price direction. For traders who may have missed an entry opportunity on a breakout, they should watch for the stock's price to retreat on declining volume. That may offer a second entry opportunity to enter a trend move at a lower price.

Rules of Thumb for Volume Analysis

Like most technical analysis tools, volume analysis relies on some common understandings of what changes in volume mean. Here are some guidelines:

1. If prices close up for the day on higher volume than yesterday, it often is a sign of institutional buying. That's bullish. The higher the stock closes in its daily range, the more significant the buying pressure.

2. If the range of the day is wide and the stock gives up most of its intraday gains and closes near the bottom of the range, distribution has occurred. That's bearish.

3. A close lower than the previous day's close on an increase in volume over prior-day volume is called a distribution day. Net selling by the smart money appears to be occurring. That's bearish.

4. If the price range of the day is wide and the stock regains most of its intraday losses and closes near the top of its range, accumulation has occurred, negating the session as a distribution day.

5. The weaker the volume relative to the average daily volume, the less significant the price move for that day. The greater the volume, the greater the likelihood that the trend will continue in the same direction as the high-volume bar. If you are holding a long position, you want to see the price move up on strong volume, while pullbacks should occur on light volume. Gains on light volume and pullbacks on heavy volume in an uptrend would be bearish.

6. Heavy volume with little net price change after an extended run or near new highs indicates churning and could signal a top, particularly if this continues to occur over several bars.

Volume-Based Analysis Tools

There are a wide variety of volume-based analysis techniques that the technical analyst can employ to sharpen his or her ability to trade the markets more effectively. In this section, we will explore three different approaches to volume analysis.

On-Balance Volume

In the 1960s, investment guru Joe Granville introduced a new technical analysis tool he called On-Balance Volume (OBV). This tool keeps a running total of up volume minus down volume to indicate the strength or weakness of the price movement at any point in time by highlighting the amount of volume supporting the move.

To calculate the OBV line, Granville examined each price bar to determine if its close was higher than the previous bar's close. If it was, then that bar was labeled an "up" bar. If the bar's close was lower than the previous bar's close, it was labeled a "down" bar.

A running OBV total is then maintained by adding or subtracting each bar's volume, depending on the direction of the market close. If the bar is an up bar, we take the amount of volume associated with that price bar and add it to the running OBV total. If the bar is a down bar, we take the amount of volume associated with that price bar and subtract it from the running OBV total. The resulting OBV indicator is then plotted as a line graph across the bottom of the price chart.

> **TA Intelligence**
>
> The OBV indicator is useful in determining if more investors are buying or selling a security. This information can confirm that a change or continuation of price trends is coming.

Using On-Balance Volume

The OBV line has the virtue of tending to lead price. Consequently, traders look for situations where the OBV line begins diverging in direction from price. If price is in a downtrend and the OBV has also been in a downtrend but now begins to turn upward, it is a sign of hidden strength in the market that often leads to a change in price trend from down to up. Conversely, if price is in an uptrend and the OBV has also been in an uptrend but now begins to turn downward, it is a sign of hidden weakness in the market, usually leading to a change in the price trend from up to down.

To more quickly identify turns in the OBV line, traders often draw a trendline on the OBV line just like on a price chart. Any time there are divergences between the direction of the OBV and the prevailing direction of price, traders should be on the alert for a potential trend change in price.

Figure 12.6 is a daily chart of the S&P 500 Index displayed along with its OBV line. Note the upsloping trendline above the price bars and the downsloping trendline above the OBV line during December. The declining OBV was revealing hidden weakness in the S&P that led to a major decline during the first quarter of 2009.

In early March, while price was declining steeply, the OBV leveled off, revealing the growing strength of the smart money buying into the decline. This flattening of the downtrend forecast the strong rally beginning during the March and April period of 2009.

Over the years, the OBV concept has spawned a number of modified and improved versions of this indicator, including Elder's Force Index, the Williams Market Facilitation Index, the Chaikin Money Flow Index, the Twiggs Money Flow Index, the Arms Index (TRIN), and the Herrick Payoff Index. These additional volume-based analysis tools are beyond the scope of this book but are referenced in Appendix B for those traders wishing to learn more about them.

Figure 12.6

A daily chart of the S&P 500 Index with its OBV line.

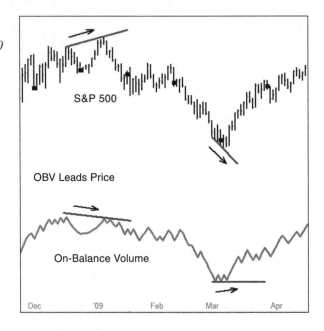

S&P 500

OBV Leads Price

On-Balance Volume

Dec   '09   Feb   Mar   Apr

Info/Tips _____

Technical analysis is ripe with tools to help you make better trades. As you become more familiar with the basic tools, you'll want to explore the more complicated possibilities.

The Volume Oscillator

In Chapter 9, we described the Moving Average Convergence/Divergence (MACD) tool, which is a very effective oscillator in detecting changes in price trends. It is driven by the difference between two moving averages of different lengths. The MACD concept can also be applied to a volume chart, in which case it is referred to as the volume oscillator. It turns out to be very useful in measuring changes in volume that can give us a clue as to the strength or weakness of the existing trend.

The volume oscillator measures the distance between a fast- and slow-moving average of volume. This distance, the fast-moving average of volume minus the slow-moving average of volume, is then plotted as an oscillator. Like other oscillators, it will move up and down on either side of a centerline as the difference between the two moving averages changes from a positive number to a negative number and back again.

Using the Volume Oscillator

 If prices are in a strong uptrend or downtrend, the volume oscillator should be rising. When the oscillator is trading with a positive value (that is, above the zero line), it is a sign that volume is increasing and that there is enough market support to continue driving the price in the direction of the current trend. Near the end of the trend, the oscillator will begin flattening and then will reverse its direction.

When the volume oscillator is trading below the centerline, it is a sign of decreasing volume support for the current trend. In an uptrend, increasing price accompanied by decreasing volume is always a bearish sign. If the volume oscillator drops below its oversold zone while prices are trending upward, the end of the uptrend is almost inevitable.

Similarly, in a downtrend, lower prices accompanied by decreasing volume is always a bullish sign, as the fearful bulls have all left the scene licking their wounds and the greedy bulls have not yet stepped in to begin buying. Once the volume oscillator drops below its oversold zone while prices are trending downward, the end of the downtrend is in sight.

Figure 12.7 is an example of the volume oscillator in action below a corresponding daily chart of the Dow Jones Industrial Average. To illustrate the use of the volume oscillator, we have drawn thick vertical lines on the chart showing the point in time where the volume oscillator crossed above its zero line, indicating that a trend (either up or down) is underway. A thin vertical line is drawn to indicate when the oscillator crosses below its zero line, signaling a weakening or disappearance of the trend.

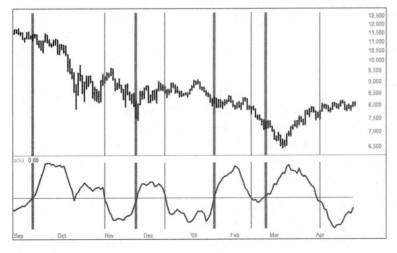

Figure 12.7

An example of the volume oscillator.

The oscillator did a good job of identifying the downtrends occurring in October 2008 and February 2009. It also identified the beginning of the shallow uptrend in December

def•i•ni•tion

Sensitivity setting is a term used to describe how aggressive or conservative a technician is when determining what conditions must be met for the chart to indicate a significant action.

2008. During the March–April period of 2009, we saw a sharp reversal from a strong downtrend to a strong uptrend, and the oscillator stayed above its centerline because the trend in both directions was quite strong.

A typical *sensitivity setting* for the volume oscillator is 14 bars for the fast average and 28 bars for the slow average. Less conservative traders often use lower settings such as 5 bars for the fast and 20 bars for the slow-moving averages.

The Arps Radar 1 Fear-Greed Index

In 1996, Jan Arps' Traders' Toolbox introduced a new volume-based oscillator called the Fear-Greed Index. This tool displays the relative strength of the bulls and bears at any point in time.

It accomplishes this task by combining price and volume information into one oscillator that provides an insight into volume-based forces that drive and lead price movement. To do this, it keeps track of the amount of volume it takes to move price up compared to the amount of volume it takes to move the price down an equal amount at any specific point in time.

 The Fear-Greed Index does this by calculating the relative friction of the market in the bullish direction as compared to the friction in the bearish direction. For example, if it takes half as much volume to move the price up one point than it does to move the price down one point, then we can say that there is 50 percent less friction to the upside than to the downside. Thus, the bulls have more power to move the market than the bears do at that particular time.

Imagine trying to push a boulder. It takes a great deal of effort to move it when the ground is dry. Now make the ground and the boulder more slippery by adding a little water to the ground in front of the boulder and the friction is reduced, making it easier to move the rock. In the markets, if it takes 10,000 shares to move a stock down one point and only 3,000 shares to move a stock up one point, then the bulls are overpowering the bears: there is less friction to the upside than to the downside.

The Arps Radar 1 Fear-Greed Index tracks this bull-bear imbalance and plots it as a set of histogram bars in its own subgraph. When price moves up on less volume than the volume required to move the price down, it means that there is reduced friction to the upside—greed is overpowering fear. To indicate this, the histogram bars extend upward from the zero line. The stronger the fear-greed imbalance showing increased bullish activity, the taller the histogram bars are.

On the other hand, if it takes less volume to move the price down than it does to move the price up, it means we have reduced friction to the downside. In that case, the indicator bars will extend downward from the zero line. The stronger the fear-greed imbalance showing increased bearish activity, the longer the indicator bars pointing down.

Figure 12.8 illustrates the behavior of the Fear-Greed Index in an uptrend. On the left side of the chart, before the beginning of the major uptrend, we see a double bottom pattern being formed by price. The downward-pointing indicator bars signify that the bears are in control. However, shortly after the double bottom, the bulls begin to outnumber the bears and drive the index above the zero line. At that point the bulls have clearly taken over control, and the uptrend continues to strengthen on increasing strength in the Fear-Greed histogram bars.

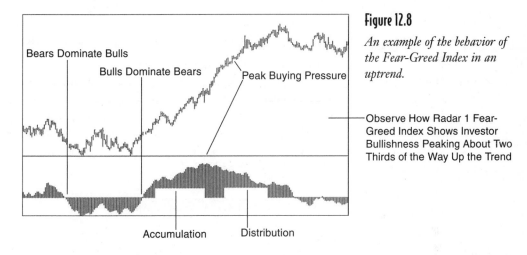

Figure 12.8

An example of the behavior of the Fear-Greed Index in an uptrend.

Observe How Radar 1 Fear-Greed Index Shows Investor Bullishness Peaking About Two Thirds of the Way Up the Trend

Note that the peak buying pressure does not occur at the peak of the trend. The buying pressure begins tapering off about two thirds of the way up the trend while the price is still continuing to work its way upward. This is typical of the Fear-Greed Index. Its behavior at this point signifies distribution by the smart money that is beginning to take its profits. The dumb money is rushing to get on the train after it has already left the station. By the time the smart bulls have gotten rid of all of their shares, the bullish pressure subsides, prices level off and begin to weaken, and the Fear-Greed Index drops below zero.

The Fear-Greed Index serves as an excellent trend exhaustion and reversal indicator in all kinds of markets. It is a powerful *leading indicator* because it usually begins to turn before

def•i•ni•tion

Leading indicators signal changes before they occur. Leading indicators are highly valued by technicians. However, they are not as certain as indicators that plot what has just happened. Still, leading indicators are valuable trading tools.

the price does. It reveals the exhaustion of the bulls or bears while the price is still moving up or down of its own momentum. If a sudden move in price is not confirmed or antici-pated by a similar move in the Fear-Greed Index, it usually means a fake-out swing has occurred and represents a move to be ignored or faded.

The Fear-Greed Index often creates a characteristic double peak or double valley pattern that diverges from price prior to a major price reversal. When a Fear-Greed Index indica-tor valley is shallower than its predecessor while the corresponding price valley is deeper than the price corresponding to the prior indicator valley, a diverging condition exists that generally signals an imminent price reversal to the upside. Conversely, when a Fear-Greed Index peak is lower than its predecessor while the price corresponding to the most recent Fear-Greed Index peak is higher than the price corresponding to the previous Fear-Greed Index peak, a diverging condition has occurred that generally signals an imminent price reversal to the downside. If the pattern is a smooth up-and-down curve uninterrupted with a minor dip, on the other hand, chances are the existing trend will continue further.

In Figure 12.9, an example of the Fear-Greed Index in a downtrend, we see an initial mildly bullish phase indicated by the upward-pointing bars in the indicator. When the bars begin pointing downward the bears have taken over from the bulls, and as the market decline accelerates, the bearish down-pointing bars grow longer. Despite a sharp rally in the middle of the downtrend, the Fear-Greed Index bars continue to point downward, confirming that the downtrend is still intact, offering sellers another opportunity to add to their short positions.

Figure 12.9

An example of the Fear-Greed Index in a downtrend.

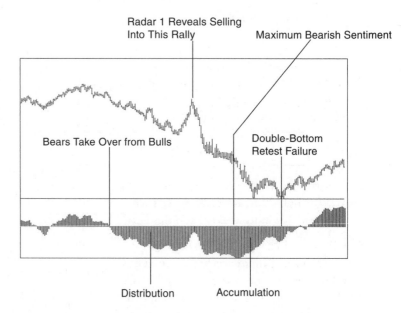

Maximum bearish sentiment occurs at about three quarters of the extent of the entire downtrend. At this point, the indicator reveals that the bulls are beginning to step in and take over from the bears. Price puts in a double bottom retest failure while the indicator shows a bullish divergence from price. When the indicator again crosses above the zero line, it represents an ideal buying opportunity.

For more information about the Arps Radar 1 Fear-Greed Index, go to www.janarps.com.

The Least You Need to Know

♦ Volume fuels the market moves. Volume analysis can tell traders whether or not it is the right time to change their market position.

♦ Market volume is affected by the behavior and expectations of greedy bulls, fearful bulls, greedy bears, and fearful bears.

♦ A healthy uptrend will see expanding volume on up days and contracting volume on down days.

♦ Volume usually increases as the price breaks out of a formation or pattern, and a large increase in volume provides a strong buy signal.

♦ OBV is one tool for combining price change with volume behavior to determine the strength and validity of a trend.

♦ The Arps Radar 1 Fear-Greed Index measures bullish or bearish strength by keeping track of the amount of volume it takes to move the price up compared to the amount of volume it takes to move the price down an equal amount at any specific point in time.

Volume Float Analysis

In This Chapter

- ◆ Understanding float analysis
- ◆ Using float boxes for better trades
- ◆ Float channel lines for support and resistance
- ◆ Trading float box breakouts
- ◆ The importance of follow-through days

In 2000, market technician Steve Woods introduced the concept of volume float analysis to the technical analysis community as a new method to combine volume, time, and price to identify stocks ready to make a major move. The Woods Cumulative Volume Float Indicators, more commonly referred to as "float charts," help to give visual form to the expression, "The smart money buys at the bottom and sells at the top; the dumb money buys at the top and sells at the bottom." The smart money traders are those who buy and sell at exactly the right time; the dumb money traders are those who buy and sell at exactly the wrong time.

Float charts also are an effective way to give visual form to such important technical terms as accumulation, distribution, support, resistance, bottoms, and tops. According to Woods, accumulation occurs when the smart money is buying and the dumb money is selling. Distribution occurs when the smart money is selling and the dumb money is buying. Support is a price level where there are more buyers than sellers and prices stop declining. Resistance is a price level where there are more sellers than buyers and prices stop rising. Bottoms are the lowest price levels reached in a market swing. Tops are the highest price levels reached in a market swing.

As technical indicators, float charts often lead or coincide with significant changes in a stock's price direction and thus serve to identify high-potential buying and selling opportunities.

Float Chart Parameters

While most stock charts focus on a stock's price and the volume of shares traded, float charts also incorporate something called a stock's float number, or floating supply of shares. The float number represents the total number of shares of a specific company actually available for trading. A stock's float is defined as the difference between the total number of shares outstanding and the number of shares owned by insiders. The easiest way to think of this is to imagine a company that comes public and issues a large number of shares. Of those shares, it sells some to the public, and the company insiders keep the rest. The shares that are sold to the public and are actively being traded are commonly referred to as the floating supply of shares, or simply the float. The rest of the shares, which are closely held, are not included as part of the float as they are normally not being actively traded.

The Float Box

The principal indicator used in float analysis is known as the float turnover box, or simply the float box. It is displayed on a price chart as a rectangle whose top and bottom are shown as two heavy horizontal lines. The horizontal width of the box represents the amount of time it has taken for the cumulative total number of shares traded to equal the total number of shares in the floating supply. This process is referred to as one float turnover. The upper and lower boundaries of the box reflect the highest and lowest prices reached by the stock during the time interval of the most recent float turnover. The box represents the shortest amount of time that a stock's float could completely change ownership. Thus, it gives us a way of estimating the time it would take for a complete turnover of ownership of the stock to occur.

A stock's current float box is plotted on the far right of a price chart. It gets replotted and moves to the right on a day-to-day basis. To calculate the horizontal length of the float box we start at the right end of the chart and record the volume associated with the current price bar. We then add the previous day's volume, and that total is, in turn, added to the next previous day's volume, and so on, backward in time until the cumulative total is equal

to the number of shares in the stock's floating supply. We then look back over that time
interval and find the highest price and the
lowest price reached during that time interval.
We then draw the horizontal top and bottom
lines of the float box through those two price
levels over the period of time represented by
the float turnover period.

The float chart software that calculates the
float box on a stock chart offers the user the
ability to perform historic analysis to calculate
and plot a float box starting from any bar in
the past. When the box is moved back in historical studies, it can illustrate how the float
box appeared at the time of long-term tops and long-term bottoms.

Info/Tips _____

Stocks that are actively
traded—that have heavy daily
volumes—may turn over their
float in a matter of days. Other
stocks, particularly those with very
large amounts of stock outstanding,
may take much longer to generate
sufficient trading volume to turn
over their entire float.

For example, Figure 13.1 displays a weekly float chart of Ralph Lauren Polo (RL), which
in 2007 had a floating supply of 58,300,000 shares. The float box at the top of the chart
was created by adding volume cumulatively starting from the bar of July 27, 2007, backward to the bar of May 4, 2007.

Figure 13.1

*A sample weekly float chart
of Ralph Lauren Polo (RL).*

The following table contains the volume numbers for each week during this time span and
the cumulative totals that were used to construct the float box.

Week Ending	Number of Shares Traded	Cumulative Total
1) 7/27/07	5,559,100	5,559,100 is < 58,300,000
2) 7/20/07	2,669,200	8,228,300 is < 58,300,000
3) 7/13/07	3,324,900	11,553,200 is < 58,300,000
4) 7/06/07	2,022,400	13,575,600 is < 58,300,000
5) 6/29/07	3,693,900	17,269,500 is < 58,300,000
6) 6/22/07	6,548,800	23,818,300 is < 58,300,000
7) 6/15/07	3,729,600	27,547,900 is < 58,300,000
8) 6/08/07	5,088,600	32,636,500 is < 58,300,000
9) 6/01/07	6,816,500	39,453,000 is < 58,300,000
10) 5/25/07	3,981,200	43,434,300 is < 58,300,000
11) 5/18/07	3,586,700	47,020,900 is < 58,300,000
12) 5/11/07	3,714,500	50,735,400 is < 58,300,000
13) 5/04/07	5,698,500	56,433,900 is < 58,300,000
14) 5/11/07	4,358,800	60,792,700 is > 58,300,000

It is during the fourteenth week of the backward count that the cumulative total volume traded equals the float number, and by the end of that week it has exceeded 58,300,000 shares. On a weekly chart, the float box is therefore created from the beginning date of July 27, 2007, over to the week ending May 4, 2007. The upper and lower lines of the box are then placed at the highest and lowest prices during the 14-week time frame.

The float box is an easy way to show where the change of ownership occurred right at the top as the smart money was selling its shares to the dumb money. The principle is similar for stocks making bottoms after long-term price declines. Right at the bottom, the dumb money sells its shares to the smart money. The smart money accumulates the floating supply of shares when they are the biggest bargains. Once the float has been accumulated, any new demand drives the price of the shares higher.

The float chart of Trina Solar Ltd. (TSL) in Figure 13.2 is an example of accumulation at the bottom of a down move. By adding cumulatively the number of shares traded during the 13-day float box period at the bottom of the move we can see that the number of shares traded equals the number of shares in the float. This is an excellent example of the case where the smart money is buying from the dumb money.

Heads Up

Float boxes illustrate what happens when traders think with their guts instead of their heads. Fear is a powerful emotion that can make traders do exactly the wrong thing at the wrong time. Float box indicators offer visual proof of frightened traders. Fear of loss or fear of not getting in on a good thing shortens many traders' careers.

Figure 13.2

An example of an accumulation at the bottom.

The Float Channel Lines

The second part of float analysis is the creation of two channel lines: the 100 percent and 50 percent float channel lines. These lines are used to find support and resistance levels where a stock's price is likely to change direction. The 100 percent float channel lines are created by using the total float number; the 50 percent float channel lines use one half of that number. Both the 100 percent and 50 percent float channel lines are created by plotting the prices represented by the upper-right corner and the lower-right corner of the float box as it is plotted each day on a day-to-day basis. The resulting channel lines show the tracks the float box has made in the past. The easiest way to understand how the float channel lines are created is to think of the float box as a railroad car that moves forward each day by laying down new track. The tracks then trail behind the float box as it moves forward day after day.

TA Intelligence

Support and resistance are key technical analysis concepts that show up in a number of commonly used indicators. Resistance indicates previous prices at which buyers quit buying. Support indicates previous prices at which sellers quit selling. Neither are made of stone, but when they are breached it often indicates the beginning of a new price move.

For example, consider Figures 13.3 and 13.4 which are both based on the same weekly chart of Ralph Lauren Polo (RL). Figure 13.3 shows the 100 percent float channel lines, and Figure 13.4 shows the 50 percent float channel lines. The 50 percent channel lines are shown as dotted lines to distinguish them from the 100 percent lines, which are solid lines. Notice also that the gray float boxes on both charts are in their most recent position, at the far right of the chart. In normal practice, the 50 percent float box (as seen in Figure 13.4) is not shown. It is only shown here to demonstrate how the 50 percent float channel lines are based on the upper-right and lower-right corners of the 50 percent float box. Ralph Lauren Polo's float is 55.9 million shares, so the 50 percent float box would be based on 27.95 million shares, which is one half of 55.9 million shares.

Figure 13.3

An example of 100 percent float channel lines.

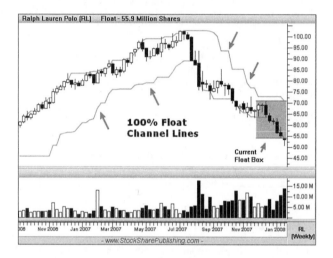

Figure 13.4

An example of 50 percent float channel lines.

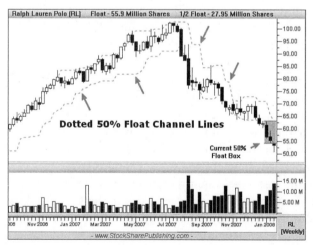

Normally the 100 percent and the 50 percent channel lines are not isolated on separate charts but instead are placed together in one integrated format. They have only been separated here to clarify how each is made. So let's look at a normal float chart that combines them together.

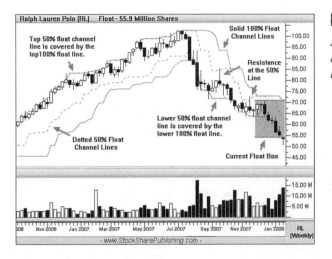

Figure 13.5

An example of 50 percent and 100 percent float channel lines.

Figure 13.5 shows the 50 percent and the 100 percent float channel lines as well as the 100 percent float box, which is at the far right of the chart. Notice that whenever the 100 percent channel lines overlap the 50 percent line, the solid line is given preference, and it covers the dotted line and hides it from view. When a stock is trending higher, the dotted lower 50 percent line is visible, and when a stock is trending lower, the dotted upper 50 percent line is visible. Also notice that the 50 percent float box has been removed from the chart. There is no need to see it because it is the channel lines that are useful. The current 100 percent float box, on the other hand, is always plotted on a float chart. This is because it gives us an easy way of looking at the current status of the stock. It is especially valuable for analyzing breakouts and breakdowns and the volume behavior within the float box.

Potential Buy and Sell Signals

Imagine the price of a stock going lower and lower over several weeks. As the price dropped, it would continually break below the lower line of its float box. If you were convinced that the company had a great future and that the decline in its price was only temporary, then you would be looking to see the stock's price turn around and head higher.

Info/Tips _____

Knowing when to enter and when to exit are among the most important decisions traders make. The decision when to buy and sell has an important and obvious influence on whether you make money on a trade or not. Technicians look for indicators that will help them with this decision. Float boxes are one of those indicators.

But how would you determine a good entry point to buy the stock? Float charts can help you find potential entry points because, if the stock is going to turn around and head higher, it will have to stop going through the lower line of its float box, and it will have to break out above the top of its float box. This would potentially indicate that the stock had been accumulated by the smart money and was now headed higher. This is exactly what happened with Trina Solar (TSL). After a long decline, its price pierced the top line of its float box (see Figure 13.6).

Figure 13.6

An example of price piercing the top line of the float box.

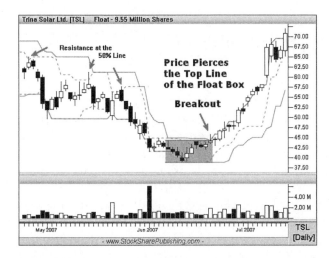

Now imagine the price of a stock going higher and higher over several months. As the price rises, it continually breaks above the top line of its float box. If you were convinced that the company had a bleak future and the stock's high price was only temporary, you would be looking to sell the stock when its price turned around and headed lower.

But how would you determine a good entry point to sell the stock? Float charts can help you find potential sell points because, if the stock is going to head lower, it will have to stop going through the upper line of its float box, and it will have to break down below the lower line of its float box. This would potentially indicate that the stock had gone through distribution to the dumb money crowd and was now headed lower. This is exactly what happened with Ralph Lauren Polo (RL). After a long rise, its price pierced the lower line of its float box (see Figure 13.7). This was a signal that the stock was no longer breaking above its float box but was now breaking below it.

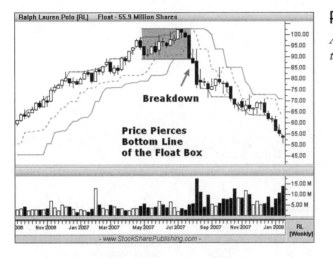

Figure 13.7

An example of price piercing the lower line of the float box.

False Breakouts and Breakdowns

If all we had to do to make money using float charts was simply wait for a stock in a down trend to break out above the top line of its float box and then after a big price rise simply to sell it when it broke below the lower line, then float charts would be the holy grail of all technical analysis indicators. Unfortunately, making money in the stock market is not that easy.

Just because a stock breaks out above its float box after a long decline doesn't mean its price will continue to move higher. In fact, breakouts often have a tendency to do just the opposite. Look at Figure 13.8 of U.S. Steel (X). From what we've discussed so far, it looks as though it is headed higher because it has just broken out above a float turnover box at a long-term bottom. Now look at Figure 13.9, 13 days after the initial breakout. U.S. Steel was 45 percent lower!

The same is true for stocks that break below the lower line of the float box after a long price rise. Look at Figure 13.10 of AMR Corp. (AMR). It looks as though it is headed lower because it has just broken down below a float turnover box after a long price rise. Now look at Figure 13.11. Sixteen days after the initial breakdown, AMR Corp was 34 percent higher!

Figure 13.8

An example of a false break-out at the bottom.

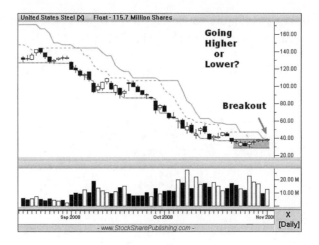

Figure 13.9

An example of a false break-out going lower.

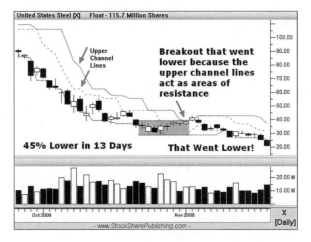

Figure 13.10

An example of a break below the float box.

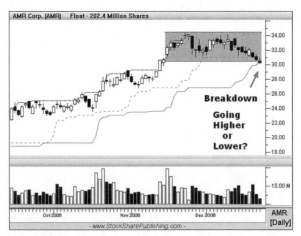

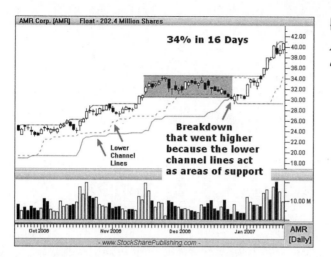

Figure 13.11

An example of a false break-down.

Solving the False Breakout Dilemma

The solution to the false breakout dilemma can be summed up in one word: patience. When a breakout or a breakdown occurs, the key is to *wait for at least one or more days of confirmation in which the stock has what is called a follow-through day on high volume.*

A follow-through day on high volume occurs when a stock's price direction is confirmed by volume that is substantially greater than its average float volume. The average float volume is the average number of shares traded per day during the period of one float turn-over. For example, if a float box is 20 days long and during the 20 days, 200 million shares traded, the average float volume would be 200 million shares divided by 20, or 10 million shares. Thus, if the price breaks out of the float box, wait to see if a follow-through day occurs where trading significantly exceeds 10 million shares before taking the trade.

Two examples of follow-through days on increased volume that led to large profitable moves can be seen in Figures 13.12 and 13.13.

As shown in the preceding examples, float charts are an exciting new charting tool that can give us a better insight into the relationships between volume, price support, and price resistance. As a result, float charts are rapidly gaining popularity as a valuable tool to help investors and traders in their search for profitable trades. You can find more information about float charts at www.floatcharts.com.

Figure 13.12

The breakout above AEM float box is confirmed two days later on above-average volume.

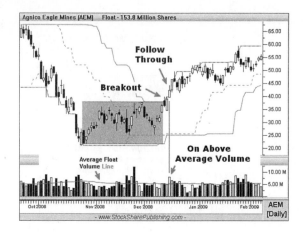

Figure 13.13

After the breakout above LVS float box, two follow-through days on above-average volume confirm its validity.

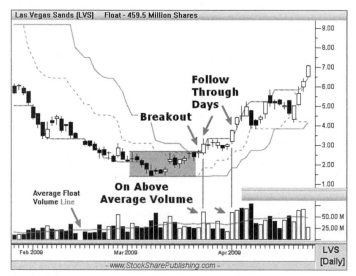

The Least You Need to Know

◆ Float analysis integrates price, volume, and time information to identify potential buy and sell points.

◆ A float box defines the price and time interval representing one turnover of the entire number of tradable shares in a company.

◆ Price breakouts of a float box on high volume represent attractive buy and sell levels.

◆ Both 100 percent and 50 percent float channel lines often locate the exact areas that a stock's price will reverse direction.

14

Meeting Support and Resistance

In This Chapter

- ◆ Understanding support and resistance

- ◆ Using support and resistance for better trades

- ◆ The importance of round numbers

- ◆ Support and resistance tools

The price level where prices stop and reverse direction is referred to as either a resistance level or a support level. If prices are moving up and then reverse direction to the downside, the highest price point reached is called a resistance level. If prices are moving down and then stop and reverse direction to the upside, that lowest price point reached is called a support level. A common analogy is that resistance is the ceiling and support is the floor. However, as you will learn in this chapter, that analogy oversimplifies an important concept of technical analysis. A more realistic view is that support and resistance levels note where buyers and sellers have achieved a balance of strength. Support levels represent prices at which the buyers have matched the strength of the sellers. Resistance levels represent prices where the sellers have matched the strength of the buyers. This equilibrium may not last long. Traders capture profit opportunities when they can anticipate a change in direction of prices. Understanding support and resistance gives you a trading advantage.

What Is Support and Resistance?

When prices are moving upward and they then stop and reverse to the downside, the market is said to have encountered "resistance" at the level where price reversed direction. At the resistance level, the sellers have gained more strength than the buyers, driving prices down. When the selling pressure begins to wane because the price has dropped below an attractive level for sellers, the stock encounters the "support" level. At this price, buyers are attracted to the stock and begin to push the price back up. It can be compared to two armies battling, in which the defending army has been falling back but then gains reinforcements to the extent that its strength exceeds that of the attacking army and thus begins pushing the attackers back.

 As an example, Figure 14.1 shows IBM rallying from a price of 101 to 104. It then pulled back and found support at 102.40 before resuming its upward journey to beyond 104.

Figure 14.1

An example of the support line on an IBM price chart.

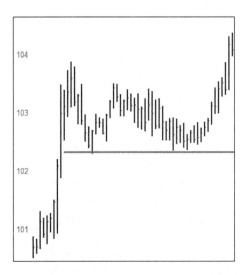

Being aware of the existence and location of key support and resistance levels is an important ingredient to successful technical analysis. The significance of support and resistance levels to traders is that prices have a tendency to return to those levels more than once over time.

When prices approach an important support level, traders become extra vigilant to look for signs of a potential reversal in price direction. If prices break through a key support or resistance level, it is a signal that the supply-demand balance has changed from the previous time prices reached that level. A breakout above resistance is an indication that demand (the bulls) has gained the upper hand. A breakout below support, on the other hand, shows that supply (the bears) has won the battle.

The interesting thing about support levels is they can transform into resistance levels, and resistance levels can transform into support levels. When price crosses below a support level, that support level becomes a resistance level, and when at some later time the price rises again, it often encounters resistance to further price increases at that same level. Similarly, if the price eventually crosses above a resistance level, that level becomes a support level, and buyers will support the price if it returns back down to that new support level.

Info/Tips

There is no literal barrier to stock prices rising or falling. It is important to remember that changes in price direction (along with other factors such as volume) are where traders make or lose money.

What Causes Support and Resistance?

 Figure 14.2 illustrates how a large institutional sell order at a fixed price could establish a price resistance level.

A large player (mutual fund, hedge fund, and so on) may make a decision to reduce or liquidate its holdings in a stock—many thousand shares. It will attempt to do so at a fixed price. This large order will absorb any and all available demand. Other traders may think this big player must know something they don't and decide to sell their shares as well. Potential buyers also decide to back away in anticipation of lower prices. Increased supply and decreasing demand ultimately leads to lower prices. This process continues until the available supply of shares dwindles and cautious buyers step back in to purchase shares at what they feel are bargain prices.

In Figure 14.2, IBM shares encountered resistance at 100.8. This may well have been the result of a large institutional sell order at or near 101. The resulting significant increase in supply caused the price to sell off down to near 100. The bulls then came back into the market and again tested the 101 level but encountered heavier selling at that level. After the heavy selling was finally absorbed by optimistic buyers, the 101 resistance level transformed into a support level. Prices subsequently tested this new support level several times before finally breaking out and rallying strongly to 103.5.

Figure 14.2

An example of resistance becoming support.

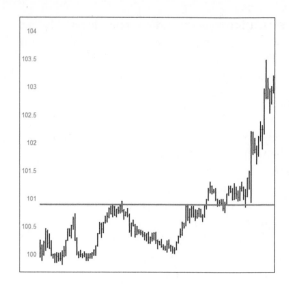

Other Causes of Support and Resistance

There are other reasons support and resistance levels occur. One big cause is that traders have memories. They remember the levels where prices stopped falling before and turned back up. Many traders are more likely to buy when prices return back down to a previous level of support with the expectation that prices will again turn up from there. Conversely, if bulls remember that prices previously found resistance at a nearby price level above the present price, there is a high likelihood that those bulls will take profits and/or sell short at or near that level.

Heads Up

Don't underestimate the impact of psychology and emotions on trading. Even professional traders are subject to these pitfalls. In the end, humans will sometimes make decisions that seem contrary to their best interests. This is amply demonstrated every day in the stock market.

Traders are also driven by pain and regret. Bulls feel pain if they buy and the price drops. They feel regret if they fail to buy and the price rises. In either case, the pain and regret turn to exhilaration if prices return to the earlier support-resistance level to give them another chance. Those with losses welcome the opportunity to escape with their shirts if prices return to their entry price. Those who missed out on the first go-around eagerly enter the market when the price pulls back to their previously missed entry price. The stronger the feelings of pain and regret by the mass of traders at that level, the stronger the support and resistance at this level will be.

Be aware that a support-resistance level is not necessarily one exact price. Rather, it is a zone around that price. When prices approach that zone from above, it serves as support. When prices approach that zone from below, it serves as resistance. The zone can be wide if the volatility is high and momentum is strong heading into it, or the zone can be narrow if volatility is low and the pace of a move into it is gradual.

The longer prices remain in a zone of support or resistance and the greater the volume traded within that zone, the stronger the emotional commitment of traders is to that price level. I liken it to a political campaign. The longer you hear each side's sales pitch, the more pronounced it becomes in your mind, and the more firmly entrenched your opinions about each candidate become.

Support and Resistance at Round Numbers

Support and resistance often occur when a key price point is reached that stimulates bulls to sell or bears to buy. Often that price point is a round number like 1,000 or 50 or another number ending in zero. These are key numbers that many traders, like sheep, will tie into. For example, "If my stock reaches 50, I'll sell," or "If the Dow drops to 6,000, I'll buy." When you start really looking, you will be amazed at how many times prices stop and reverse at round numbers. As an example, let's examine the behavior of the Dow Jones Industrial Index from 2003 to 2009.

Figure 14.3 is a chart of the Dow Jones Industrial Average weekly closes for the six-year period from 2003 to early 2009. I have drawn horizontal lines on the chart at even price increments of 1,000. Notice how prices are drawn to those even numbers and tend to find support and resistance there before they move on to the next support-resistance level.

Figure 14.3

An example of round-number support and resistance levels.

Let's follow this chart from left to right to see many excellent examples of round-number support and resistance. Beginning in 2003, prices moved sharply upward from the 8,000 level and broke decisively through the 10,000 level. However, when prices pulled back during the summer of 2004, they found strong support at the 10,000 level. That level was tested and held three times before prices moved upward and encountered resistance again near the 11,000 level in early 2005.

Near the end of 2005, prices again tested the 11,000 level and finally broke through in early 2006. Again, resistance became support as prices pulled back to the 11,000 level in mid-2006. Although prices briefly broke below 11,000, they quickly bounced back above that level and made a beeline for the 12,000–13,000 range in late 2006.

During early 2007, prices pulled back to tag the 12,000 support level. This round-number level had been passed quickly earlier in the year and needed to be tested again for validity as a support level. In the summer of 2007, prices reached their all-time peak of 14,000. I remember well the headlines at the time: "Dow breaks 14,000—headed for 20,000?" But in fact, it had taken all the energy that was left in the market to barely break that 14,000 level. Exhausted, the market began its frightening drop toward levels that had not been seen in 10 years.

Savvy traders who recognized the price patterns saw what was coming and got out of the market. Some sold short as the market exhibited a classic head-and-shoulders pattern with the neckline at 13,000 during 2007. An even larger head-and-shoulders pattern with the neckline at 12,000 developed between the beginning of 2007 and the middle of 2008. As you may recall from Chapter 5, head-and-shoulders patterns are bearish patterns foretelling further lows ahead, so if you recognized this pattern developing, you would have known that the market was likely to drop.

Info/Tips

You will frequently hear market commentators note that some event—lower than expected earnings, for example—is why a stock's price changed. What has actually happened is the news or event has changed the balance between supply and demand. A poor earnings report, for example, means some holders will want to sell because they believe the price is now too high.

Now, on the way down, previous resistance levels were becoming support levels. First came 13,000. Prices found support at this level in late 2007 before breaking it decisively in the beginning of 2008. Prices then made a beeline down to 12,000, where they again bounced sharply back up to 13,000. At this level, previous support now became strong resistance to further upward movement.

Unable to break above resistance at 13,000 in early 2008, prices dropped precipitously but again found support at a previous round-number resistance level, 11,000. A further drop in the summer of 2008 found support at the 8,000 round-number level, followed by resistance at the 9,000 round-number level before breaking down again and finding support at the 7,000 round-number level.

We can learn a number of lessons from this real-life example of market behavior:

- Markets often find support and resistance at round-number price levels. Investors and traders are very conscious of these numbers, which are widely disseminated through the media. They use these numbers as decision-making targets for buying and selling.

- Resistance levels on the way up become support levels on the way back down.

- Resistance and support levels are often tested by price several times before prices move on to new support-resistance levels.

- Savvy traders need to be on the alert when prices approach round numbers for possible reversals in direction.

Prices often test support and resistance levels by repeatedly approaching and then retreating from these levels. If prices decisively break through support or resistance levels, the levels are considered to have failed. It is not the support and resistance lines that constrain price movement—they simply reflect what is happening in the market. It is supply and demand that moves prices up, down, or holds them in a narrow range or channel.

Swing Pullback Price Projections

Some support-resistance levels are not necessarily set at previous price levels where prices had stopped and reversed before. Instead, they are predicted support and resistance levels based on the historical odds that prices will pull back against a trend at only a certain percentage of the length of the previous swing.

In Chapter 3, we learned about how prices swing and that major trends are usually interrupted by pullback swings. If we knew how large these pullbacks were likely to be, we could then wait for prices to pull back after a significant trending move and hop on board as prices resumed their longer-term trend.

History has shown that a typical valid pullback will range between 30 percent and 65 percent of the length of the previous leg of the trend. In other words, if a price upswing began at a price of 20 and ended at a price of 30, the length of that upswing was 10 points. Accordingly, based on the 30 percent to 65 percent rule of thumb, it would be normal to expect the ensuing pullback to find support at a level between 3 and 6.5 points from the beginning of the pullback. If the pullback ends up exceeding 6.5 points, the existing trend has more than likely ended, and prices will continue to move in the new direction.

Traders can take advantage of this knowledge and experience by watching for the beginning of a pullback in a trend and then placing an order to take a position in the opposite direction at a price equal to, say, 50 percent of the length of the previous swing. He would further plan to exit his position with a small loss if the price pullback exceeded 65 percent of the length of the previous swing.

Continuing the preceding example, he would place an order to buy at 5 points below the previous swing high of 30 (50 percent of the previous 10-point swing). If the trader's order gets filled at that 50 percent pullback level, he has entered the market at an advantageous price with an opportunity to be at or near the beginning of the next major move when prices turn back up in the direction of his trade. If he is wrong in his analysis, he plans to exit his position if the price pulls back more than 6.5 points from the end of the previous swing.

Figure 14.4 is a 15-minute chart of IBM. On the left side of the chart, an uptrend has occurred from a low of 91.74 to a high of 98.29. The price then pulled back to 95.79 before resuming its previous uptrend. I have drawn a sloping line connecting the low and the high of the first leg of the uptrend. I then drew a set of horizontal lines illustrating the top of the swing (0.00 percent), the bottom of the swing (100.00 percent), and three retracement levels as illustrations: 38.20 percent, 50.00 percent, and 61.80 percent. As you can see, the pullback to 96 was approximately 38 percent of the length of the first leg of the uptrend. This is well within the 30 percent to 65 percent typical range of valid pullbacks and is, in fact, an almost perfect Fibonacci ratio. The next section will explain the concept of Fibonacci ratios.

Figure 14.4

Support at 38.2 percent pullback in an uptrend.

Fibonacci Ratios

If trading pullbacks and calculating pullback ratios is going to be part of your technical analysis arsenal, then you need to be aware of another very popular method among many technical analysts to predict more accurately the levels of support and resistance for pull-backs in a trend. This method involves the use of Fibonacci ratios. Fibonacci ratios are based on the work of Leonardo Fibonacci of Pisa, an Italian mathematician who died in 1250. Fibonacci was perhaps the most gifted mathematician of his time. He had many great accomplishments but is remembered for a string of numbers (actually, the relationship of these numbers) that uncannily appear in many natural situations.

TA Intelligence
Fibonacci numbers are more than an interesting sequence. They have widespread applications in math, music, art, and architecture. They even appear in the popular book and movie *The Da Vinci Code*.

In the Fibonacci sequence, each number in the sequence is the sum of the previous two numbers. The Fibonacci sequence begins with 0 and 1. Here is the early part of the sequence:

0, 1, 1, 2, 3, 5, 8, 13, 21, 34, 55, 89, 144, 233, 377, 610, and so on.

One important fact about this sequence is that the ratio of each number to the next number in the Fibonacci series is approximately .618, or 61.8 percent, while the ratio of each number to the previous number in the series is 1.618, or 161.8 percent. Without going into detail about the math, suffice it to say that for traders the significant Fibonacci ratios are .382 (which is 1 minus .618), .50, .618, 1.0, 1.382, 1.5, 1.618, 2.0, 2.382, 2.618 ... and so forth.

The history and relevance of this sequence has filled many books over the centuries, and we don't have room for a complete description of how it fits into everything from Renaissance painting to the dimensions of the pyramids to the relationship of the distances between the eyes, nose, and mouth of the human face to modern number theory.

Suffice it to say that many technicians use analytic tools based on the Fibonacci sequence, including Fibonacci arcs, fans, retracements, channels, time zones, extensions, and clusters. Most modern trading software includes some or all of these tools, and if you pursue further education in technical analysis, they will be an important subject to master. Where I previously said that a valid retracement usually ranges between 30 percent and 65 percent of the previous swing, a Fibonacci aficionado will narrow this down to the possibility of either a 38.2 percent retracement or a 61.8 percent retracement. Whether you are a believer or not in these magic ratios, it behooves you to be aware of the potential support and resistance levels these ratios generate because the trading world is full of individuals who utilize these ratios in making their buy and sell decisions.

Floor Pivot Support-Resistance Levels

If you have an interest in day trading (that is, trading on intraday charts), you need to be familiar with a support-resistance concept known as floor pivots. This concept has been commonly used by traders on the stock exchange floors for many years; however, it can be a valuable tool for any trader. Determining the predicted floor pivot support-resistance levels for the next trading day involves a mathematical calculation using the previous day's high, low, and closing price.

The calculation of the floor pivot levels is based on the concept that the relationship of the previous day's close to the previous day's high and low has a strong influence on the price range within which the market is likely to trade and find support and resistance during the next day's trading session.

The floor pivots formula originated with traders on the exchange floors, most of whom are too busy to do sophisticated calculations during the trading day. They use this formula to calculate, after the end of the trading day, a set of predicted support-resistance price levels for the coming day.

Remember, support-resistance levels represent price levels at which the prevailing trend is likely to stop and reverse. Because most of the traders on the floor are aware of these projected price levels, the floor pivot levels become sort of a secret understanding between traders that those are price targets for the day. They are levels where floor traders, through buy and sell orders, will jointly set up resistance or support. For this reason, it is valuable for the technician off the trading floor to be aware of and know how to calculate these floor pivot levels.

The five floor pivot points are as follows:

- Resistance Level 2 (R2)
- Resistance Level 1 (R1)
- Pivot Price
- Support Level 1 (S1)
- Support Level 2 (S2)

Here is the process for calculating the floor pivot support-resistance values at the beginning of a new trading day:

♦ First you calculate a Pivot Price, which is the average of the previous trading day's high, low, and closing prices.

♦ Then you calculate Resistance Level 1 (R1), which is twice the Pivot Price minus yesterday's low.

♦ Then you calculate Resistance Level 2 (R2), which is the Pivot Price plus yesterday's high minus yesterday's low.

♦ Then you calculate Support Level 1 (S1), which is twice the Pivot Price minus yesterday's high.

♦ Then you calculate Support Level 2 (S2), which is the Pivot Price plus yesterday's low minus yesterday's high.

This gives you five levels of potential intraday support and resistance that must be recalculated at the end of each trading day for use on the next day. When prices approach these levels, traders should be cautious and not be surprised if prices stop and reverse at or near these levels.

Certain trading websites publish the floor pivot numbers each evening, and many trading software packages provide formulas for calculating and plotting these values automatically.

> **Info/Tips** _____
>
> Trading software will make all these calculations (and more) for you; however, it is a good idea to have some idea of the math behind key formulas.

Figure 14.5 shows the floor pivot levels superimposed on a five-minute chart of SPY (an *exchange-traded fund* that tracks the S&P 500 Index) covering one trading day. Each line is labeled with its name and support-resistance price level. Note that prices encountered resistance at the pivot level of 87.78 until prices finally broke through in the early afternoon.

def•i•ni•tion

> **Exchange-traded funds** (ETFs) are similar to mutual funds except they trade on stock exchanges just like stocks. Each ETF represents an equity (or bond) index and allows investors to trade sectors, sections, or the broad market.

Figure 14.5

*Example of floor pivots
support-resistance lines.*

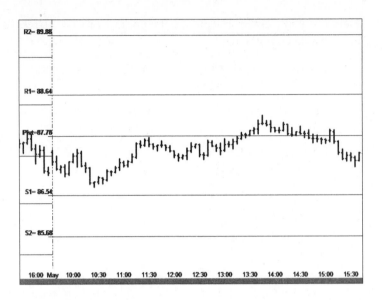

Trading with Floor Pivot Levels

The projected floor pivot support-resistance levels for the day can be used in two ways. The first way is for determining overall market trend. If price breaks upward through a floor pivot level, then the market is currently bullish and vice versa. Keep in mind, however, that pivot points are short-term trend indicators, useful for only one day until they need to be recalculated.

The second method is to use pivot point price levels to enter and exit the markets. For example, a trader might put in an order to buy if the price breaks above a resistance level. Alternatively, a trader might enter a sell order for his active trade if the price breaks below a support level.

Floor pivot formulas can also be applied to daily charts over a one-week interval to calculate projections of longer-term support-resistance levels. If a particular price level appears as a key floor pivot level on both intraday and daily charts, it offers even stronger support or resistance than on just the intraday calculations.

Using Support and Resistance Levels to Trade

The most effective use of support and resistance levels is in conjunction with some of the other forms of technical analysis described earlier in this book. These other technical indicators can be anything from moving averages, to MACD crossovers, to divergence signals, to various types of candlestick patterns.

A good place to start is to use a moving average of price to determine the strength and direction of the short-term trend. This will help you determine whether you should be buying or selling when prices approach a floor pivot price level. If the moving average indicates that the short-term trend is up, you would be more inclined to buy if the price drops and finds support at a floor pivot line. If the short-term trend is down, you should be more inclined to sell a rally when prices approach a floor pivot resistance line from below. If a divergence signal occurs near a support-resistance line, it adds credence to the likelihood that prices will reverse direction when it encounters the support-resistance line.

Many traders try to enter the market at or near the Pivot Price. If the current price is above the pivot, they buy on a pullback to a price close to the Pivot Price. If the price subsequently rallies, they may take partial profits at Resistance Level 1 and take profits on the rest of their position at Resistance Level 2.

Once price has reached Resistance Level 1, they will look to exit the remainder of their position at the Pivot Price if prices again drop instead of continuing to rise. This is just good risk management.

Similarly, if the current price is below the pivot, traders look to sell short on a move up to a price close to the Pivot Price. If the price subsequently drops, they may tack partial profits at Support Level 1 and take profits on the rest of their position at Support Level 2.

And again, if prices reverse back up after passing below Support Level 1, traders would look to exit their position at breakeven if prices should rise to the Pivot Price.

In conclusion, floor pivots are yet another useful tool that can be added to any trader's toolbox. The formulas, along with the software to calculate them, give traders the power to quickly calculate levels that are likely to slow or reverse price movement.

Jackson Probability Zones

A very useful extension of support-resistance concepts is a technical analysis method referred to as Jackson probability zones. They are named after technical analyst J. T. Jackson, who pioneered their use in the early 1990s. Jackson did extensive research looking at the relationship between the closing price of the day before and the opening price of the current day. He discovered that the relationship provided a statistical method of predicting probability zones to predict where prices would trade during the coming day. These probability zones gave traders an idea of how successful a trade might be in a particular zone.

Jackson zones describe areas where price trends may reverse or continue and assign a probability to the likelihood of that happening. These areas occur around and between the floor pivot points. Remember the five floor pivot points mentioned earlier in the chapter.

Jackson established six zones based on the floor pivot points:

- ◆ Zone 1 is below Support Level 2.
- ◆ Zone 2 is between Support Level 2 and Support Level 1.
- ◆ Zone 3 is between Support Level 1 and the Pivot Price.
- ◆ Zone 4 is between the Pivot Price and Resistance Level 1.
- ◆ Zone 5 is between Resistance Level 1 and Resistance Level 2.
- ◆ Zone 6 is above Resistance Level 2.

The zone probability calculations are based on two numbers: the zone of the previous day's close and the zone of the current day's opening price. The math behind the zones is significant, but fortunately trading software will make the calculations for you. The end result looks like Figure 14.6, which is the same chart as in Figure 14.5 but with the Jackson probabilities added.

Figure 14.6

Example of Jackson zones probability levels.

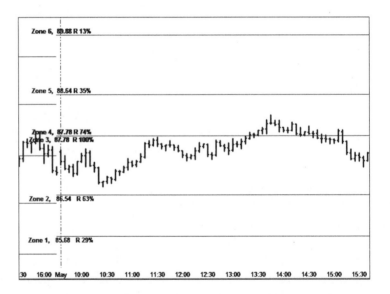

The zone probability predictions appear on the chart as soon as the market opens for the current day. The labels designate the zone number, the price at the zone boundary, and the probability that the market will reach that zone boundary at some time during the current trading day.

What the zones suggest are probabilities that price will touch one of the six zones during that trading day. This information, along with other indicators, confirms the high probability that the price will continue on its trend, move sideways, or reverse.

> **Heads Up**
>
> Most technicians like to use two or more tools to confirm the direction of their trade. Two indicators pointing toward the same price direction do not guarantee that is what will happen. However, two (or more) agreeing indicators add a degree of confidence to trading decisions.

For example, Figure 14.6 shows the following zone probabilities:

- A 29 percent chance the price will touch or penetrate Zone 1.

- A 63 percent chance the price will touch or penetrate Zone 2.

- A 100 percent chance the price will touch or penetrate Zone 3. (After all, this is the zone in which the opening price occurred, so there is a 100 percent chance that price would trade in this zone for at least one bar.)

- A 74 percent chance the price will touch or penetrate Zone 4.

- A 35 percent chance the price will touch or penetrate Zone 5.

- A 13 percent chance the price will touch or penetrate Zone 6.

So, for example, if at the opening of the trading day shown in Figure 14.6, a trader observed that the opening price occurred in Zone 3 and that there was a 74 percent chance that prices would reach Zone 4 at some time during the day, he might wait until he observed the price beginning to rise within Zone 3 and then buy in Zone 3 with a profit price objective in Zone 4.

It should be noted that Jackson zones were created to help day traders, so you must recalculate them each day. (Actually, my trading software does the heavy lifting.)

Jackson zones, like other technical analysis tools, give you confidence in your trading decisions. If several indicators point to the same conclusion about where prices are going, you can be confident you are making an informed decision. Technical analysis isn't perfect; however, it certainly gives you a better chance to make the right decisions.

To be used effectively, Jackson zones require more study than is possible in this book; however, you now have a better idea how they and other support and resistance analysis tools can improve your trading success. You can find more information about Jackson zones probability analysis tools at www.janarps.com/catalog/. Search for "Jackson Zones" and double-click on the graphic.

The Least You Need to Know

- Support and resistance provides traders with key information to make better trades.

- The price level where prices stop and reverse direction is referred to as either a resistance level or a support level.

- Prices have a tendency to return to support and resistance levels more than once over time.

- Markets often find support and resistance at round-number price levels.

- A typical swing pullback support-resistance level will range between 30 percent and 65 percent of the vertical length of the previous swing.

- Jackson probability zones give traders an idea of how successful a trade might be if entered at a particular price level.

Part 3

Time to Trade

The charts and indicators of technical analysis provide you with important information that can improve your trading profits—but only if you actually put this information to use. This part describes how you can begin to use technical analysis in making trading and investment decisions and what kind of support (computers, software, data services, and so on) you will need to improve your profitability as a trader or investor.

Chapter 15

Setting Up Your Trading Office

In This Chapter

- ◆ Your trading office
- ◆ Money requirements
- ◆ Hardware considerations
- ◆ Trading software

Learning technical analysis is an interesting academic study, but its purpose is to help you make better trades and increase the odds that you will be successful. Trading with technical analysis is where you put what you have learned into practice. You will learn a great deal more by using these tools to make actual trades. If some of the techniques seem hazy when reading about them, they will come into sharp focus when you apply the tools to real-world trading situations. Before you can actually begin to trade with technical analysis, you'll need to acquire the necessary equipment, services, and software. Many of these decisions are personal preference; however, there are some considerations to factor in before you begin assembling your trading office.

Putting Lessons into Practice

We study technical analysis because we are interested in making more intelligent trading and investment decisions with our hard-earned capital. We recognize that technical analysis tools can help us in identifying profitable entry and exit points that can improve the return on our investing capital.

So to put into practice all that you have learned in the previous chapters, you will need to set up some kind of a trading office. The nice thing about trading or investing with technical analysis is that it is a job that can be performed anywhere that is convenient to you, from anywhere in the world with a connection to the Internet. You can take your work with you on the road, if you choose. You can live where you want, and you don't have to commute long distances to get to your job. You can start and stop your work any time you want. You can wear what you want, even trade in your pajamas if you so choose.

To set yourself up for trading, you will need the following:

- Money to invest. This should only be money that you can afford to lose if you fail to make sound trading decisions.

- A quiet location to perform your technical analysis and trading activities. Your trading office can be as simple as a laptop computer on the kitchen table or as complex as a dedicated room filled with computers and multiple display screens. Many beginning traders just find a quiet nook in their home where they can set up a computer to monitor the markets.

- An adequate personal computer—the more RAM memory and number of on-board processors the better.

- A high-speed Internet connection to acquire data and place orders.

- A data feed service to obtain price data in accordance with your trading style (i.e., intraday, end-of-day only, stocks, futures, Forex).

- Technical analysis software for your computer that can collect and store price data, create price charts, and calculate and display analytic information.

- An order-entry capability to transmit your trading orders and *fills* to and from your broker.

def•i•ni•tion

Fill is the completion of a trading order. For example, if you enter an order to buy 100 shares of IBM and are matched with a willing seller, your order has been filled. What you paid for the 100 shares is known as the fill price. Your buy order was filled, and the seller's sell order was also filled by the same transaction.

♦ Adequate time to perform your technical analysis and trading activities, whether during the day, in the evening after your day job, or just on weekends.

♦ A brokerage account.

♦ A means of tracking the balance in your trading/investment account and recording your trading results.

Money to Invest

Adequate money to invest is the first and most important component of any and all investing programs. Without adequate capital, you reduce your chances for success. How much capital you need to get started is a personal decision that is dependent on how much and how often you intend to trade. Another consideration is whether you intend trading to be your "job" or simply a way to improve your investing.

Many people use technical analysis to trade for a living; in other words, they become full-time traders. If you plan on trading as a full-time occupation, your capital needs are substantially greater than what a part-time trader will need. Trading for a living is like operating a small business. Undercapitalization is one of the primary causes of failure in small businesses and for beginning full-time traders.

You must consider that, in the beginning, you will have more losing trades than winning trades. That is part of the price you must pay to learn this new profession of full-time trading. Money discipline (cutting losses quickly and letting winners run) will play heavily into whether you survive the first year of full-time trading.

If you plan on becoming a day trader (most successful day traders use technical analysis), know there are some regulatory requirements you must meet. Regulators consider you a "pattern day trader" if you trade four or more times during a five-day period or if your broker considers you a pattern day trader based on your trading history. Regulators require pattern day traders to have a minimum of $25,000 equity in their accounts at the start of each trading day.

As a practical matter, if you plan on trading as a full-time profession, you should begin with at least $50,000 in cash that you can afford to lose and not disrupt your life. For example, you should not put your home or your retirement at risk. Your family should not unduly suffer if you lose every penny of your starting capital.

If you plan on only trading part time (after your day job), you can start with much less capital, but it still needs to be money you can afford to lose. Give yourself a chance to succeed by beginning with a large enough capital stake to weather trading mistakes, which will surely come in the beginning as you learn.

Info/Tips _____

Before you invest a lot of money in a new computer, practice as best you can with whatever system you have access to. Get a feel for what software you want to use and then make sure your new computer (if you need one) matches your trading strategy.

Your Trading Computer

The first thing you will need for serious technical analysis work is a Windows-based personal computer. With very few exceptions, almost all technical analysis software is written for the Windows platform. There are almost no technical analysis programs available for Apple computers. However, modern Apple computers can run Windows-based programs. There may be some performance issues to consider, and finding support for problems may not be the best.

The type of computer hardware you will need is going to depend on the amount of real-time analysis you are going to be doing. Most trading software includes information about the minimum amount of computing capacity required to run the software efficiently.

If you are going to study the markets on the weekend, simply analyzing daily data, just about any modern computer will suffice. However, if you are planning to create live charts updated in real time on a second-by-second basis, then the more computer power you have, the more responsive your computer will be to the demands placed upon it. The critical components in computer selection are the processing chip speed and capacity, the amount of random access memory (RAM), and the amount of hard drive storage space.

Processing chip speeds and capacities continue to increase at an exponential rate, so any recommendations made at the time of writing this book will be obsolete within a matter of months. At the time of this writing, dual- and quad-core processors are becoming commonplace and should be incorporated into your technical analysis computer. These multi-core processors are really two or four computers in one, with each core capable of sharing a portion of the total computing load of the computer. Processor speeds are constantly increasing. The higher the processor speed, the more efficient your computer will be in analyzing the mountains of data coming in over your Internet connection.

The amount of RAM, or computer memory, is very critical in any TA computer. Ideally, it should be as large as your computer can handle. If budget is a constraint, go with at least 1 gigabyte of RAM. Memory upgrade is the most cost-efficient way to improve your computer's performance. Be sure the computer you use has the capacity to add additional memory if needed.

Although computers that will do the job adequately are easily available from many different computer manufacturers and distributors, there are several companies that specialize in building computers specifically designed and optimized for technical analysis applications. Two popular suppliers are XView Technologies, Inc. (www.Xview.com) and Sonata Trading Computers (www.tradersworld.com/computers). Both companies provide excellent products and service.

Make sure you add a battery backup to protect the computer against power surges, spikes, and outages. It keeps the computer running and allows you to get into and out of trades during a power outage. Keep your computer free of viruses by using the latest virus software. Also use a defragmenter to keep your hard drive running smoothly.

Your High-Speed Internet Connection

The quality of your Internet connection is another extremely important factor to consider in setting up your trading office, as it affects the timeliness of the price data you are receiving from the data provider. Access to broadband Internet service is a must for the serious technical analysis–based trader, especially if you are going to be an intraday trader. A slow Internet connection can lead to lagging data. That can cost you money in the form of less advantageous entry and exit prices.

For most traders, this means a cable or DSL connection from a reputable provider with a good record of keeping the connection active. You will need to research what options are available where you live and trade. Remember, if you are planning on trading from different locations, you need an alternative way to achieve a broadband connection. Wireless hotspots at coffee shops and other public places may not always offer the speed of connection you need.

You should also know that using a public network (such as found in a coffee shop or airport terminal) can be a security risk. These networks are seldom secure, which means a hacker could capture account data while you are using such a connection.

Your Data Feed

The data feed is the lifeblood of any TA software. If you are going to be doing real-time technical analysis, choosing a high-quality source of streaming price data will help ensure that your investment in your technical analysis software is not in vain.

Data feed services maintain massive computerized "server farms" in various secure geographic locations around the world. These server farms store tick-by-tick historical price data on everything that is traded on the world's stock, futures, Forex, and options exchanges. The data services have the capability of providing this historical price information to you, for whatever time period you request, on a second's notice. The historical data is streamed to your computer over the Internet on demand by your charting software.

Data feed services also provide you with real-time streaming price data for any financial instrument of your choosing. These data allow your charting software to update your chart every time a trade occurs somewhere in the world on the financial instrument you are following.

Data feed services generally give you the choice among three types of service: real-time data, delayed data, or end-of-day data. Real-time data is the most expensive because it is being provided for you on a second-by-second basis as the actual trades occur and are being recorded by the exchanges. Data feed services generally charge around $100 per month to provide you with real-time data service. Many brokerage firms offer free or low-cost data feeds as an incentive if you agree to place a minimum number of trades per month through them.

Delayed streaming data, usually delayed by 15 or 30 minutes, is provided at a lower price by data feed services and can be used by traders who are only interested in charting longer time periods or who are doing simulated trading where they do not need up-to-the-second data.

Heads Up

Use caution when subscribing to a data feed. Some services (typically those in the very low price ranges) offer streaming quotes; however, what you are receiving are quotes that are delayed by an exchange. Although the numbers change frequently, you are not receiving live quotes. Trading off these numbers can be hazardous to your bank account if you are attempting to trade in real time.

End-of-day data is the least expensive, as it presents only the day's open, high, low, and closing prices and daily volume at the end of the trading day, after the markets have closed. This type of data can be sufficient for traders who are only interested in studying daily, weekly, or monthly charts.

Your decision about the level of service is an important one. If you subscribe to a data feed that does not match your trading pattern, you will suffer the consequences. If you buy a service that is delayed when you need real-time, tick-by-tick information, you will have little chance for success. On the other hand, if some form of delayed information suits your trading needs, paying for real-time data feeds will be a waste of money.

The data feed services obtain their data from the world's financial exchanges, and each exchange generally charges a user fee for the data, which is passed on to the data user. The fees are usually relatively nominal, only a few dollars per month per exchange, but they can add up if you follow many different financial instruments traded on many different exchanges.

Among the major sources of streaming price data available to technical analysts are eSignal (www.esignal.com), TradeStation Securities (www.tradestation.com), Genesis Financial Technologies (www.genesisFT.com), Bloomberg (www.bloomberg.com), and Reuters (www.reuters.com).

Your Technical Analysis Software

The principal tool of the technical analyst is his trading software. The amazing growth in inexpensive desktop computing power over the last decade has given the average home-based trader the ability to access really powerful software that was previously only affordable to large money managers or brokerage firms. Nowadays, relatively inexpensive, PC-based technical analysis software enables anyone to analyze thousands of stocks or trading instruments in a matter of seconds to search for predetermined conditions and parameters.

What Your Technical Analysis Software Can Do

Most technical analysis software packages have the ability to perform many or all of the following functions:

♦ Create a variety of types of real-time price charts on many different financial instruments based on price data provided by the data feed service

♦ Apply selected built-in or third-party technical analysis tools to the price charts

♦ Scan a large list of financial instruments for those meeting selected technical analysis criteria

♦ Interpret and display the behavior of the price charts based on the technical analysis tools applied in a color-coded manner easily understandable by the user

♦ Provide action recommendations (such as buy, sell, hold) based on the analysis criteria

♦ Prepare and/or automatically enter orders to buy or sell selected financial instruments based on the analysis criteria

♦ Keep track of orders placed or filled, show their current profit or loss position, and maintain an accounting record of closed and open trades

♦ Provide a vehicle for the user to design, program, and apply his own custom analysis and trading tools to the price charts

♦ Provide the ability to test and evaluate the relative profitability of selected custom trading strategies

Choosing the Right TA Software for Your Needs

Your choice of technical analysis software will depend a lot on your needs and trading style. Almost all technical analysis software packages can plot stocks, futures, Forex, and index prices and have the capability to apply and display most of the standard technical indicators such as trendlines, moving averages, MACD, Stochastics, and RSI.

Info/Tips _____

Many trading platforms will let you generate practice trades using their software to get a feel for how their system operates using actual historic prices for practice trading so that you get a feel for what the real thing is like.

There are dozens of different technical analysis software packages on the market today, each with its own strengths and weaknesses. Some have the capabilities to perform all of the functions listed at the beginning of this section, but many limit their features to only some of those listed. You will need to decide for yourself which features are the most important to your particular charting and trading needs and then focus on evaluating the software that provides those features and services. Of course, the more features the software offers, the more expensive it is likely to be.

Some TA software providers—for example, TradeStation, Metastock, and eSignal—package their TA charting software with their own proprietary data feed service. Others, such as MultiCharts and NinjaTrader, do not provide their own data feed service but instead utilize data that the user can subscribe to from numerous different third-party data feed services.

Some TA software providers sell their software outright, while others offer their products on a monthly or yearly lease basis. Most offer a free or low-cost trial period, usually one month, during which you can test the product to determine if it is right for you. Some brokerage firms offer free TA software to clients who execute a given minimum number of trades per month. There is at least one source of completely free basic TA software on the web for analyzing stock prices: www.freestockcharts.com.

Technical Analysis of Stocks and Commodities, a leading industry magazine (www.traders.com), produces an annual Readers' Choice issue in which subscribers rate the various TA software offerings and brokerage firms on the basis of a wide selection of criteria. This is a good source of information about which platforms and services are considered most useful by traders who use them every day.

There are also websites, such as www.elitetrader.com, that provide frank and honest reader feedback on their experiences with many of the TA software packages currently in the marketplace.

Based on the Readers' Choice 2009 survey, Worden Brothers' Telechart Gold Service (www.support@worden.com) is rated #1 by users of introductory-level charting services, and AmiBroker (www.amibroker.com) is rated #2. For more advanced users who demand a greater degree of functionality and flexibility from their TA software, TradeStation (www.tradestation.com), eSignal (www.esignal.com), and Metastock (www.equis.com) all receive high ratings. A newcomer on the horizon, MultiCharts (www.tssupport.com), is also receiving significant plaudits for its advanced design.

Web-Based TA Charting Services

The web is a wonderful source of technical analysis information. If you are a casual investor and have minimal charting and data needs, there are a number of free or relatively low-cost sites on the web that can provide you with all of the price information and charts you would need for basic technical analysis. These charting sites provide end-of-day data at little or no cost, and in many cases they will also provide intraday data delayed by 15 or 30 minutes.

There are limitations to this form of service, including the timeliness of the data provided and limited access to advanced technical analysis tools, but these websites serve as inexpensive alternatives for the beginning technical analyst.

Two examples of web-based technical analysis sites are Yahoo! Finance (finance.yahoo.com) and www.StockCharts.com. These and similar websites provide the capability of creating charts and adding the common technical analysis tools without the necessity of acquiring and installing your own charting and technical analysis software on your computer.

Television in Your Trading Office

There are at least two cable TV channels that provide information exclusively about the worldwide financial markets: CNBC and Bloomberg TV. Many traders keep a TV set in their trading room tuned to one of these two channels all day long in order to stay current on the latest financial news. Personally, I recommend against it. Although I do have a TV in my trading office, I keep it switched off unless my charts signal an unusual event occurring and I want to determine if the anomaly is news driven, such as a terrorist attack, an assassination, or a major economic announcement.

The rest of the time, in my opinion, having the TV financial channels on during trading hours is usually more of a distraction than it is helpful. The financial news reports are filled with opinions and rumors designed to fill up the time during the day. As technical analysts, we need to focus on what the charts are telling us about the particular financial instruments we are following, not what some talking head thinks is supposed to happen.

Internet Chat Rooms and Forums

Doing technical analysis by yourself can be a very lonely business. Many traders and investors have discovered that by joining one or more Internet chat rooms populated by fellow traders with similar specialized interests, they can all share their ideas and observations. As a result, all participants can improve their ability to apply technical analysis to their trading and investing.

The web abounds with trading chat rooms. Just about every TA special interest group and trading platform has its own chat room or forum where participants can discuss chart signals and software settings, compare notes, or alert one another on stocks and futures contracts on the move or likely to begin moving. Participants can share their favorite charts as well as data and research from their favorite sources.

Conversations between participants can be typed, spoken over a microphone, or transmitted via live video. It gives all participants the opportunity to pool their senses and resources so that, in effect, the combined effort of many becomes greater than the sum of the parts.

As one member of a forum group wrote: "One brain and a pair of eyes and ears are fine, but there is little doubt that there is strength in numbers. This extends from the initial learning phase right through to the expert professional level."

Heads Up

Be very careful in chat rooms and forums because they are favorite lurking places for scam artists and people selling something. Some chat rooms and forums are moderated, meaning someone is filtering out the objectionable material; however, others you may visit are wide open where anyone can say anything.

TA Seminars and Webinars

One of the best ways for budding technical analysts to sharpen their skills is to attend trade shows and workshops sponsored by some of the major trade associations and software providers. The major technical analysis industry show is the Traders' Expo (www.tradersexpo.com), which generally occurs three times per year: once on the East Coast, once in the central United States, and once on the West Coast. The Money Show (www.moneyshow.com) is another producer of regular technical analysis trade shows.

Many technical analysis software companies provide a regular schedule of seminars and workshops around the world. One of the most complete selections of trader education is provided by eSignal (www.esignallearning.com/seminars).

As an alternative to live trade shows, there is a growing trend toward web-based seminars, or "webinars," both free and paid, aimed at students and practitioners of technical analysis. The great advantage of webinars is that participants do not have to travel great distances to the convention sites and pay for hotel accommodations and other travel expenses. Webinar participants can watch and listen to a series of presentations by industry veterans and watch their slide or live presentations on the web over a multiday period. Archived copies of the presentations are also available for subsequent review by attendees.

The TradersWorld Online Expo (www.tradersworld.com) is an excellent example of an online webinar presented over a four-day period once or twice a year.

There is also the shadier side of TA seminars. There are a few unscrupulous, quick-buck artists who travel from city to city offering get-rich-quick TA seminars and workshops. Their sole purpose is to sell you overpriced and relatively useless trading software for thousands of dollars. Before investing your hard-earned trading funds with any software seller or expensive seminar entrepreneur, do your due diligence. A good place to start is to check them out on www.elitetrader.com.

> **Info/Tips**
>
> There are no magic answers or insider secrets to successful trading, despite what you may see in your e-mail inbox or online. Successful traders work hard for their success. Be wary of shortcuts and workshops that offer "proven" trading strategies. Lucky traders are those who work harder than their peers.

Maintaining a Trading Journal

Many technical analysts and traders keep a diary, or journal, of their trades. The journal provides a record of the thought processes that led them to make that particular trade. By keeping accurate records of the reasons for their entries and exits, traders create a powerful tool for looking back objectively at past trading decisions to recognize problem areas as well as strengths in their trading habits.

By identifying common denominators in their bad trades, traders can more easily recognize their weaknesses and learn which types of trades best match their abilities and personality. By keeping a journal, they can learn from the past instead of mindlessly repeating the same mistakes over and over again. A journal also helps traders to clarify where their strengths lie. The objective of reviewing one's journal regularly is to learn to do more of what works and to avoid what doesn't.

What should your journal contain? Obviously you will want to include the date and time, information about your entry price and exit price, and the outcome of the trade. But the information that will really help you the most addresses subjects like where you got the idea for your trade, your expectations for the trade, and how the outcome compared to your expectations. Often it is this incidental information that provides you with the greatest insights upon rereading at a later time.

You can keep your journal in a hand-written spiral notebook or in a spreadsheet format on your computer. Dr. Alexander Elder, trading teacher and author of the book *Come Into My Trading Room*, offers an excellent trading diary template for Microsoft Outlook called "AK47" that you can order through www.elder.com. In the words of Dr. Elder, "Learn from your profits and losses. Keeping a diary and learning from your trades is as close as you can come to a guarantee of trading success …. [A trading diary] helps you to learn and succeed. It helps you become free …."

The Least You Need to Know

- ◆ Technical analysts who trade need a dedicated work area—many set up a work area in their homes.

- ◆ Selecting the correct computer, data feed source, and trading software is the most important initial step in establishing your trading work area.

- ◆ Industry conventions, seminars, and chat rooms can be valuable resources for the technical analyst to polish his trading and analytical skills.

- ◆ Keeping a trading journal can help the technical analyst become a better trader.

Chapter 16

Trading Using Technical Analysis

In This Chapter

- ◆ Making better trading and investment decisions
- ◆ Determining your class of investment
- ◆ Choosing a trading time frame
- ◆ Technical analysis tools

Technical analysis is just an interesting academic exercise unless you put it into practice. Technical analysis gives you the tools to make better buy and sell decisions. How you use these tools is up to you. They will fit any trading style you choose, from long term to day trading. Your first decision is whether you are an investor or a trader. The difference is important. Although you can use technical analysis for either trading or investing, the tools better serve traders for reasons already covered or those you will discover in this chapter. Using technical analysis to improve your opportunities for profit in the market makes sense. The jargon and number of tools may seem overwhelming; however, when you see the real-life examples of how technical analysis works, you may be surprised at how logical it all is.

Trading vs. Investing

Now that we have covered the fundamentals of technical analysis, it's time to address how you can apply technical analysis techniques in making better trading and investment decisions. There are many different trading decision-making styles, and each person needs to match his trading style to his personality as well as to the amount of risk capital he has available in his account.

Do you consider yourself an investor or a trader? Most people who own stocks think of themselves as investors. However, if you knew that big winners in the markets call themselves traders, wouldn't you want to know why? Simply put, they don't invest; they trade. People who think of themselves as investors typically make money in bull markets and lose money in bear markets. This is because they encounter bear markets with fear and trepidation and do not plan how to respond when they are losing. Most of them hang on to their losing positions way too long, so they continue to lose. They may have some idea that the alternative to losing money when markets go down involves more complicated trading transactions like "selling short," but they don't understand it and don't care to learn.

The public often sees investing as "good" or "safe" and trading as "bad" or "risky," and thus many people are reluctant to align themselves with traders or even seek to understand what trading, as opposed to investing, is all about. A trader typically has a clear plan to put capital into a market in order to achieve a single goal: profit. Traders usually employ technical analysis techniques to help them make their trading decisions. Traders don't care what they own or what they sell as long as they end up with more money than they started with. They are not investing in anything. They are trading. It is an important distinction. Actually, when you come right down to it, people who refer to themselves as "investors" are also traders. They make a decision as to when to buy and when to sell, and that is all that trading is, after all.

As we have learned in earlier chapters, technicians focus on price and volume patterns and behavior that reflects a change in the balance between demand (buyers) and supply (sellers), driven by the powerful emotions of greed and fear. Being able to identify these characteristic patterns gives the technician a trading advantage. He or she will have a higher probability of making the correct trading decision, thereby increasing his profitability.

We have seen that markets do not travel in a straight line. They have a tendency to trend for a while, then pull back or move aimlessly sideways, to be followed later by either resumption or reversal of the earlier trend. As many of us have learned firsthand to our dismay, "buy and hold and hope for the best" is not

Info/Tips

One of the biggest mistakes investors (and traders) make is assuming the market or an individual stock will continue in the same direction indefinitely. Technical analysis can help you spot price reversals in advance—a big advantage.

necessarily the best way to manage our investments. The world has changed. It is not a buy-and-hold market anymore. As we have seen, the markets go up slowly and can come down fast. Sadly, anyone who bought stocks any time after 1997 and held on to them through the end of 2008 would have seen all of their paper profits generated over those 11 years evaporate. To make money in today's markets, you need to be nimble, to learn how to sell short as well as buy long, to trade with a game plan, and to be disciplined.

What to Trade

As a technical analyst and trader, the first decision you need to make is what class of investment you want to follow. You can follow stocks. You can follow exchange-traded funds (ETFs). You can follow futures. You can follow foreign exchange (Forex). Any or all of these choices must be weighed in light of your time availability, your interest and knowledge about the particular investment medium, your available capital, and your risk tolerance level.

Stocks

When the average person hears the word "trading" in financial context, he or she usually thinks of trading in shares of stock. The stock market is, after all, where shares of public companies worldwide have been bought and sold for hundreds of years. It is in this environment that you can participate in the fortunes of one or more of thousands of companies whose shares are publicly traded.

One of the biggest challenges to the stock trader, however, is selection—choosing which stocks out of the huge universe of available companies is the best investment at any particular time. Some technical analysts focus their activities on only one or two companies' shares and follow their gyrations intensively. Most, however, have a tendency to diversify their holdings, spreading their risk over a variety of companies and industries. Technical analysis can help in identifying those stocks and industries that are poised to move or are already making a strong move.

When you are considering acting on a stock recommendation, pull up a daily, weekly, or monthly chart of that stock and study its past behavior under differing market conditions. Look at not only the price behavior but also the volume behavior relative to the price movements.

Is the stock currently trending, consolidating, or oscillating? Where has support or resistance occurred in the recent past? Is it making new highs or new lows? How is the stock behaving relative to its moving average? Are key oscillators in overbought or oversold territory? Are oscillators diverging from price?

Many technical analysis software programs provide the ability to scan large numbers of stocks for particular technical patterns that give the user the power to quickly narrow down the list to only those that meet specific criteria.

Mutual Funds

As a popular investment option, you have probably already heard plenty about mutual funds. Chances are you own a mutual fund in your retirement plan or brokerage account. But do you know what a mutual fund is and why so many people own them?

A mutual fund is an investment that allows a group of investors to pool their money and hire a portfolio manager. The manager invests this money in stocks, bonds, or other investment securities according to the style dictated by the fund's prospectus. The beauty of a mutual fund is that you can invest a few thousand dollars in one fund and obtain instant access to a diversified portfolio.

> **TA Intelligence**
>
> Mutual funds are very attractive, offering professional management and instant diversification of some kind. However, you pay a price for that expertise in the form of fees, which can exceed 2 percent per year. High fees are among the most common reasons mutual funds fail to deliver the expected results.

Many investors don't have the resources or the time to buy individual stocks. Investing in individual securities, such as stocks, takes not only resources but a considerable amount of time. By contrast, mutual fund managers and analysts wake up each morning dedicating their professional lives to researching and analyzing their holdings and potential holdings for their funds.

There are many types and styles of mutual funds. There are stock funds, bond funds, sector funds, money market funds, and balanced funds. Within just stock-based mutual funds there are a variety of types, from those that seek aggressive growth to those looking for both growth as well as income in the form of regular dividends. There are also a variety of sector funds that invest in specific industries such as technology, energy, or communications.

As with individual stock selection, to apply technical analysis to the purchase and sale of mutual funds, the best time frame to look at is weekly or monthly charts to identify possible changes in their long-term trends. Before you decide to invest in a particular mutual fund, create a set of percent change charts, described in detail in Chapter 4, in order to compare each fund's performance to that of several different mutual fund candidates to determine which is currently the strongest and which is moving up through the pack.

Mutual funds are not ideal trading vehicles because many limit the extent to which you can trade in and out of them, and the process of buying and selling them is often quite onerous and paperwork intensive. Nonetheless, technical analysis can help investors make a judgment as to which has the best chance of meeting their financial goals.

Exchange-Traded Funds (ETFs)

A relatively new variation on the mutual fund concept is the exchange-traded fund, or ETF, first introduced in 1989. ETFs are an investment vehicle that is traded on stock exchanges just like shares of stock. However, unlike shares of stock in a single company, shares of an ETF are based on a basket of company shares in a particular industry such as biotechnology or homebuilders.

There are also ETFs based on commodities, such as crude oil or precious metals, as well as ETFs based on broad market indexes like the S&P or NASDAQ indexes. There are even ETFs based on international country-specific markets, such as Chinese, Indian, or Brazilian market indexes.

The very first ETF traded in America (and the most widely held) is the Standard & Poor's Depository Receipt (SPDR), dubbed the "Spiders." Other common ETFs are the QQQQ, based on the NASDAQ 100 index (these ETFs are dubbed "Qubes"), and the DIA, based on the Dow Jones Industrial Average, referred to as the "Diamonds."

The great advantage of trading ETFs over individual stocks is that a trader or investor can gain exposure to an entire industry group or stock index with the same ease as he would have in buying shares of stock in a single company, without the complexities and regulatory limits of trading in mutual funds.

The important fact for the technician is that ETFs follow the same principles of technical analysis and the relative balance between supply and demand as shares of individual stocks. Accordingly, ETFs are favored by technicians as a way to broaden their market focus.

Unlike mutual funds, which can only be bought or sold at the end of the trading day at the mutual fund's closing price, ETFs are continually priced throughout the day and can be bought and sold at the current market price at any time during the trading day. As publicly traded securities, ETF shares can be purchased on margin and sold short and traded using stop orders and limit orders, which allow investors to specify the price points at which they are willing to trade.

Another interesting feature of index-based ETFs is that many of them offer both bull and bear versions. A bear ETF is structured such that its price goes up as the value of the index goes down. In this way, traders who are reluctant or unable to sell short can still profit from falling prices of the related index by purchasing a bear version of the ETF.

Finally, there are leveraged ETFs, which are a special type of ETF that generates returns that are more sensitive to market price changes than nonleveraged ETFs. For example, a 2X Bull DIA ETF would be structured to achieve daily returns twice as great as those of the Dow Jones Industrial Average in an up market. Conversely, it would also lose value twice as fast as the Dow Jones Industrial Average in a down market. A 2X Bear DIA ETF, on the other hand, would behave in exactly the opposite manner, gaining twice as much value in a down market and losing twice as much value in an up market. This means you get twice the bang for your buck without using margin. This is truly market magic and provides great flexibility and trading opportunities to followers of technical analysis.

Heads Up _____

Although ETFs offer many opportunities for traders, don't let the basket of stocks lull you into complacency. Some funds, particularly the leveraged ones, can move swiftly against you. You still need all of your technical analysis skills to be successful.

Futures

A very popular trading vehicle for technical analysts is the futures contract. A futures contract is a publicly traded financial contract between two parties who agree to buy or sell an asset for future delivery at a particular price. That asset can be an agricultural product such as corn, wheat, or cattle, or it can be a physical asset such as gold or silver. It can also be a financial instrument such as U.S. Treasury bonds or the most popular futures instrument of all, an entire stock index.

Stock index futures contracts, such as those on the S&P, NASDAQ, or Dow Jones indexes, give the trader the ability to make an investment in an entire market with a relatively small amount of money. These are "leveraged" contracts, which mean that a relatively small percentage move in the underlying market is translated into a much larger percentage move in the futures contract based on that market.

Trading futures requires that you deposit money, known as a margin deposit, with your broker, who holds that money for you as security against losses in your trading account. When you enter into (buy or sell) a futures contract, your broker will set aside an amount equal to the margin deposit as collateral against losses from your trade. If your trade is profitable, your profit is credited toward your required margin deposit, thus freeing up additional purchasing power to enter a new futures position.

The ins and outs of futures trading are beyond the scope of this introductory book about technical analysis, but there are many excellent books on the subject included in the reference list of Appendix B. Suffice it to say that the futures markets are an extremely liquid, diverse set of meeting places for manufacturers, speculators, exporters, importers, farmers, and investors. Thanks to modern technology, futures prices are seen throughout the world, so a trader in Texas can match a bid from another trader in Australia.

Why should a technical analyst trade in futures? For leverage and liquidity. Futures markets are among the most active trading markets in the world. The nominal value of futures contracts traded in the futures markets worldwide dwarfs the value of stocks traded in the stock markets worldwide. Because of the huge volumes traded, futures contracts exhibit characteristic technical analysis patterns on shorter as well as longer time frames as the crowd moves into and out of positions day in and day out. It thus behooves the trader who uses technical analysis to consider the futures markets as a trading vehicle, but only after fully understanding this market, which has its own set of rules that govern trading.

Foreign Exchange (Forex)

The foreign exchange market, referred to as the Forex, or currency market, is a market in which participants buy, sell, exchange, and speculate on currencies worldwide. The Forex market is made up of government banks, private banks, corporations, speculators, and investors. The Forex market is considered to be the largest financial market in the world, processing trillions of dollars worth of transactions each day. The Forex market is not dominated by a single set of market exchanges, but consists of a global network of computers and brokers from around the world.

Prior to the 1970s, currency exchange rates were fixed in accordance with the *Bretton Woods system*. However, the Forex market that we see today started evolving after 1971, when countries around the world began abandoning Bretton Woods and adopting floating currency exchange rates.

The foreign exchange market is unique because of its geographical dispersion, its round-the-clock activity, its very high leverage, and its participation by governments around the world. For technical analysts, though, it is just another market that trends and consolidates and responds to human emotions and thus can be traded and charted just like stocks and futures contracts.

def•i•ni•tion

The **Bretton Woods system** was an international monetary agreement adopted by most of the world following World War II. One of the key features was a commitment by countries to tie the exchange rate of currencies within a few percentage points of the value of gold.

What Time Frame to Trade

Once you have decided what markets to trade, the second decision you need to make is the time frame you want to follow. Are you going to be a long-term trader, an intermediate-term trader, a day trader, or a very-short-term scalper? Although the same kinds of chart patterns occur in all time frames, your time availability will control which charting and trading time frame style best suits you.

No matter what time frame you choose to trade, you can apply the principles of technical analysis equally to weekly charts as to daily charts or intraday charts of any market, whether it is stocks, futures, Forex, or indexes. Technicians don't trade stocks or futures; they trade people. The human emotions that drive people to make buying and selling decisions are the same in all time frames.

Are you only able to study your charts on the weekend and make your trading decisions on a long-term basis? In that case, you must focus your attention on monthly, weekly, and daily charts. Are you willing and able to study your charts every night after work to make trading decisions for the next day? In that case, daily and intraday charts will be your focus. Or are you willing and able to watch your charts during every trading day and make minute-to-minute buy and sell decisions? In that case, daily and intraday time frame charts will be your focus.

No matter what time frame you are going to trade in, you will want to follow not only the chart of that time frame, but also of at least one or two higher time frames to confirm the longer-term direction of the market. For example, if you are trading on a daily chart, your odds of success will be greater if the direction you are trading is consistent with the overall trend of the weekly and monthly charts. Similarly, if you are taking trades on the basis of a possible trend signal on a 15-minute chart, the odds are more in your favor if the direction you are trading is consistent with the trend of the 45-minute and daily charts.

Your Trading Style

Next there is the question of your trading style. Do you want to be a trend trader, a swing trader, an oscillation trader, or all of the above? Many technical analysis techniques apply to all of these trading styles, but some techniques work more effectively than others in particular circumstances. As a novice technician you might experiment with each of these techniques, but it is usually better if you ultimately settle on a specific niche, matching your investing knowledge and experience with a style to which you feel you can devote continuing research, education, and practice.

Trend Trading

Trend trading seeks to capture the majority of a trend, up or down, for profit. One of the most famous sayings in technical analysis is, "The trend is your friend." Trend traders want to know one thing: is the price moving in an uptrend, a downtrend, or sideways? Clearly, if you can identify the beginning and the end of a trend, you can very profitably ride that trend for all it's worth. However, that is not always so easy to do.

One of my favorite sayings is, "You don't know you're in a trend until you're in a trend." In other words, it takes skill, experience, and good technical analysis tools to distinguish, with a high degree of probability of success, the beginnings of a likely strong price trend as opposed to a brief price surge or pullback.

Another of my sayings is, "Every trader needs a trend to make money." If there is not a trend after you buy, then you will not be able to sell at higher prices. So it's important to identify a valid trend as early as possible and then get on board.

Attempting to pinpoint the beginning of a trending market as it is happening is not easy. When trends begin, they often arise from a flat market that doesn't appear to be trending in any direction. The trick is to take a small, "toe in the water" position early on in a market that is showing signs of trending to see if the trend does indeed mature and get big enough to make big money. Trend traders typically wait for the trend to shift, then they follow it and add to their positions as it extends. Good trend traders make a conscious effort to only take trades that exist in the midst of quality trends.

Tools to Identify the Beginnings of Trends—Oscillator Reversals

Before a trend can begin, there has to be a change in direction, such as from down to up or sideways to up in the case of a new uptrend. One indication most likely to alert you first to a possible beginning of a new trend would be the reversal from an overbought or oversold reading of a leading oscillator, such as RSI, MACD, or Stochastics.

Sometimes the first reversal turns out to be a false alarm, so traders often wait for a divergence signal to occur between one of these oscillators and price before considering entering a trend trade. If the price is making lower valleys, for example, while the oscillator is making higher valleys, that's when the hairs on the technician's neck begin to rise as he anticipates an imminent reversal in trend direction to the upside.

Breakaway Gaps

A breakaway gap also frequently accompanies the beginning of a significant trending move. A breakaway gap up occurs when the low price of a new price bar near the low of the previous downtrend is significantly higher than the high of the previous price bar. Conversely, a breakaway gap down occurs when the high price of a new price bar near the high of the previous uptrend is significantly lower than the low of the previous price bar.

Let's look at an example of the signs leading to a change in trend direction as just described.

Figure 16.1

An example of divergent trend reversal.

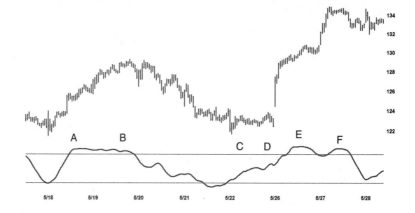

Figure 16.1 is a 15-minute chart of Apple Computer (AAPL). The Stochastics oscillator, with its overbought and oversold horizontal lines, is plotted below the price chart. Notice how effective such an oscillator can be to anticipate price direction changes. For example, between points A and B the Stochastics oscillator is above the overbought line, showing that we are in a steady uptrend. At point B the Stochastics oscillator crosses below the overbought line, suggesting that the uptrend is about to end and a new downtrend is about to begin.

After having previously crossed below the oversold line, at point C the oscillator crosses back above the oversold line, indicating the likely end of the downtrend. Between points C and D we see a divergence between the oscillator and price. The oscillator is rising while the price remains in a horizontal congestion zone, indicating possible behind-the-scenes buying by the smart money and warning us of an impending price move to the upside.

A breakaway gap on the price chart between points D and E signals the beginning of a strong uptrend move as the oscillator moves into the overbought zone, confirming a strong uptrend underway.

At point F, the oscillator peak is lower than its predecessor at E while price has paused in its up move, signifying potential exhaustion of the uptrend.

Candlestick Pattern Signals

Candlestick pattern analysis is another excellent method for identifying trend reversals (see Figure 16.2). For example, a doji candlestick pattern during a strong trend move often signals the end of a trend. Remember, as explained in Chapter 8, a doji bar is a Japanese candlestick bar that has a very narrow real body and a long wick, signifying a lack of commitment to the previous trend on the part of traders.

Doji bar

Figure 16.2

An example of the doji candlestick reversal pattern.

Tools to Identify Trend Continuations—Flag Patterns

Most strong trends are interrupted by at least one pullback where it "takes a breath" before resuming its trending move. Such a pullback often takes the form of a "flag" or "pennant" pattern, as described in Chapter 9. This is an ideal spot for trend traders to take or add to their positions in the direction of the main trend. History has shown that the chances of the pullback turning into a major trend direction reversal are much lower than the odds of a major trend continuation move occurring after the pullback.

As we described in Chapter 6, such a pullback often defines the approximate halfway point in the main trend, so we can use the length of the first leg, the "flagpole," as a guide to predicting the approximate length of the anticipated second leg of the trend.

Info/Tips

Trend traders know that prices will not continue in the same direction forever. Technical analysis gives them the tools to not only spot the trend, but also to be alerted when it shows signs of reversing.

Figure 16.3 is an example of a trend continuation after a flag pattern occurs when prices pause to take a breath before continuing in the direction of the previous trend.

Figure 16.3

The trend continuation flag pattern.

Parallel Moving Averages

As the trend matures, if 100-bar and 200-bar simple moving averages move in a more or less parallel direction, the chances are good that the trend will continue in the direction of the moving averages for some time longer. Once the moving averages cross, the trend has ended. Figure 16.4 illustrates this concept on a chart of the Dow Jones Industrial Average.

Figure 16.4

Dual moving averages confirming a trend continuation.

Exiting a Trend Trade

The basic trading strategy that trend followers try to follow is to cut losses and let profits run. A skilled trend trader knows when to get in and when to stay out. Even more importantly, he must know when to get out once he's in. If he recognizes that he is wrong, he exits immediately. He views a loss as a cost of doing business as a trader.

One of the safest ways to exit a trend trade is to plot a 30-bar moving average of the price lows in the case of an uptrend (see Figure 16.5) or a 30-bar moving average of the price highs in the case of a downtrend (see Figure 16.6). If the closing price of a bar penetrates one of these average lines, the trader should exit his trade.

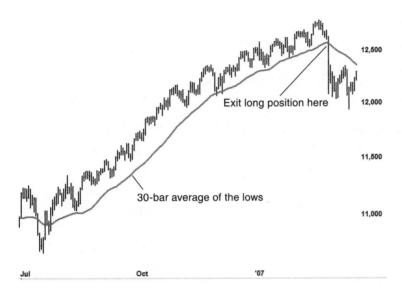

Figure 16.5

An example of exiting an uptrend at the 30-bar moving average of the lows.

Figure 16.6

An example of exiting a downtrend at the 30-bar moving average of the highs.

Trend traders go with the flow. They leave their personal or fundamental opinions at the door. Their philosophy is, "Do you want to be right, or do you want to make money? If you want to make money, go with the flow."

Oscillation Trading

Identifying a trend and getting on board early is a key strategy of technical analysis. However, history has shown that prices move in a nontrending, sideways direction more of the time than they move in a trending mode. It is during these times of sideways movement that the trend-following traders must stand aside and bide their time.

When the market is moving sideways, the oscillation traders take over from the trend traders. Oscillation traders trade the oscillating price peaks and valleys within a horizontal trading channel. They will buy when prices approach the lower boundary of the channel, and they will sell when prices approach the upper boundary of the channel. They discontinue their oscillation-trading mode if prices break outside of the channel and begin to trend.

The more times the price has changed direction at the boundaries of a sideways channel, the more powerful is that boundary and the higher the probability that prices will find support or resistance at those boundaries. To make money with oscillation trading, the trading channel must be sufficiently wide so that the profits to be made from successful trades would be several times larger than the potential losses that would be incurred by exiting the trade if the price breaks through the channel.

Figure 16.7 is an example of a series of oscillation trades. In contrast to many other charts in this book, I have plotted this particular chart as a candlestick chart (see the explanation of candlestick charts in Chapter 3) to better highlight where each bar's prices opened and closed and to display the tails, or "wicks," of the candlestick bars to illustrate how the prices frequently penetrated but failed to close outside the support and resistance lines. I have also manually drawn a series of horizontal lines to illustrate where prices found significant support and resistance.

In Figure 16.7, the stock first encounters resistance at 64.9. The price then declines to 64.3. When the price has a 2-bar rally to 64.6 and then drops down again to 64.3, that price becomes a support level. At 64.3 would then be a price level where oscillation traders would consider buying the stock, then looking to exit their long position and sell short when prices return to the level where the price previously found resistance around 64.9.

Oscillator traders would then look to exit their short position and buy the stock again where prices found previous support around 64.35. This level is tested twice before again reaching 64.9 after a bit of a struggle. At this point, if the oscillation trader went short again, he would quickly exit his position on the next bar when it was clear that a breakout of the 64.9 resistance level had occurred.

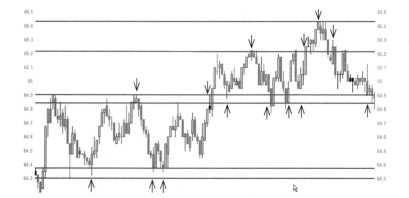

Figure 16.7

An example of oscillation trading.

The 64.9 resistance level now becomes a potential support level, and when prices pull back to that level and reverse, the oscillator trader will again buy. Prices then rise and hold at the 65.2 level for the second time, making that a new resistance level. The old resistance level of 64.9 now becomes a support level, and the oscillation trader may buy there and sell out when price once more approaches the 65.2 resistance level.

When prices finally break out of the 65.2 resistance level, they find new resistance at 65.42, a level where four bars in a row were unable to penetrate, thus creating a new resistance level. At this point, the bears gain control and prices drop back to what now has become a support level around 65.2. The price vacillates for several bars before continuing its downward journey to the next support level of 64.9.

Thus, in what appears to have been a sideways market, the oscillator trader has been able to enter numerous profitable trades by repeatedly buying near support and selling near resistance.

In addition to candlestick charts, the type of technical analysis tools used by many oscillation traders to sharpen their entries and exits are, naturally, oscillators such as Stochastics, RSI, MACD, and %R. Oscillation traders use these tools to identify overbought and oversold conditions and diverging patterns that would signal an impending reversal in price direction. They also look for characteristic candlestick patterns such as dojis, hammers, and engulfing patterns to identify potential price tops and bottoms within the trading channel.

Oscillation trading works great when the market is moving sideways, but it obviously crumbles when the market goes into a trend. If the market breaks out of a channel and keeps moving in the direction of the breakout, it becomes a favorite setup for the trend traders. The trend-following traders want the market to get moving in one direction before they hop on board. As the market is moving up, they buy, which is the exact opposite of what the oscillation trader is doing. Although chewed up in oscillation, trend traders enjoy the large profits of the trend. You can refer to Chapter 13 on float analysis for more information about trading channel breakouts.

Swing Trading

Rather than looking only for longer-term trends to trade, swing traders focus on trading the secondary price fluctuations that occur in a market. Swing traders try to anticipate the most probable future direction of price movement by looking at the relative length of successive price upswings and price downswings. With this information, they project where the next price swing is likely to end. Swing traders often employ the swing pullback price projection concepts described in Figure 14.4. They buy on a given percentage pullback of the previous swing, looking for a breakout beyond the end of the previous swing.

Swing trading principles apply to all time frames and all markets. In contrast to day traders, who usually are out of the market by the end of the trading day, swing traders frequently hold their positions anywhere from several days to several weeks as they trade on the basis of daily or weekly movements. Figure 16.8 illustrates a series of swing trades over several days each.

Figure 16.8

An example of swing trades.

Day Trading

Day trading has seen an explosive growth in popularity in recent years since access to second-by-second price data for every market in the world has become available at a reasonable price to anyone with a personal computer and a high-speed Internet connection.

Day traders operate on an intraday time horizon, generally exiting their positions by the end of the trading day to avoid the uncertainties associated with unfavorable overnight news events that could have a major impact on the price of their holdings the next day.

Most day traders use some form of technical analysis to make their trading decisions as they follow the short-term trends up and down during the course of the trading day. Day trading is particularly popular with traders who trade the futures markets because of the short time horizons and high leverage that futures markets offer.

Scalping

A scalper is an individual who makes dozens or hundreds of trades per day, trying to "scalp" a small profit from each trade. A scalper has to be attuned to the subtle ebbs and flows of market action and is quick to follow them. He is satisfied to take quick profits of a few tens or hundreds of dollars on each trade and is quick to exit the moment a trade goes against him. Scalping has been compared to picking up nickels in front of a steamroller. You have to be nimble to avoid being crushed. Clearly, commissions take a significant bite out of the scalper's small profits, so most scalpers trade on the exchange floors as members of the exchange who pay miniscule commissions.

The Least You Need to Know

- ◆ Traders apply technical analysis to any investment and trading vehicle, including stocks, mutual funds, exchange traded funds, Forex, and futures contracts.

- ◆ Traders utilize various trading styles, including trend trading, swing trading, oscillation trading, day trading, and scalping.

- ◆ Oscillation traders buy support and sell resistance in sideways markets.

- ◆ Swing traders trade the secondary price fluctuations that occur in a market and often hold their positions overnight.

- ◆ Day traders operate on an intraday time horizon, generally entering and exiting their positions the same day.

- ◆ Scalpers are usually traders who do extremely short-term trades, generally working on the exchange trading floors.

Chapter 17

Entry and Exit Order Basics

In This Chapter

- ◆ Entering and exiting positions
- ◆ Buy/sell orders
- ◆ Different types of orders
- ◆ Using the best tools

Technical analysis tools will not be of much help if you aren't able to translate the information to actionable buy or sell orders. The importance of getting into and getting out of a position at the correct time cannot be overstated. In fact, one of the underlying purposes of technical analysis is to signal you when to buy or sell. Fortunately, there are numerous tools traders use to execute buy and sell orders at the best possible moment. Traders can also use certain orders to protect from loss or to secure a profitable trade against the market turning against them. This chapter will give you a full arsenal of trading orders to help make you successful.

Types of Orders

If you are new to technical analysis, it's important to become familiar with the types of orders you can use to enter and exit your trades. Understanding how different types of entry and exit orders function and their intended purpose will help you to incorporate them more effectively into your trading activities.

These are the most commonly used types of orders:

◆ Market orders

◆ Limit orders

◆ Stop-loss orders

◆ Stop limit orders

You may find that these order types are all that you will ever need. Many professional traders use these four types of orders to fulfill all of their trading requirements. Later we shall discuss some of the order types that are either more complex in structure or are designed for specific entry and exit situations.

Note: your broker and the type of order entry platform you select for trading determines the menu of order types available to you. However, the four basic order types will be available on all trading services.

Market Orders

A market order is an order to execute your trade, whether a buy or sell order, at the best available price at the earliest opportunity once received. During trading hours, a market order will always be filled as quickly as possible. In today's markets, the order, once sent from your trading computer, will generally be executed within seconds electronically over the Internet. Market orders generally go to the head of the line in the sequence of filling orders.

Market orders offer several advantages. They help improve a trader's execution speed and decisiveness. By always having your order entry platform set to enter market orders, you simply click your computer mouse to get in or out of a trade. No fumbling with entering execution prices or choosing other order types from a drop-down menu.

Trading with only market orders allows the technical trader to devote all of his or her attention to chart analysis and can facilitate a critical learned skill in trading: the ability to quickly "pull the trigger" when it's time to enter or exit a trade. The main disadvantage of trading with market orders is that you transfer control of your "fill" price to the market. Your order will be filled at the best possible price, but that may not be the price you wanted.

With the advent of electronic exchanges, greater regulation, and a highly competitive environment for brokerage accounts, there is less need to worry about market makers and brokers holding market orders and filling at a less favorable price. Now "bad fills" are primarily just the concern of intraday traders who trade large positions in which a few cents on a stock price or one or two ticks on a futures contract can greatly impact the profit or loss on a trade. If you consistently receive bad fills or a significant delay in executing your market orders, discuss this with your broker and consider a change if there is not a valid reason. In some highly volatile markets, such as the futures markets, it's not uncommon for fills on market orders to be one or two ticks away from the desired price. Scalpers and large position traders use limit orders (see the next section) to address this issue.

It's important to be aware that in fast market conditions caused by a market-moving event, such as a key economic release or a Federal Reserve interest rate announcement, market orders can expose you to an unfavorable fill considerably away from your expected price that cannot be controlled by a broker or an electronic exchange.

In general, however, you can confidently expect market orders to deliver the price you wanted or very close to it.

Limit Orders

A limit order designates the specific price at which you are willing to buy or sell. On a buy limit order, the limit price represents the most you are willing to pay. Usually the order is placed below the current market price, but it is often placed at or close to the market price to ensure receiving a good fill price to enter a long position or close out a short position.

Conversely, on a sell limit order, the sell limit price states the lowest price at which you are willing to sell your security. A sell limit price should be entered above or at the current market price. Unlike a market order, limit orders are not guaranteed to be filled. The market can touch your buy limit price, for example, and not fill your order if there is more demand than supply at that specific price. However, if the price drops below your buy limit order price, your order must be filled at your limit price or better. As long as the order is not cancelled, an open limit order can be filled at any time when the market returns to your price point, such as during choppy market conditions.

It is possible that a limit order may be filled at a more favorable price than requested. A better price fill, however, may not always be a gift. Often it turns out that the price just continues to move in the direction against your purchase or short sale, indicating that your trade call was incorrect.

Limit orders are perhaps the most common type of order used in today's highly liquid markets since they assure the trader exact profit and loss control on his trading transactions.

The precise entry and exit price control that motivates traders to use limit orders can sometimes be a disadvantage. Let's say you have identified a support level, and thus you resolve to go long at that level by entering a standing buy limit order at that price. Then later the market again declines but just misses the support level or touches it briefly but does not fill your order and then takes off on an explosive rally. The desire to only go long with a limit order at the exact low, or lowest risk/highest return price point, can result in missing the profitable move.

Similarly, let's say that you had a nice profit in a stock and determined only to sell at a previously established high, so you enter a "profit target" order: a sell limit order at your profit target price. However, the price doesn't quite reach your sell limit price and then drops and completely erases your paper gain. Despite the satisfaction gained from nailing the best entry and exit prices, it often pays not to be too greedy with your entry and exit targets.

Market-If-Touched Orders

Instead of using a limit order, one other way to enter on a buy order below the market or a sell order above the market is to use an order type known as a market-if-touched (MIT) order. As the name implies, a market-if-touched order becomes a market order once a specific price is touched. It is most often used to initiate a position. The reason a trader might utilize a MIT order is to guarantee that he will enter the market at or near the MIT price, whereas with a straight limit order, depending on the available supply or demand at that price, he may not be filled unless the price actually crosses through his limit price.

> **TA Intelligence**
>
> Technicians must understand the often unintended consequences of using a certain order to get in or out of a position. Special orders are powerful tools, but be sure you understand all the possible outcomes before using these orders.

The ability to be flexible is important in many aspects of trading. The degree of volatility and liquidity in your chosen trading vehicles at any given time will impact whether you should employ market orders, limit orders, or MIT orders. Always be open to change how you trade, depending on market circumstances.

Stop Orders

A stop order can be either a buy stop order or a sell stop order. In a buy stop order, you select a stop price above the current market price. If the market rises and touches your buy stop price, the order becomes a market buy order, and you will be filled at whatever the market price is after your stop is touched.

Conversely, in a sell stop order, you select a stop price below the current market price. If the market drops and touches your sell stop price, the order becomes a market sell order, and you will be filled at whatever the market price is after your stop is touched.

Note that the difference between a sell stop order and a sell MIT order is this: sell stop orders are placed at a price below the current market price to sell at market if the price touches the stop price. Sell stop orders are usually used to exit a long position when the market starts moving against it. In contrast, sell MIT orders are placed at a price above the current market price to sell at market if the price touches the MIT price. They are usually used to enter a short position.

Similarly, buy stop orders are placed at a price above the current market price to buy at market if the price touches the stop price. They are usually used to exit a short position if the market moves up instead of down. Buy MIT orders, on the other hand, are placed at a price below the current market price to buy at market if the price touches the MIT price. They are usually used to enter a long position on price pullbacks in the trend.

Stop Limit Orders

A stop limit order combines a stop order and a limit order to gain greater control over the fill price received. It requires the entry of both a stop price and a limit price. Once the stop price is hit, the limit price designates the least you will accept on a sell stop limit and vice versa on a buy stop limit order. The stop and limit price can be the same price, or the limit can be a price a few ticks away from the stop price to decrease the possibility that the price would jump right over your stop limit price like a forest fire jumping over a road. Thus, the downside of a stop limit exit order is the possibility, when used to exit a position, that the order will not be filled and that the market rapidly moves away from your maximum loss target.

Using Stop Orders to Minimize Losses

Stop orders are used for several reasons. The most common reason is to minimize the potential loss on a long or short position that goes against you. For example, if your trading rules require you to not risk more than 5 percent of the price on any one trade, you would enter a sell stop order 5 percent below each long position or a buy stop order 5 percent above each short position. Most traders believe in entering actual stop orders, known as "hard" stops, on their positions as opposed to "mental" stops, in which they pre-determine that they will exit at a specific price point to limit a loss but don't actually enter the order until the price reaches that level. The problem with mental stops is that human nature enters the picture and traders end up rationalizing and "hoping" that prices will return to a profitable level but end up risking more than they planned.

Heads Up _____

Traders who attempt to keep track of orders in their head may be in for a rude awak-ening. Prices can move swiftly in one direction, and the smart trader knows where to put a "stop" to the decision. Relying on stops that only exist in your head is dangerous and should be avoided.

Using Trailing Stop Orders to Protect Gains

Stop orders can also be used to protect a gain on an open position. Unlike a market order that requires you to constantly watch your chart and be ready to pull the trigger, with a stop order you can enter it and let the order do the work.

Traders frequently use a "trailing stop" to follow a profitable price move and lock in prof-its as their positions gain profitability. Trailing stops work like this: initially, after a buy entry, for example, you enter a sell stop order below the entry price in order to minimize your loss if the trade goes against you. Once the trade becomes profitable, you then cancel the original stop order and replace it with a new stop order at, for example, your entry price. At this point, the worst that can happen is that you break even.

Then, as the price continues to rise, you will from time to time cancel your current stop order and place a new order at a higher price to lock in more profit. The secret to this technique is not to move your stop too close to the current price, where it will take you out on a small pullback before continuing in the direction of the major trend.

Info/Tips _____

When using an automatic trailing stop, you must remember to cancel it if you exit the position manually, or you could accidentally be entered into the market in the direction of the stop.

Some computerized trading platforms offer a convenient automatic trailing stop option that constantly moves your stop a user-controlled distance away from the most profitable price reached thus far.

Using Stop Orders to Enter the Market

A stop order can also be used to automatically put you into a trade. This method is often used to trade breakouts out of resistance or support levels, for example. In this form of trading, a buy stop order is placed above a key resistance level and/or a sell stop order is placed below a key support level to initiate a position in the direction of the breakout. This way, you use price momentum in your favor to enter a market already moving in your chosen direction.

Order Management

To summarize basic order mechanics, enter a position with a market or limit order. Then protect against a greater-than-acceptable loss by entering a stop or stop limit order. When your profit target is reached, exit your position with a market or limit order. Incorporate other order types as your trading strategy and style dictates.

All buy and sell orders fall into two broad categories: day orders and good-till-cancelled (GTC) orders. Day orders automatically expire at the end of the trading day if unfilled, whereas GTC orders remain in effect until cancelled by the trader. When you enter your order, you must always specify whether it will be a day order or a GTC order.

Keeping track of your filled and unfilled orders is an ongoing job for traders and especially demands keen attention from active traders who place many trades. In addition to efficiently capturing profit targets and minimizing losses, you must utilize good order-management skills to eliminate the possibility of double fills and other unintended trades.

At times you may have reasons to exit a position before it reaches an existing limit order (profit target) or stop-loss order (maximum loss target). If the price of your new order is close to that of your existing open order, it is a good practice to cancel your open order first to eliminate the possibility of a double fill. Also, make it a habit to immediately cancel unfilled orders on trade setups that you decide to abandon; otherwise, you may find yourself unexpectedly in an unwanted position. Most order entry platforms have a one-click option to "cancel all outstanding orders." In choosing how you want to manage orders, consider the speed of the market and your individual execution skill.

> **TA Intelligence**
>
> Practicing with a simulator, available on most charting software packages these days, is an excellent way to develop your order management technique and build execution skill.

Other Special Order Types

Automated trading systems and large institutional trading desks often use complex entry and exit order strategies that are beyond the scope of this book. The following sections, however, discuss a few additional order types used by discretionary traders.

Fill or Kill

This order instructs the broker to immediately fill an order at a stated price or cancel the order if he is unable to fill it promptly. This order has the immediacy of a market order, but you have control over the fill price.

One Cancels the Other (OCO)

To avoid the possibility of a double fill, this order combines two orders on one order ticket. For example, an OCO order could consist of a limit order to buy at a price below the market and a stop order to buy at a price above the market. Once one side of the order is filled, the other, unfilled side of the order is simultaneously cancelled.

Reversal Stop

Commonly referred to as a "stop and reverse" order, a reversal stop order instructs the broker to close the current position when the stop price is hit and enter a new position in the opposite direction. In other words, this is an order to trade two lots in the opposite direction for every one lot currently owned. Traders find this order type useful in expected range-bound markets to trade both swing directions and "double up," for example, reversing from a long position to a short position.

Proper Stop Placement

One of the biggest challenges traders have in the market is using stop orders correctly. Many novice traders have no idea how to use stops to prevent large losses. Even if they do, they often do not understand where to put them and consequently end up getting shaken out of their positions. After a while, they get frustrated and may stop using stops altogether. That sets them up for a very dangerous situation.

First of all, you should be aware of the fact that, if you don't use stops, you are in danger of having your trading position one day crash on you. For example, imagine if you owned shares of Bear Stearns stock in 2008 and held on while it dropped like a rock and eventually went bankrupt, and you didn't use a stop-loss order. You would have seen your stock go from 30 to 0 in a matter of days. I'm sure it happened to many people who owned it above 30 and who could not conceive of it falling so far so fast. But it happened. And in fact, stocks frequently do drop suddenly and dramatically. That's why you use stops—they help to protect you from unexpected price shocks.

There is really no excuse for holding through such a drop, and the only reason people do is because they don't use sell stop orders. Traders may not know how to use stop orders, or they are afraid they'll get whipsawed: that is, they are afraid that they would get taken out of their position at the very low of the move only to see the stock rally sharply.

It's important for you to remember that the key to making money in the market is to cut your losers. At the same time, you want to let your winners run. Everyone knows this, and it sounds like a simple concept, but many investors and traders simply don't know how to do it.

> **Info/Tips**
>
> Novice traders focus on making the most possible profit and forget to protect themselves against a big loss. Suffering big losses not only reduces your investment capital but is also discouraging. Cut your losses and preserve your investment capital.

Stops as Part of Your Exit Plan

When your technical analysis tools tell you it is a propitious time to make a trade, the first and most important step before you ever take the trade is to have an exit plan in place. This allows you to plan your exit, whether profitable or unprofitable, in a calm and disciplined manner away from the pressures of the moment of decision.

An exit plan should include both an initial exit strategy after entry if the price immediately goes against you and also a strategy for following a profitable move with a trailing stop. Finally, you should have a profit target point in mind.

Your initial potential exit should be a stop order fairly close to your entry price. Now here's the problem: what is close for me may be quite different from what you consider to be close. You may be willing to risk $500 on a position and consider that amount to be "close" to your entry, while I may define "close" as only risking $50. This step of setting stops is one of the most subjective and difficult parts of successful trading. If we set our stop too close when we buy a stock, the price could dip, we would be stopped out of the position (our broker would sell the stock at the stopped price), and the stock could then turn back up just as we supposed it might when we took the position in the first place. On the other hand, if we set it too far away we may be risking more money than we can afford to lose.

Your initial exit stop may be set at a fixed distance away from your entry price, or it may be based on the penetration of a nearby trend line or a support or resistance level. It could be based on an indicator crossover or any one of a number of other tools. The objective is to remove emotion from the exit decision. If you are incorrect in your entry decision, you should be out of the position quickly with a relatively small loss in most cases. First and foremost, you need to protect your priceless trading or investment capital. That gives you the capability to come back and try again another day.

Establishing an initial exit stop addresses the first part of the exit plan. Now, assuming you have correctly predicted the direction of the price move, you may then follow the move with a trailing stop or use a trend line or a moving average or one of a large variety of other techniques to trail the price with a stop while letting your profits run.

How far away you set your stops from the current price is a question of price volatility. Volatility is a measure of how "noisy" stock movement is. That is, how much the price wiggles while moving in a trending direction. The more volatile prices are while in an overall trend, the wider your stop will have to be to avoid being stopped out prematurely.

One way to estimate volatility is to calculate the average range (the length) of the price bars. You will want to set your trailing stop some multiple of average range away from the bar price so as to put it far enough away to avoid the noise and preclude you from being taken out of your position before the trend has run its course.

The important point to remember is that you can't expect to set the same trailing stops in a volatile market as you would in a calm market and get the same results. You must be willing and able to adapt your stop strategy as market volatility changes.

There are a number of volatility-based stop tools available on most charting and trading platforms, such as Welles Wilder's Parabolic stop and the generic percentage trailing stop. You can also use one of the more sophisticated adaptive trailing stop tools, such as the Arps Trender, available from Jan Arps' Traders' Toolbox at www.janarps.com.

Figure 17.1 illustrates the application, the Arps Trender, to a daily chart of Microsoft. Note that the stop line first follows the price downward until the price bar on March 10 closes above it. The stop line then changes direction and follows the price upward through the course of the entire rally, staying just far enough away to avoid the random noise.

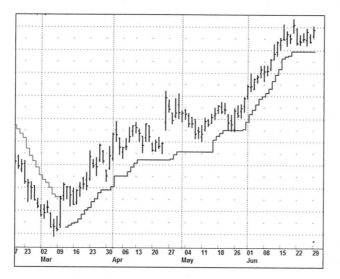

Figure 17.1

A trailing stop example, the Arps Trender.

Stop Placement Guidelines

Some traders abide by strict stop placement guidelines, whereas others have a flexible approach dictated by the particular trade setup and the current volatility of the instrument they are trading. As in many aspects of trading, find what best suits your trading style and individual risk tolerance.

Enter stop orders immediately after your entry order is filled on all orders, regardless of how confident you are about the trade setup, your execution skill, and the risk of the trade.

Never let a winning trade become a loss: raise your stop-loss order to breakeven at the earliest opportunity or take your profit once the trade makes significant signs of reversing. Keep in mind that you can always reenter for a continuation trade. On the other hand, unless you have the uncanny ability to buy at the exact bottom of a move and sell at the exact top, it's normal for a long trade initially to have a small positive move and then to reverse to a small loss before the anticipated trend finally takes hold. So use smart stop placement to give the trade some "breathing room" at the beginning.

Enter a "hard" stop on all trades as opposed to using a "mental" stop. In a mental stop, the trader plans (hopes) to exit a losing position at a specified price manually. Traders often use mental stops in the belief that they can exit a failing trade in time and also to avoid a practice known as "running the stops," where large professional traders hit the obvious stop price points and then reverse the market back to the original direction for easy money. Needless to say, it can be very frustrating to take a stop loss and then see your position immediately or eventually recover fully. Having no stop, however, exposes the trader to a potentially larger-than-expected loss in the event that the market reverses with a sharp move through the stop price or the trader fails to exit in time and then the market trends strongly against his position with no significant reversals.

Here are a few common mantras in trading: "Let your profits run, cut your losses short." "Plan your trade and trade your plan." "Never let a winner become a loser." And so on. These sayings have evolved to help traders deal with the mental challenges of trading. Once you have adequate experience and methodology, it is often said that trading is 90 percent mental. Trading with sound and proven technical analysis techniques can help to remove emotions from your trading decisions.

The Least You Need to Know

- ◆ Market orders are executed immediately at the best available price at the time the order is entered.

- ◆ Limit orders are only executed at a price no worse than the limit price specified.

- ◆ Stop orders and MIT orders become market orders when the price specified is touched. Buy stop orders are always placed above the current market price, whereas buy MIT orders are always placed below the current market price and vice versa for sell stop and sell MIT orders.

- ◆ Stop orders become market orders when the price specified is touched. They are usually used to limit losses in a trade that does not go as expected or to protect a winning trade from turning into a losing trade.

- ◆ Most successful traders use trailing stops to prevent winning trades from turning into losing trades.

- ◆ Proper stop management gives traders the power to let their profits run while cutting their losses short.

Chapter 18

Developing a Trading Plan

In This Chapter

- ◆ The value of a trading plan
- ◆ Structuring your trading plan
- ◆ Contents of a trading plan
- ◆ Managing your trading capital

It may be a cliché, but you should plan your trades and trade your plan. A trading plan helps keep emotion out of trading decisions, which is a major advantage over most traders who are making it up as they go along. A trading plan is your road map, especially when things don't go as planned. A written trading plan and a trading journal can help you become a better trader. You hold yourself accountable for success or failure and learn as much from your mistakes as from your successes. Money management is a critical part of any trading plan. Your plan and the accompanying journal of successes and failures sharpen your trading skills.

Your Trading Plan

The world has changed—it is not a buy-and-hold market anymore. You need to be nimble, trade with a plan, and be disciplined. If you are flying by the seat of your pants, your emotions can easily override your better judgment and force you into a reactive mentality, such as selling only after a significant decline. To win in the business of trading, just like in any other business, you need to have an edge. With technical analysis, that edge is the use of your analytic tools to buy a stock in the very early stages of a new uptrend, for example, and to sell it in the very late stages before the price trends down. It helps if you become an expert at a small number of patterns in the markets and then exploit those patterns when they reappear.

In order to effectively manage your emotions when trading, it helps to have a written plan that you can review regularly to stay focused on your goal of trading success. Your trading plan can give you a clear vision for a trade, including how much of your capital to risk, where to enter, where to take profits, and where to exit if the trade goes against you.

There are several reasons to have a trading plan, but probably the biggest is the way that it simplifies things. Decision making becomes very clear cut. The trading plan defines what is supposed to be done, when, and how. Just follow the plan. The plan serves as a roadmap to entering and holding, profit taking, or cutting losses. Writing down your plan gives you an immediate edge over most traders and investors.

Whenever you plan a trade, you should have two goals: to make money and to become a better trader. Your trading plan can be very useful in helping you to understand the reasons for any performance problems you are experiencing (and to highlight what is working for you). It gives you the ability to measure your performance in a very clear, straight-forward manner on a running basis.

Just as you use a map to determine the route to an unfamiliar destination and to follow the progress that has been made along your planned route, your trading plan gives you benchmarks for use in following your progress in the execution of your plan. From this experience, you can learn from your mistakes and successes and thereby improve your trading abilities as time goes on.

For example, if you are experiencing losses beyond what would be expected by following the plan, there are only two possible reasons. Either you are not following the plan, or there is a problem with the trading system. That's it. Without the trading plan, resolving performance issues becomes a much more complicated process.

Info/Tips

Your trading plan won't be of much value if you dash it off in 10 minutes and then stick it in a file and forget it. Spend some time formulating the plan and then integrate it into your daily routine. Some traders find a quick review before each trading session helps them stay focused until the plan is a natural part of what they do each day.

Contents of a Trading Plan

A trading plan usually consists of four parts:

1. Rules for entry

2. Rules for exit

3. Money management rules

4. Selecting a trading strategy

In addition to these four parts, you should have a methodology for recording your trading decisions.

Rules for Entry

The first part of your plan addresses your entry rules. The key to good entries is putting on trades where there is a relatively low risk compared to a relatively high reward. Your entry rule should also include a clear reason for a price move in the expected direction. You may want to include which technical analysis tools and indicators you will rely on for trading signals.

Rules for Exit

The second part of your plan addresses your exit rules. For your exits, you must first define an initial loss exit point for your trade in case you are mistaken in your assessment of the expected price direction and the trade begins to lose money. This is the point where you say, "I'm going to cut my losses and move on to the next trade," rather than hoping the trade will suddenly become profitable. You will also need a trailing stop technique to protect your profits and limit your potential loss as the trade goes in your direction. And finally, you will need to define a profit target where you would expect to exit your position with a profit. Your profit target does not need to be an unchangeable hard and fast number; it can change as conditions change, but it gives you a way to evaluate the probable reward-to-risk ratio and thereby make a determination if the gain to be made from the trade is worth the potential risk of loss. While your profit target may change in the happy event you pick a rocket going up, your exit strategy should be written in stone. Once this mark is hit, you are out of the trade.

Info/Tips _____

When preparing your trading plan, you will need to determine what type of orders you will use to enter and exit your trade. For entries, many traders prefer to use limit orders rather than market orders. This way their risk and reward is clearly defined on entry. When exiting, on the other hand, many traders prefer to use stop orders to protect profits if the market turns against them and limit orders to exit at their profit target. If you need to exit quickly, a market order would be your best choice as compared to the risk of losing even more money with a missed limit order.

Money Management Rules

In your plan, you must also define what percentage of your capital you will commit to each trade. This is different for each trader, but somewhere between 2 percent and 20 percent would be a typical amount. For example, if you commit 10 percent of your capital to a trade, a 20 percent loss on that position would represent a 2 percent loss on your entire trading capital. Your goal should be to keep your risk per trade at 2 percent or less of your portfolio value in order to avoid being wiped out completely by a string of consecutive losses.

Your plan should specify the maximum number of positions you can comfortably focus on at the same time. If your portfolio is too big, it's easy to lose focus, which could lead to the possibility of missing an exit on a trade at a critical point in time. A comfortable maximum might be 6 to 10 different positions at one time. Beginners will want to start with even fewer positions until comfortable with monitoring more trades.

Selecting a Trading Strategy

Finally, you must decide on the strategy or strategies you will use to identify trades with a high probability of profit along with an acceptable level of risk. That means you should only consider trades with relatively small capital exposure (risk) and pass up any trade setup, no matter how good it looks, if the risk is more than allowed by the trading plan. Generally, you should look for opportunities with at least a 3:1 reward-to-risk ratio.

TA Intelligence

Shorting is an acceptable and potentially profitable strategy if you follow the indicators. Betting a stock is going to fall because "it feels like it" is a recipe for failure.

Be as willing to trade the short side of the market as the long side. There should be no reason to fear "shorting" a stock or futures contract. Take a look at any price chart, and the likelihood is that you will see that moves down are usually faster than moves up. This should alert you to the fact that there is a real trade opportunity there.

With respect to the mechanics of shorting, it is no different than going long except that you sell the instrument now with the intent of buying it back later at (hopefully) a lower price. If the price falls when you are long, you lose, and if the price rises when you are short, you lose. The margin requirements are the same. Make sure you study your markets carefully, but if the signal is calling for a short position, don't be afraid of it.

Once you have clarified all of the preceding aspects of your trading plan, you are in a much better position to control your emotions when trading. Make sure to review your plan on a regular basis to reinforce your good trading habits.

Writing Down Your Trading Plan

Every trader has a little bit different way to set up his or her own trading plan. One good way is to use a spreadsheet format. You can create this spreadsheet yourself, or as a worthwhile alternative, you can purchase a ready-made trading plan worksheet. One of the best is the AK47 trading plan form available from www.elder.com. The AK47 worksheet is set up so that for each trade you make you can enter, along with your entry price and stop levels, your reasons for taking the trade, the results, and what you learned from the experience.

Your first part of the plan should address what markets you are going to trade. Stocks? Futures? ETFs? Forex? Once you decide, you need to stick with your chosen market long enough to gain sufficient expertise rather than giving up and looking for the next great thing.

For example: I will focus on trading stocks on a daily chart that have an average daily volume turnover of at least XXXX shares. I will look for both long and short setups to follow the market in whichever direction it decides to move. I will only take trades consistent with the direction of the medium-term trend, as defined by the 200-day moving average. My setup will be a pullback of price into its moving average. My trigger will be a zero-line crossover of the MACD oscillator signal line after the pullback. I will not take a trade without a proper setup and trigger signal.

For each trade, I will invest no more than 15 percent of my total trading capital. I will risk no more than 2 percent of my total trading capital on any one trade and will use good-till-cancelled stop-loss orders to ensure that I do not hold on to my position beyond my stop-loss point.

I will look for flag and pennant pattern projections and previous support and resistance levels to determine my initial profit target. When prices have reached the half-way point to my profit target, I will exit one half of my position on a limit order and move my stop-loss exit order to my entry price, thus guaranteeing, at worst, a profit on one half of my original position and a breakeven trade on the other half. I will enter a limit order to exit the remainder of my position at the profit target.

After entering the trade, I will record the reasons for taking the trade and my expectations for profit. Upon the completion of my trade I will record where I exited, the reasons for the exit, and whether or not the trade worked out in accordance with my expectations. I will rank my trades as follows:

♦ Successful exit at profit target

♦ Exited at a different price from profit target but profitable

♦ Exited at breakeven

♦ A losing trade at a different price from my stop

♦ Taken out of the trade at my stop level

♦ Impulsive exit at a loss

My trading plan will also include a remarks column where I can elaborate on what I learned from this trade. For example, I may have entered on a specific signal but exited too late or too early because I wasn't paying attention or I was too hopeful or too scared or second-guessed my analyses. This way, I hold myself accountable and will hopefully learn from my mistakes by regularly reviewing the results of past trades. I must remember that it is not my entry that makes or loses me money but rather where I exit relative to my entry!

Heads Up _____

Your trading plan is only as good as you make it. Write it as if you were going to show it to a banker to apply for a loan. Better yet, give a trusted friend or colleague a copy of the plan and ask him or her to go over it with you once a month or so. This way, you are holding yourself accountable to another, which will make fudging on the plan more difficult.

Applying Your Trading Plan

What else can a beginning technical analyst do to ramp up as quickly as possible on the road to becoming a successful trader? First of all, there is no substitute for real trading and market experience. You can "paper trade" for months, but when you've got real money on the line, it's different. Stuff just sinks in to your brain and is not forgotten when you're making or losing real money.

It can be quite useful to your growth as a technical analyst/trader to attend some good seminars or webinars and listen to the best technical analysts in the world explain why they are successful. The trading magazines and trading websites listed in Appendix B often carry schedules of upcoming seminars and webinars.

You should read some good books by successful technical analysts and traders. Not only do you need to know the markets, you also need to know how the successful traders trade them. There are scores of books on the subject of technical analysis, and many of the best are in our list of recommended books shown in Appendix B.

For example, in his book *Trading in the Zone*, Mark Douglas writes, "You must be rigid in your rules and flexible in your expectations. Most traders are flexible in their rules and rigid in their expectations." There is a great deal of wisdom in that statement. If you are rigid in your expectations, you often tend to form a market bias based on your expectations and hold to that bias regardless of what the chart is actually telling you. You will buy a stock when good news is released, then stubbornly hold on to it even though the chart and your technical indicators tell you that the price is dropping and no sign of a reversal is in sight.

This leads to the second problem, being flexible instead of rigid in your rules. Indeed, most traders do not even have a trading plan with a clearly set forth set of rules to trade by. Oh, they will say they use stops and profit targets, but few actually have and follow specific rules set forth in a well-written trading plan. Even if they do, many traders often treat them as being optional, which defeats the whole purpose of even having a trading plan.

Yes, trading requires you to be flexible. However, all of the expected flexibility can be defined as part of the rules in your trading plan. For example, in your rules you can define what constitutes a change in market direction and then address how you would react to such a change. Your rules might call for exiting your entire position, exiting half, or moving your stop closer in that situation. The point is, you have predefined your action in the event of a change in circumstances, and you do not have to make that decision impulsively in the heat of the moment.

Traders should follow the saying, "Plan your trade and then trade your plan." If you violate any of your trading rules, make yourself take a break. If you love trading, having to be away from it should feel terrible. You will avoid being put in the penalty box at all costs.

Money Management

As we have stressed before in this book, the goal of technical analysis is to allow the investor or trader to improve his trading effectiveness and thereby become more profitable in his investment activities. An important aspect of this process is intelligent money management.

Money management represents the administrative side of the trading plan. It addresses the question of how best to employ the capital available to you in the most effective manner possible with the goal of maximizing your profitability while at the same time protecting your precious capital by minimizing the risk of ruin. No technical trading strategy will produce consistently profitable results in the long run without also incorporating a systematic approach to money management so as to maximize your return on investment while minimizing your risk.

Info/Tips

Most brokers have good reporting tools to let you know where you are with the money in your trading account. However, if you find yourself unsure of your balance because commissions, fees, and such are not posted in a timely manner, it's time to find a new trading platform. Don't rely on any accounting of your capital but your own. That way, you will always be confident where you are financially.

For example, many investors got very badly hurt in the bear market of 2008–2009 by holding on to their positions and hoping for a reversal while the market sank to ever lower lows. Typically, in such a situation people first think that the initial drop is just a regular pullback. Then they vow to sell on the next rally. Then the market falls, and they feel they cannot afford to sell this cheap—while the market continues sliding, decimating their account.

As the preceding example illustrates, the essence of money management is managing risk. Wise money management is the basis of any trading strategy and is what ultimately will distinguish a successful trader from a consistent loser. Many a trader has fallen to the wayside trying to make a bundle in one trade when he probably would have been better off making small, steady gains and working his way up the wealth ladder.

The subject of money management includes consideration of the following factors:

- Deciding on the optimum amount of money to commit to any one trade relative to your total available trading capital

- Protecting your profits from erosion

- Avoiding turning a small losing position into a big losing position

- Determining when and how to increase the size of your cash commitment when the odds are in your favor (that is, when and how to add to a winning position when you are risking the "house's money")

- Recognizing the importance of taking some of your winnings off the table after a profitable streak

There is no "holy grail" in trading. However, if there were one, I think it would be having a sufficient amount of money to trade and taking small risks. Many successful traders initially wiped out small accounts early in their careers. It was only after they became adequately capitalized and learned to take reasonable risks that they survived as long-term traders.

Your Emotions and Money Management

One reason why successful trading can be so difficult to achieve is the emotions wrapped up in the money we trade. If in our minds we are equating the money on the next trade with the money needed for the car payment, the kids' tuition money, or the mortgage, we are on a sure path to trading failure. If it is money we can't afford to lose, it is money we simply can't afford to trade. If we attach our emotions to the money at risk, we are much more likely to commit trading errors, which is as bad a malady as having a bad system to follow.

Here's how one trader uses visual imagery to help him recognize and accept the risk of loss when taking a trade: When I begin to plan out a trade, I use a visual cue that helps me stay within the loss parameters I have set for myself. I view my trading account as a checking account, and when I am planning my trade and filling out my trade sheet (which I always do before I enter any trade), I literally write a check out in the air, right in front of myself, for the amount that the potential trade will cost my trading account if my stop loss is reached. If the check that I write out is for an amount more than what is my maximum acceptable loss on any trade, I do not take the trade.

The act of writing the check out in the air forces me to confront the size of the potential loss before the trade is entered. And writing this check before each trade is entered has an added benefit: As I write the check, I simply consider that I have just spent that amount out of my trading account. I assume that money is gone, even before the trade is entered!

Sound crazy? By assuming the stop-loss money is gone, I have also dealt with any emotions associated with the trade if it turns into a loser: I've already lost that money, right? But if it turns into a winning trade, I not only get the profits I accrue in the trade, but I get the initial stop-loss money check back as an added bonus! Try it. You might find it helps you limit the size of your losses and makes it easier to deal with your losses.

Determining the Correct Reward-to-Risk Ratio

If you are trading according to your plan, you should only take trades that have a risk/reward ratio of at least two dollars gained for every dollar risked. Thus, if on average you are risking $100 on every trade, your winning trades should average at least $200 at the end of each month. If your monthly reward-to-risk ratio is higher than 2:1 and you make winning trades 50 percent of the time, you are well on your way to becoming a profitable trader.

Heads Up _____

It has been said that the best way to make money in the stock market is to not lose it. This may sound odd, but if you manage your losses (keeping them small), your profits don't have to be "home runs" to earn you a good living.

Limiting the Damage to Your Account from Losses

We also need to set some rules limiting our maximum allowable losses over a fixed period of time. For example, these rules should address the following:

♦ The maximum amount of money you are allowed to lose on any one trade

♦ The maximum amount of money you are allowed to lose in any given week

♦ The maximum number of losing trades you are allowed to have in a week before you stop trading for the rest of the week

♦ The maximum number of consecutive losing trades you are allowed before you stop trading for the rest of the week

♦ The maximum number of losing trades in the same direction you are allowed to take in a week before you stop trading

If you violate one of your trading rules, you will take some days off, staying away from the markets entirely. Does that sound restrictive to you? It's meant to be restrictive. There should be hard limits on every aspect of your trading. If you start to lose money and it turns into a series of losers, you want hard limits in place so that the damage to your account is limited. If you break one of your trading rules, you are either out of control or you are very tired and ragged and badly in need of an emotional or physical break.

Pat Yourself on the Back

A very important part of the overall trading plan should be to reward you. Here's how one trader set up his trading plan to reward himself:

♦ Once I am up $500 on a single trade, I will put a trailing stop order $250 below the highest price reached to protect a portion of that profit.

♦ Once I reach my predetermined profit target, I will close the trade and take the money.

♦ If I am up more than $5,000 for the month, I will put a profit floor of $2,000 below the cumulative profits for the month to protect a portion of those profits. If my cumulative monthly profits drop through that level, I will stop trading with real money for the rest of the month. I will only "paper trade."

♦ If I am up more than $10,000 for the month, I will take the rest of the month off, stay away from the trading screen, and do something I enjoy other than trading: take a vacation, sleep late and read books, or do something else fun.

♦ If my account is up for the month, I will withdraw at least 20 percent of my profits for that month and put the money in the bank or a savings account to use for something other than trading.

Trading is hard work! When we get it right, it is important to internally recognize that we did something special. Look at what we accomplish by taking some money off the table and paying ourselves:

♦ We remove a portion of our risk.

♦ We create a cash flow for our family.

♦ We create a sense of accomplishment, which allows us greater confidence in our system.

♦ We have justified our hard work and turned our trading money into spending money.

Too many traders open a brokerage account, fund it, and forget it. Once they send their money into cyberspace, it no longer feels real. It takes on the effect of being a game. They watch their accounts go up and down. They add to their positions as the account balance goes up, only to take a loss and watch the account balance zoom back down—it's the ultimate "yo-yo" effect. However, the simple act of physically paying themselves by withdrawing some of their profits changes everything from being a game to being a legitimate business and attaches a value to their trading.

If you have never tried this, I urge you to do this one simple thing: After your next winning month, contact your broker and withdraw some funds from your account. It doesn't matter how small or large the amount, just do it. Make sure he sends you a check, not wired funds. Once you get the check, deposit it in an interest-bearing checking account. I guarantee you will feel better about trading and technical analysis than you ever have. It will probably make your spouse happy, too!

The Least You Need to Know

♦ A written trading plan helps you to stay focused on your goal of trading success. In addition, it helps you learn from your mistakes and successes and thereby improve your trading abilities as time goes on.

♦ A skilled trader should only take trades where there is a relatively low risk compared to a relatively high reward.

♦ One of the keys to profitable trading is limiting the damage to your account from losses with well-placed stop-loss orders.

♦ A skilled trader should be as willing to trade the short side of the market as the long side.

♦ Allocate only a small fraction of your trading capital to each trade.

♦ When you have a profitable month, pay yourself by withdrawing some money from your account and putting it in the bank.

Part 4

Trading Mechanics

Knowing your best opportunities to seize a profit or avoid a loss is the real value of technical analysis. Timing in trading is everything, and technical analysis gives you an edge that can mean the difference between profit and loss. This part completes the picture by walking you through the actual process of trading, including developing a trading plan, understanding the types of entry and exit orders skilled traders use, and knowing when to pull the trigger.

Chapter 19

Making the Trade

In This Chapter

- ◆ Entering and exiting trades
- ◆ Best entry positions
- ◆ Trading strategies
- ◆ Exiting a trade

Now that you have learned about many of the different chart patterns, analytic tools, and setups, you can start to work identifying good buying and short selling opportunities. Rather than blindly depending on your broker's advice, you can now quickly see which of your potential trades have a high probability of success and which ones are very likely to give you an ulcer.

When you look at a historic price chart that displays a major advance, in hindsight you will see that there were a few points in time that would have been the perfect place to take a position. Selecting the best (or a very good) point to enter and exit a trade is the essence of technical analysis. Technical analysis helps you increase the probability that your entry and exit points will assure you of a profit. These ideal entry and exit points are what we are now going to focus on.

Ready, Aim, Fire!—Planning and Entering a Trade

There is a four-step process every trader should go through before actually pulling the trigger.

The Trend Confirmation (Ready)

Plan to take trades only in the direction of the longer-term trend. An excellent method to ascertain whether the short-, medium-, and long-term trends are confirming one another is to watch multiple moving averages. If they are moving up or moving down together, you can feel more confident about the direction and strength of the trend.

Figure 19.1

Short, medium, and long moving averages confirm the trend direction.

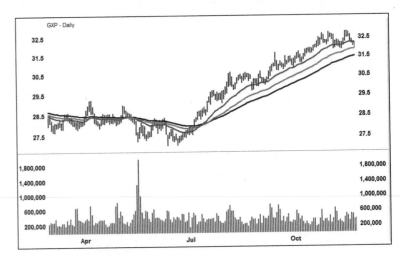

The Setup (Aim)

Once you have confirmed the overall direction of the trend, look for a specific price pattern consistent with the direction of the overall trend to set up your entry. For example, you may want to wait for price to encounter a support or resistance level and enter on the "bounce back" from that level into the direction from which it came. Alternatively, your plan may be to wait for a breakthrough, a support or resistance level, followed by a pullback to that level, at which point you would look to enter on a stop order if price bounces off that level back into the direction of the original breakout.

You may want to look for particular volume patterns to confirm the price patterns you are seeing. Are you seeing a "climax volume" up bar where the volume and the bar's range are both very large, or a high-volume "churn" bar where the volume is high but the bar's range is relatively small, or a low-volume and small-range bar indicating a lack of demand?

A high-volume large-range bar whose close is lower than the open often confirms a top, while a high-volume large-range bar whose close is higher than the open often confirms a bottom. The important thing is that you have a plan of entry, as well as a contingency exit strategy, before committing to take the trade.

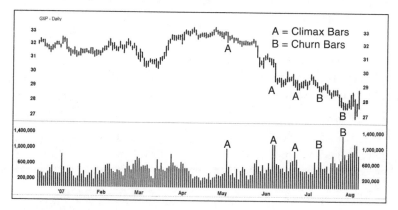

Figure 19.2

Climax bars and churn bars.

The Entry (Fire!)

Once you have established your plan, place an order to enter the market on a limit order or a stop order consistent with your setup strategy. As soon as your entry order is filled, enter a protective stop order to exit your position consistent with your contingency plan to exit if you are wrong in your assessment of the upcoming direction of the market.

The Plan to Manage Your Trade (Confirm)

Follow winning trades with a trailing stop and set a reasonable profit target. Always keep in mind what your reward-to-risk ratio is going to be before taking a trade. Remember, there are two aspects of risk to consider:

1. Risk in terms of a specific individual trade.

2. Risk as a percentage of your trading capital.

In terms of individual trade risk, a good rule of thumb is not to risk more than one third of your anticipated minimum profit. Thus, if your analysis shows a potential $300 move in your favor, do not risk more than $100 if price moves the wrong way. With respect to the second consideration, risk as a percentage of your trading capital, the most important criterion is not to deplete your trading capital below some acceptable minimum. Otherwise, you are out of the trading game and no longer able to take new positions. Most professional money managers recommend that you risk no more than 1 percent to 3 percent of your trading capital on any one position.

The Exit

Remember, it's not where you enter that generates your profit—it's where you exit! Establish a profit target price and place a limit order to exit your position with a profit at that price. This profit target order may be changed as the trend develops, but having one in place gives you the discipline to keep an attractive profit from turning into a loss because you were too stubborn or too greedy to take it when you had the opportunity.

As the trade becomes profitable, replace your protective sell stop with a trailing stop that you raise, but never lower, as prices continue to rise. For example, some traders ratchet up their trailing stop at a price one tick below the lowest low of the most recent three price bars.

As soon as your trailing stop rises to the level of your entry price, exit one half of your position. This way you have locked in a profit. At worst you will exit the other half of your position at a breakeven.

Exit the balance of your position at your profit target. You are not likely to pick the exact top of the trend, but your odds of the trend continuing without a new pullback are decreasing significantly. Don't try to pick exactly when a market is ready to turn around. Too many traders, novice and pros alike, will try to make the decision when a trend has played itself out, and will continue to try to make money against the trend. The market is not going to turn from a trend up or down just because you want it to, or think that it should. Let the market tell you when the trend has ended and then get on the right side.

Info/Tips

When the trade is done, don't look back to what could have been. Spend a few minutes analyzing each trade to determine how you could have done better, and then forget the trade. Dwelling on past success or failure won't help you become a better trader.

No One Is Perfect

Keep in mind that no trading strategy is perfect. However, basing your trading on some simple rules and logic helps to stack the odds in your favor. Even the big gambling casinos don't win all the time. They do well over time, though, because they understand that they don't always have to win. They just need to stick to their rules that give them an edge, which means betting against people who don't have the edge. In the preceding example, we are looking to buy when things are on sale. Our buy signal told us objectively that someone was selling after a decline in price and selling within the context of an uptrend.

This can only be the action of unsophisticated sellers. A consistently profitable trader does not sell short after a small decline in price within the context of a major uptrend.

Order Types to Use to Enter or Exit a Position

Different entry and exit strategies require different types of orders. For example, if you plan to buy a stock on a breakout, the best type of entry order to use is a buy stop order. With a buy stop order, you will automatically be entered into your position when and if the price has some momentum in the direction of your entry, even if you are away from your computer and your charts. With this type of order, you avoid the frustration of missing a trade because you were not watching your charts when the big move started.

Your best decisions are usually made when the markets are closed, late at night or on weekends—a time when you can calmly study the charts and decipher their message without distractions and then enter one or more resting orders before the market opens to buy or sell at your chosen price. That's where resting buy and sell stop orders are useful. They will automatically be executed without you actually having to be there watching the market to enter the trade.

There is one problem with a regular buy stop order, however. Let's say you have studied your charts during the evening after the markets have closed and determined that ABC stock, which closed at 11.75, shows the possibility of breaking out above resistance at 12.00. So before the market opens the next morning, you enter a stop order to buy if the price breaks out above 12.00 and reaches 12.10. Then, just before trading begins, good news is announced on the stock, and as a result the price gaps up from yesterday's close of 11.75 and opens at 15. So now, instead of buying it at your perfect entry price of 12.10, you suddenly find yourself owning the stock at a price of 15. Although the trade may ultimately work out anyway, a price of 15 was not where you had wanted to enter the position. For one thing, your reward-to-risk ratio is now much lower than it was when the price was around 12.

In view of this potential issue, many traders do an end-run around the problem. They enter a buy stop limit order. This order instructs the floor broker to buy if the price reaches your stop level, but at a price no higher than the specified limit price. So, for example, if you entered an order to buy 100 shares of ABC at 12.10 stop 12.20 limit, you know you will not buy at a price any higher than 12.20. If the price jumps to 15 on the open, it will have skipped over your limit price of 12.20, the maximum price you are willing to pay, and you will have eliminated the ulcer factor because you won't have to worry about ending up paying a much higher price than you had bargained for.

Here is another situation traders often encounter: Suppose you entered a stop order on a Monday morning, and the price didn't reach your stop price that day. Normally, your order would expire at the end of the trading day. Then you get busy and forget to reenter your order on Tuesday, and of course, Murphy's Law being what it is, that's the day that the price breaks out. Your order isn't in, and the price ends up running away from you. There's an old cliché that says, "The market will do what you expect but not when you expect it to." So be prepared for this eventuality.

Consequently, after you do your homework and plan your trades, you should enter your stop limit orders as good-till-cancelled (GTC) orders. This means that your order remains active until you specifically cancel the order or it gets filled, whichever comes first. Just be careful to keep good records. It's your responsibility if you forget to cancel the order, and you end up getting filled days later on a GTC order.

Using GTC stop orders to enter and exit the markets is useful in several ways. First of all, this type of order eliminates the need for you to have to watch the market closely during the day, allowing you to focus your attention on other things (such as your day job, for example). Secondly, you will be making fewer emotionally driven decisions in the heat of the moment that you may regret later. It's crucial that you learn to trade in a disciplined, relaxed manner. The more structured your trading decisions and the less subject to judgments and emotions, the more profitable you will become. You must avoid at all costs the twin demons of fear and greed. Fear causes you to panic and sell at the bottom, while greed motivates you to buy right near the top.

TA Intelligence

When you begin using technical analysis in your trading, it may be useful to keep a "cheat sheet" that describes the features of the orders you may use in a given trading day. This cheat sheet can be on paper or in an electronic file on your computer. Double-check your orders against this cheat sheet to be confident you are using the correct order type.

When you place your order, be sure to place it carefully and deliberately. If you place your orders over the telephone, the most important thing is to *listen* carefully when the order is repeated back to you. Be sure you are not hearing what you want to hear; instead, listen to what is actually being said. If you said "buy" when you meant "sell" or vice versa, and the order is read back to you, you may often believe you heard correctly—until the order is filled and you realize you made a mistake. That may cost you. Even if you gave the order correctly, if the clerk or broker wrote it down wrong, he or she will read it back the way he or she wrote it. The same caveat applies if you enter your order electronically. If you don't catch the mistake … it is your mistake!

If your plan is to sell and you mistakenly place the order as a buy (or vice versa), correct your error the moment you realize what you have done. Your error usually ends up costing you more money if you wait to see if the market will help you get out of your mistake with a profit or less of a loss by turning back in the direction of your erroneous order.

Pyramiding—Adding to an Existing Position

"Pyramiding" or "scaling in" refers to adding more shares to a profitable position. The idea is that, when you first take a new position, you enter with only a portion of the money you plan to commit to the position so that if you are wrong you don't risk too much. Then, if the price moves your way, you can add to your position. That way, only if you are right will you have your maximum-sized position. Putting the ratios in your favor can make you a more profitable trader.

So, for example, if you believe you are at the beginning of a sustained uptrend, begin by committing 50 percent of your planned investment in the trade to a long position and enter a stop-loss order below your entry point. After the move in your direction has begun, move your stop-loss order to protect yourself against loss on the existing position, commit another 30 percent to the position, and move your trailing sell stop order to protect some more of your profits. If the trend continues in your direction, add the final 20 percent to your position and move your stop-loss order up again. Your pyramid is now complete. From this point on, keep moving your trailing stop up incrementally as price moves up to protect more and more profit.

A pyramid should always begin with the largest incremental capital commitment first, then adding a decreasing amount with each additional purchase. *Never* build an inverted pyramid, with the smallest cash commitment first and then increasing quantities with subsequent additions of capital. By adding to your winning position in progressively smaller increments, you have kept your average entry price relatively low, and even if the market pulls back, the damage to your account should be minimal. Conversely, if you build an inverted pyramid, you are raising your average entry price substantially, which can mean that a small reversal in the trend direction can erase all of your gains in the trade and, in many cases, much more.

Reviewing Your Trades

Have an end-of-day routine to review your trades and to evaluate whether you have followed your plan. If a trade was closed during the day and was a winner, review the data you had when you made the trade to see if there was anything at that time that you may have overlooked that could have helped you maximize your profits on that particular trade.

If the trade was a loser, ask yourself if, based on the available data and research that you performed at the time, you would have still made the trade. If you can answer "yes" to that second question, then you made a good trade even if it was a loser.

Also determine if you correctly placed your stop order and if there was any way you could have cut your loss even further. After you have reviewed the trade and learned from it, then forget that particular trade. There is nothing you can do to change the results now, good or bad, and your attention needs to be focused on preparing for the next trade. Move forward in your education and trading, not backward. Planning your potential trades for the next day will give you a more balanced market feel and allow you to be relaxed and confident as you follow your profitable game plan the next day.

Success in the markets comes by minimizing risk. Unfortunately, too many traders look at the market only from the viewpoint of maximizing reward and end up taking unnecessary risks to achieve it. Ignoring a stock's technical position just because it has strong fundamentals can easily result in a quick loss.

Cutting losses short is crucial for long-term investment success. Look at it this way: Taking a trading or investment position can result in only one of five eventual outcomes. We can make a large profit, make a small profit, break even, have a small loss, or have a large loss. If we can possibly eliminate one of these outcomes, obviously the large losses, then we're left with the other four. Over the years the small profits, small losses, and breakeven positions will offset one another, leaving us with the enjoyment of occasionally booking the large profit. That's what we are after, and that's why avoiding large losses is such an important part of anyone's trading plan.

Adequate Capital

Be sure your trading business (and never forget to treat it as a business and not as a game) is adequately capitalized. Undercapitalization is one of the biggest reasons why many traders fail. When you are trading with your fingers crossed because you have placed yourself in a position where a few losses can wipe out your entire capital reserve, your trading becomes desperate. When you are trading with very little equity, you have become a gambler instead of a businessman. You are simply hoping to hit the jackpot. Never risk more than you can comfortably afford to lose and still have sufficient capital left in reserve to regain your profitability.

Many traders' emotions tend to move to extremes. On one end you have greed, usually associated with a top (nobody left to buy), while at the other extreme you have fear, usually associated with a bottom (nobody left to sell). The two emotions have quite a different effect on your body.

Greed involves the feelings of increased material wealth. When you are anticipating large profits, you feel exhilarated; the endorphins are racing through your body. You can do no wrong, and you are mentally spending the wealth you expect to generate.

Fear, on the other hand, is something unpleasant you feel in the pit of your stomach. It affects your world outlook, your health, and your ability to behave rationally. Hope often accompanies fear. Hope that things are bound to get better before they get any worse. Hope that we will be given a second chance to redeem our bad investment decision before it devours us. As a result, many traders in a losing position hang on way too long, hoping and expecting that prices will rebound and prove them correct. Unfortunately, in most cases, such feelings result in even larger losses until, at last, in a fit of frustration, the losing trader capitulates and "throws in his cards."

Info/Tips

Technical analysis can do many things for your investment success. One of the most important characteristics of technical analysis is removing emotion from the investment decision.

On the other hand, when you have had several profitable trades in a row, you can easily become overconfident, and you may also start to overtrade your account or begin deviating from your research and plan. You begin to feel that you can take more risks because you deserve the big money (greed again). Be sure to stay with your plan so that you will have the pleasure of seeing your account continue to grow. Don't throw all that away! If you shoot for the big hit, you will likely lose. Remember to stick to the plan and look for steady growth in your equity. If you are making a 10 percent return per month, consider this: where else can you generate a 120 percent return annually? It is the methodical trading that will keep you on track toward profits if your plan is working. There is a saying in the markets: "Bulls and bears make money … pigs get slaughtered!" By the way, don't forget to take a break from trading from time to time, particularly if you start to feel over-stressed or you could suffer a losing streak.

How to Exit a Position

Traders don't make money when they enter a position; their profit depends on where they exit their position. Good exits are the key to successful trading. That's why no entry should ever be made until and unless you have in mind an exit strategy. Without a good exit strategy, the likelihood of success is greatly reduced.

When you initially enter a trade, you should always have a predefined stop-loss exit close to your entry in order to limit your loss if prices fail to go your way shortly after your entry. That way, you know right away how much money you will lose in any given trade.

Then you should continue your exit plan by following behind a positive movement in price with a trailing stop loss order to protect at least a portion of your accrued profits.

If your initial entry quickly leads you into a losing position, don't fall for the old saying, "If you liked it at the higher price, you've got to love it at this price." The fact is, you were wrong in your first assessment, so what makes you believe that you will be right by adding positions? You don't want to put yourself into a position where you lose a substantial amount of money because you are fighting the market, hoping it will soon turn in your favor. Now, if you really believe that you are right but are just off a little in your timing, go ahead and stay with your current position (unless you get stopped out by that carefully placed stop), but don't add to it until it begins moving in the right direction.

The Least You Need to Know

- ◆ A well-planned and executed trade will include a setup, a trigger, an entry, and an exit strategy.

- ◆ Three good opportunities to enter a trade are on breakouts from a consolidation area, pullbacks into consolidation after a breakout, and pullbacks into the moving average after a significant trending move.

- ◆ Don't buy below a declining moving average or sell short above a rising moving average.

- ◆ Smart traders use good-till-cancelled stop limit orders to enter a position.

- ◆ When you add to a profitable position by "pyramiding," always make each subsequent addition smaller than the previous addition to limit your risk.

- ◆ It's crucial to keep your losses small and to let your profits run.

Chapter 20

When to Buy or Sell

In This Chapter

◆ Mental preparation

◆ Market internals

◆ Systems trading

◆ Backtesting and optimization

How can some investors be so right and yet so wrong? As with many things in life, timing is critically important to profitable trades. Finding a company that has all the important attributes of a great stock is only one half of the trading equation. A company may be fundamentally great—low debt, plenty of free cash flow, dominating market position, and so on—but unless you buy it at the right time, you may have to wait for a long time before realizing a profit. Technical analysis is about timing when you buy and when you sell so that your chances of a profit are at their highest. It doesn't get much more basic than this: technical analysis helps you buy low and sell high (or sell high and buy low).

Overcoming Your Fears and Inhibitions

Having knowledge about a stock's fundamentals can certainly help you in your decisions about what to buy or sell. Fundamental information like earnings, capital structure, return on equity, and debt ratios all certainly have an effect on stock valuation over the long term. However, this information often has little bearing on when price movement will occur.

Even though a company may be a great company fundamentally, that doesn't necessarily guarantee that its stock will perform well after you buy it. It's when you buy and when you sell that determines whether you will profit from your investment or not.

Market fundamentalists teach you to do plenty of research on a stock before buying it. You are taught to make sure that the company has good earnings and management, is a leader in its industry, and has a stock price that is in an uptrend. However, where do you think the price of the stock is when all of these criteria are met? Generally, all of this public information is already incorporated into the current price of the stock. Accordingly, when you buy, you are simply paying those who bought before you. To buy at that point in time completely goes against how you make money buying and selling anything and can carry a very high risk.

You must not lose sight of the fact that, when you buy, many other buyers have to come in after you at a higher price or there is no chance that you will profit from your purchase. Similarly, if you sell short, many other sellers have to come in after you at lower prices or there is no chance that you will profit from your short sale. That is why technical analysts focus on methods that can help you buy and sell before others do and at price levels where the risk is relatively low.

Oftentimes this means buying at or near the end of a downtrend, when the news is bad and the crowd is hesitant about entering the market. For many, this is completely contrary to their emotional makeup. We naturally tend to run away from things that make us fearful and are drawn to things that make us feel good. As technicians, we must learn to overcome these inhibitions to profitable trading and investing.

Heads Up

Following the crowd can get you run over when the smart-money investors anticipate a reversal. By the time the crowd realizes what is happening, smart-money investors have locked in their profits. As the crowd scrambles to catch the trend that is already underway, slow movers are left behind. It is better to anticipate than to react to price reversals.

Opportunities in Selling Short

Many traders and investors have a gut-level reluctance to sell short. But if you look at any chart of any market, the likelihood is that when the price makes a correction in a bull market or when a bull market turns into a bear market, the move down is usually faster than the move up was. It is important to realize that there are real trade opportunities there.

As for the mechanics of selling short, it is really no different from buying long except that you sell first, with the intention of buying it back later at a lower price. If the price falls when you are short, you win. If the price falls when you are long, you lose. It's as simple as that. You have to learn that you can make or lose money on both sides of the markets and that they don't always go up.

Markets spend much of their time consolidating and resting between surges up and down. Traders who wait for a move and then have to chase it will always be at a disadvantage compared to traders who get in before the move takes place. The key is to be able to anticipate the direction of the next move.

Market Internals

Tools that are useful to the trader in evaluating the health of the entire market are called "market internals."

Market internals comprise a group of indicators and indexes disseminated by the various stock and futures exchanges that measure the health of the trend of the markets as a whole. Some also reveal the current trend in the sentiment of the market participants. Such information helps a smart trader to see what's going on beneath the surface.

There are basically two types of market internals: those that deal directly with the stock market by keeping track of the health, quality, and strength of a trend in the major averages, and those that deal with investor sentiment, primarily by keeping track of the relative number of bullish and bearish stock options that are being traded. Each of these groups is important to the technical analyst.

For example, market internals can tell the analyst whether more money is flowing out of a bull market while price is continuing to rise, which is bearish, or whether more money is flowing into a bear market while price is continuing to fall, which is bullish. They can also tell the analyst whether price is going up but an increasing number of traders are hedging their long positions with options, which would be bearish.

Since traders generally look to capture moves in the direction of an established trend, market internals can help them estimate the chances of the major averages moving mostly higher or lower in the near future. If the trader determines that the market has better odds of moving higher rather than lower, he or she will attempt to capitalize from this bullish sentiment in the markets. The same is true for a bearish outlook.

In this section, we will be looking at some of the more popular market internal indicators: the TICK index, the TIKI index, the TRIN index, the TRIN/Q index, and the VIX index. Learning how to read and interpret these indicators can give you a much better feel for whether the predominant pressure in the markets is generated by buyers or by sellers. This can be an important factor in helping you to decide at any time whether to focus on buy setups or sell setups and whether to focus on setups that do best in choppy markets or on setups that do best in trending markets.

The TICK Index

The New York Stock Exchange (NYSE) disseminates an indicator called TICK (symbol: $TICK). This indicator calculates the difference between the number of stocks on the NYSE that are increasing in price and those that are decreasing in price.

By watching the trend of the TICK index, we can gain an excellent leading indication of market direction.

Keeping track of changes in the TICK is one way to measure the relationship between the buying and selling pressures in the overall stock market at any point in time. If the TICK reading is 375, for instance, then there are 375 more stocks on the NYSE moving up than moving down. This is a bullish indication. If the TICK is reading at -375, on the other hand, that would be an indication that the bears are stronger than the bulls and that the market is weakening. Thus, you should focus on taking long positions when the TICK is above zero and on selling when the TICK is below zero.

If the TICK remains positive on the day, the chances are that the bullish momentum will continue into the next day. If the TICK remains negative on the day, the chances are that the bearish momentum will continue into the next day.

TICK values above 800 or below -800 are an indication that the market is excessively overbought or oversold and thus ripe for a reversal in direction (see Figure 20.1). So if you are in a long position when the TICK begins to rise above 800 or in a short position when the TICK begins to fall below -800, you should consider lightening up on your positions or closing them entirely in anticipation of a reversal.

Although this indicator is based only on the stocks trading on the NYSE, it can nevertheless be used as a barometer for stocks trading on all U.S. exchanges.

Info/Tips

Market internals, like many other technical analysis indicators, should be used in conjunction with other tools to gain a stronger sense of which direction money is flowing. As part of your technical analysis toolkit, market internals should be near the top.

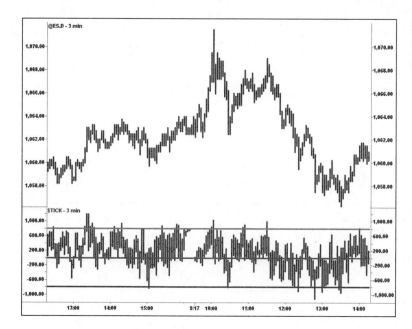

Figure 20.1

TICK indicator and market reversals.

The TIKI Index

The TIKI index (symbol: $TIKI) is similar to the TICK, but it measures the difference between the number of stocks moving up and the number of stocks moving down of the 30 stocks making up the Dow Jones Index rather than the entire NYSE, as the TICK index does. In a manner similar to the TICK, the TIKI shows whether there are more individual Dow stocks with increasing prices or decreasing prices. Since the TIKI includes fewer stocks than the TICK, it often reacts faster than the TICK and thus may signal a pending change in trend direction before the TICK reacts. Since the TICK and TIKI are usually displayed as a bar chart, both can be interpreted like a price bar chart, using concepts such as support and resistance and trend lines (see Figure 20.2).

The TRIN Index

TRIN (symbol: $TRIN) is an acronym that stands for "The Trading Index." It is also referred to as the Arms index, since it was invented by Richard Arms. The TRIN measures internal market strength or weakness by looking at changes in the amount of volume flowing into declining stocks compared to the amount of volume flowing into advancing stocks (see Figure 20.3). If it shows that there is more volume going into stocks that are dropping in price than rising in price, it is a sign of internal weakness in the markets. If the broad market is rising at such a time, it is a warning sign that you should be exiting your long positions and looking for short-selling opportunities.

Figure 20.2

TICK vs. TIKI indicators and market reversals.

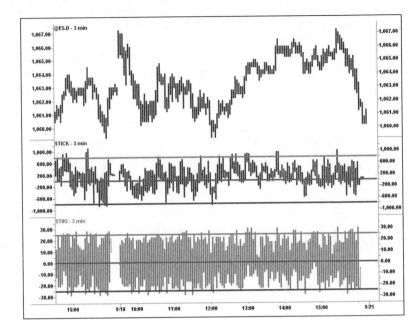

Figure 20.3

The TRIN indicator.

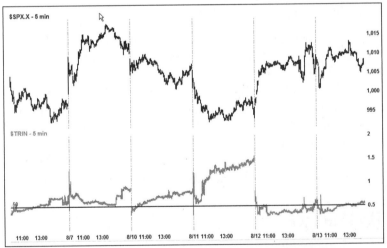

In contrast to the way the TICK displays its information, a falling TRIN value shows us that more volume is flowing into advancing stocks than declining stocks and thus the bulls are beginning to take control. A rising TRIN value signals that the bears are beginning to take control.

The absolute value of the TRIN is not nearly as important as the direction of its trend. If the TRIN is trending higher and making higher highs on the day, you should ignore all long setups. If the TRIN is trending lower and making new lows for the day, you should ignore all short setups.

Watch for days when prices gap up on the opening and the TRIN starts off low and stays low all day long. Such a sustained low reading is very bullish and should discourage you from taking any short setups. The most bullish days occur when the TRIN hovers below 0.5.

The TRIN/Q Index

The TRIN/Q index (Symbol: $TRINQ) is similar to the TRIN index, except that it is based on the NASDAQ stocks instead of the NYSE stocks. The same rules apply here as they do for the TRIN. That is, what we are really interested in is the trend of the TRIN/Q. A downtrending TRIN/Q is bullish, whereas an uptrending TRIN/Q is bearish. On days where the TRIN/Q is mixed while the TRIN is trending, pay more attention to the TRIN and vice versa. The strongest moves in the market occur when both the TRIN and the TRIN/Q are moving in the same direction (see Figure 20.4).

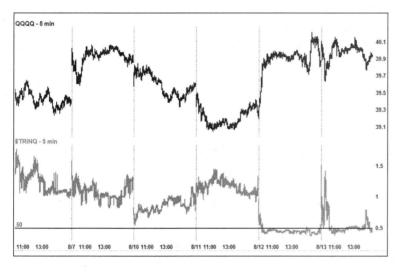

Figure 20.4

The TRIN and TRIN/Q indicators.

The VIX Index

The Volatility index, or VIX for short, measures investors' expectations as to how drastically the S&P 500 market index may fluctuate in the near future. It looks at the relationship between the number of buyers of put options, which are bets that the market will fall, to the number of buyers of call options, which are bets that the market will rise.

High VIX readings above 50 indicate fear among traders who are buying significantly more put options than call options. That's why the VIX index is often referred to as the "fear index." When the VIX is rising, it is a sign that the fear level is increasing. If at the same time that the VIX is rising the price is rising as well, it would show that even though the market looked bullish from the outside, on the inside the buyers were seething with fear and anxiety.

Just keep in mind that the VIX is basically a contrarian indicator. It tells you whether or not the markets have reached an extreme position. When that occurs, it tends to be a sure sign that the markets are about to stage a reversal. The idea here is that if the wide majority believes that one bet is such a sure thing, they pile on. But by the time that happens, the market is usually ready to turn the other way. The crowd hardly ever gets it right. It's counterintuitive, but it works most of the time, especially in volatile markets.

In mid-2007, the VIX began to rise above its normal range of below 20, which indicated increasing doubts by the smart money about the viability of the continuing uptrend in the S&P 500. On October 24, 2008, the VIX hit its historic high of 89.53, revealing a complete crisis of confidence in the market (see Figure 20.5).

Figure 20.5

High VIX reading at market bottom.

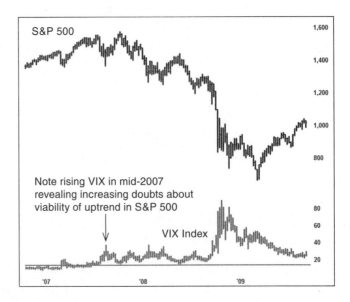

Use market internals such as the TICK, the TRIN, the TRIN/Q, and the VIX to look for clues as to the path of least resistance. When the markets are quiet, that is the best time to get into position to follow the move in the direction revealed by the market internals. Once the move takes place, the amateurs will chase it, and you can sell your position to them.

TA Intelligence

Market internals help you plot your trading strategy by suggesting where the market will be headed. Used with other technical analysis tools, market internals can be thought of as an early warning system for smart traders.

Trading Systems

In this section, we will discuss the advantages and drawbacks of utilizing a trading system. If you find yourself on a mailing list of individuals interested in technical analysis, you will undoubtedly receive unsolicited mail from people wanting to sell you a trading system or offering to manage your money for you utilizing a proprietary trading system.

The idea of using a trading system has great allure to many traders, both beginners attracted by the promises of huge profits and nonbeginners who have been trading long enough to realize that they need some help. After all, what is more appealing than having a rule-based tool that tells you exactly what to do to make big money without much effort? But be careful: don't spend hundreds or even thousands of dollars on a trading system and think you are on your way to Easy Street without thoroughly researching its results and track record.

That is not to say that trading systems do not work. The big question, however, is whether the system you select will work for you, and that may depend as much on what you bring to the system as what the system offers to you.

What Is System Trading?

System trading is a mechanical method of trading that utilizes a clear and well-defined set of trading rules to issue strict entry and exit signals based on the parameters of the system.

The trading rules of a well-designed system usually have been researched and tested to produce optimum results over a wide range of market conditions. Usually orders are placed automatically by the computer.

A trading system may be simple or complex, but whatever the design, its purpose is to eliminate discretion and the emotional element from the decision-making process. Each trade generated by a system is based on a specific set of rules and does not depend on subjective second-guessing and the usual fear/greed concerns that plague many beginning traders. As we have learned, emotion can be one of the worst enemies of any trader, so using a rule-based computerized trading system that eliminates the risk of making emotion-based decisions can in itself be quite valuable to many technical traders.

Backtesting a Trading System

Because it comprises a written set of rules, a trading system can be back tested over historical data from many different types of markets to determine its robustness and consistency in generating a profitable trading record. With a properly designed and tested trading system, you will have a good idea of how it might perform on similar data in the future.

Many charting and trading software packages offer the capability to apply a programmed system to a specific set of historical price data from many different types of markets to see how well the system would have performed in the past had it been trading based on that data. This process is known as "backtesting."

Backtesting gives us a way to determine the robustness and consistency of a trading system to generate a profitable trading record. With a properly designed and tested trading system, you will have a good idea of how it might perform on similar data in the future.

A well-tested trading system should give you the confidence to take every trading signal required by the system's rules despite the fact that a particular trade may not seem logical at the time. If you start cherry-picking to select only the trades that seem "right" or fret about what expert analysts are thinking or what the talking heads are saying to discourage you from taking the trade, you are defeating the purpose of the trading system and are wasting the money you spent on the system.

A good backtesting program will provide you with a variety of useful statistical data about the trading system you are evaluating. These data will typically include information about system profitability, maximum drawdown, average profit per trade, the number of trades over a given period of time, the percentage of winning trades, the magnitude of the biggest winning trade, and the biggest losing trade. It will also generate a graphical equity curve of theoretical profit versus time.

Profitability

The amount of profit that it will be expected to generate is, of course, what a trading system is all about and is one of the first items you will want to look at. If a system doesn't show a nice level of profitability, it is not worth much attention. But profit levels alone are certainly not the only factor to consider.

Maximum Drawdown

An equally important factor is "maximum drawdown." That is, what was the largest drawdown in your capital account during the test period as a result of a string of losses? Some trading systems with very attractive profits nonetheless have severe setbacks along the way. If those setbacks are so great that you can no longer take the pain and abandon the system, then those particular system settings are not for you. It would be better to settle for a smaller overall profit number if it means smaller drawdowns as well. This is a decision you must make based on your own tolerance for loss. Would you rather accept an 80 percent gain with a maximum drawdown of 40 percent, or would you be more comfortable settling for a 15 percent gain with a 3 percent maximum drawdown?

Average Profit Per Trade

You need to look at the average profit per trade. If the system trades a lot and the average profit per trade is relatively low, you may find that just a few larger-than-average losers, along with commissions, will eat up most or all of your profits.

Number of Trades

You may not care how many trades it takes to generate profits, but commissions, fees, and "slippage" may eat up your profits if the system makes too many trades. You can live with these costs if the profit is large enough, but if these costs are not included in the performance calculations, they can be a big factor in a marginally profitable system, so be sure to check that the test results include provisions for both commissions and slippage costs.

Percentage of Winning Trades

Many traders consider the percentage of winning trades to be one of the most important criteria in evaluating any trading system. A trading system that generates winning trades more than 75 percent of the time will attract a great deal of investor attention. It is human nature for people to like to be right most of the time. However, in the case of evaluating a trading system, it is vital to consider the size of the average win versus the size of the average loss when you look at the ratio of the number of winners to the number of losers.

Suppose you have a system where 90 percent of the trades are winning trades. Each winner earns a consistent average of $100 per trade. That sounds great, doesn't it? However, on the 10 percent of the days that this system loses money, it will lose an average of $1,000. That means for every 10 trades you make, 9 will be $100 winners, for a profit of $900. But one trade will be a loser, losing an average of $1,000. Consequently, even with a 90 percent win-to-loss ratio, with this system, for every 10 trades you take, you will typically make $900 and lose $1,000, giving you a net loss of $100. Would some people trade that system? Yes, they would. They would probably trade it until they wiped out their trading account. Why? Because they get to be right 90 percent of the time, and that in itself is very rewarding.

The point of this example is that you can still be very profitable with more losers than winners so long as you keep the losers small compared to the winners.

Best Trade, Worst Trade

Study the trading system's trading history to find the largest winning and losing trades. You may find that a system that reported profits of $10,000 made $8,000 of that gain on a single trade, for example. What if you had tested over a different time interval that had missed that one trade? Your performance and the system's performance might be far different from the excellent results shown. Or what if the system's parameters would have produced a large losing trade that is conveniently omitted by adjusting the trade history over which the tests were run? Check out those days when you know the market's volatility might have made a big difference in a system's performance and make sure they are covered in the back tests and optimizations.

The Equity Curve

 One of the most important items of information produced by a systems back test is the equity curve. The equity curve is a graph of cumulative account profits and losses over time based on following a specific rule-based strategy. When evaluating a potential trading strategy, the equity curve should be one of the first things that you look at to judge its effectiveness. It gives you a quick visual snapshot in the form of a graph of what your account balance would have been over time if you had strictly followed the given strategy.

An ideal equity curve would look like Figure 20.6. It would be a relatively smooth line heading upward, indicating a consistently profitable series of trades with few significant losses. This would be the ideal. However, practically speaking, it is not likely to be achieved very often. Figure 20.7 shows a group of equity curves of other real systems. Which ones would you choose to trade after examining these graphs of past performance?

Figure 20.6

Ideal equity curve.

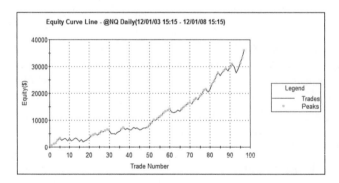

When you examine an equity curve based on historical data, there are several things you should look at. First, make sure that the curve is not just based on a time period that was particularly favorable for the system's approach. Check the trade history dates carefully to make sure that they encompass enough of a time range to cover different types of market conditions, both in bull markets and in bear markets. After all, you want to make sure the system holds up in all types of market conditions. You want the curve to be relatively smooth and steady as opposed to consisting of sudden and irregular jumps up and down.

For example, Figure 20.7A shows several profitable periods, but subsequent unprofitable periods drag the equity curve right back into unprofitable territory. Figure 20.7B ends up being profitable over the long term, but the equity curve growth is interrupted by extended periods of flat and/or unprofitable behavior. Figure 20.7C shows impressive growth over the first 100 trades or so, but then breaks down dramatically and moves essentially sideways for the balance of the period shown. Similarly, Figure 20.7D had some nice trades early on, but then failed to maintain its profitability and gradually sank into negative territory. Finally, Figure 20.7E reveals disconcertingly erratic behavior, generating attractive profits during the first half of the equity curve period, but then breaking down dramatically during the latter half of the equity curve period, followed by a final profitable surge.

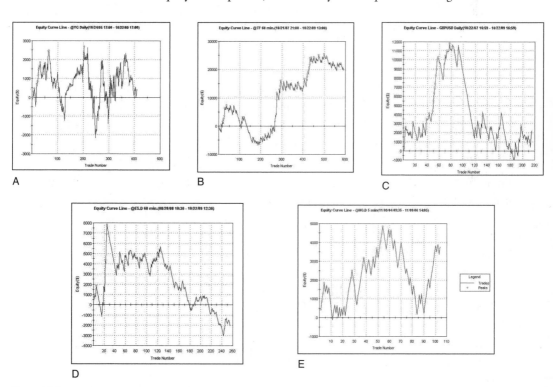

Figure 20.7

Real equity curves.

Optimizing a Trading System

Most backtesting tools also give you the ability to "optimize" the rules by changing various controlling parameters to determine the affect on the overall results. For example, let's say that you have developed a very simple strategy that buys whenever a fast moving average crosses above a slow moving average and that it exits on a trailing stop a specified number of points below the highest high achieved since entering the position. You have read an article that suggests such a strategy would work well using a length of 9 bars for the short moving average and 30 bars for the long moving average. It also recommends a 3-point trailing stop. With a backtesting program, such as is available on many different charting platforms these days, you can determine how well this set of criteria has worked over, say, the past five years on the type of investment you plan to be trading.

Now, one of the things you can do with such a system is to vary the parameters over a chosen range to see if different numbers for the lengths of the two moving averages and the stop levels might generate better results. An optimization capability in most backtesting programs can do this for you by giving you the opportunity to input a range of lengths for the moving averages and a range of levels for the trailing stop and rapidly testing the profitability of each combination.

For example, you can tell the program to vary the length of the short moving average from 9 to 20 bars and the long moving average from 21 to 40 bars and test all combinations of these lengths to see which works the best. You might also test various settings for your trailing stop from, say, 2 points to 6 points away from the most recent price extreme to see if moving your trailing stop closer to or farther away from price helps to keep you from being stopped out too early or too late. After running a series of tests, the program will give you the results in a table of all combinations of these settings over the ranges you have specified. You can then sort this table to see which combinations are likely to provide the best results.

Figure 20.8 shows a typical optimization table for a specific strategy run on a daily chart over 30 months. The first and second columns display the combination of various short and long moving average lengths used in the sample test described above. The third column displays the total net profits generated by the strategy using the combination of settings in columns 1 and 2 over the entire testing period. The columns to the right of the first three columns display many different types of diagnostic information, including total number of trades, the percentage of trades that were profitable, the greatest equity drawdown, the profitability factor, and the total return on investment. Many other measurements related to the profitability and stability of the trading system can also be added to the optimization table.

In the example of Figure 20.8, Row 1 displays the most profitable combination of moving average lengths for this particular test. The optimal combination turns out to be 18 bars for moving average 1 and 25 bars for moving average 2. That combination generated a total net profit of $37,582.50 over the period of the test. A total of 35 trades were generated, 40 percent of which were profitable. Although this example generated attractive profits, a glance at the Max Intraday Drawdown column reveals that the user would have had to endure a substantial equity drawdown of over $15,000, which would have significantly reduced the appeal of this particular strategy.

	ARPS XOVER TRADE: MA1Bars	ARPS XOVER TRADE: MA2Bars	All: Net Profit	All: Total Trades	All: % Profitable	All: Max Intraday Drawdown	All: ProfitFactor	All: Return on Account
1	18	25	37,582.50	35	40.00	-15,457.50	1.97	243.13
2	18	33	37,397.50	34	38.24	-12,842.50	2.02	291.20
3	18	35	37,397.50	34	38.24	-12,842.50	2.02	291.20
4	18	37	37,397.50	34	38.24	-12,842.50	2.02	291.20
5	18	27	37,207.50	35	40.00	-15,457.50	1.96	240.71
6	16	25	37,060.00	34	41.18	-15,257.50	2.01	242.90
7	16	33	36,875.00	33	39.39	-12,642.50	2.06	291.67
8	16	35	36,875.00	33	39.39	-12,642.50	2.06	291.67
9	16	37	36,875.00	33	39.39	-12,642.50	2.06	291.67
10	16	27	36,685.00	34	41.18	-15,257.50	2.00	240.44
11	18	29	36,232.50	35	37.14	-15,457.50	1.92	234.40
12	7	37	36,047.50	34	38.24	-12,142.50	2.02	296.87
13	18	31	35,757.50	35	40.00	-15,457.50	1.93	231.33
14	16	29	35,710.00	34	38.24	-15,257.50	1.95	234.05
15	7	25	35,532.50	35	40.00	-15,457.50	1.94	229.87
16	7	33	35,347.50	34	38.24	-12,842.50	1.98	275.24
17	7	35	35,347.50	34	38.24	-12,842.50	1.98	275.24
18	18	19	35,305.00	36	38.89	-17,735.00	1.86	199.07
19	18	21	35,305.00	36	38.89	-17,735.00	1.86	199.07
20	18	23	35,305.00	36	38.89	-17,735.00	1.86	199.07
21	16	31	35,235.00	34	41.18	-15,257.50	1.96	230.94

Figure 20.8

Example of an optimization table.

The Importance of Walk-Forward Testing

Beware of "curve-fitted" trading systems. When designing a system, many developers have a tendency to optimize the parameters for the best possible performance over a given set of historical data. If you then take that system and apply it to new data that was not used in the optimization process and examine the equity curve, you can quickly judge whether the system is truly robust or not.

A properly designed system will have predictive value and perform well on unseen, out-of-sample market data.

If you see the equity curve performance drop off noticeably based on new "unknown" data occurring after the design and optimization process, beware. This system may have been overly curve-fitted. If a trading system does not perform as well on out-of-sample trading after the optimization process, then the effectiveness and reliability of future performance of the trading system is definitely suspect.

Any well-designed trading system should first have passed a walk-forward test. The purpose of walk-forward testing is to determine whether the performance of an optimized trading system is realistic or the result of curve-fitting. To perform a walk-forward test, the developer first segments the historical data spanning the testing period into several in-sample and out-of-sample periods. He then runs an optimization over the first in-sample period to determine the optimal parameters for the system. Now he applies those optimal parameters to the system and tests it over the first out-of-sample period to see if the results are consistent with those of the in-sample period. He then optimizes the next in-sample period to provide the values for the next out-of-sample period. By continuing that sequence several times, the developer can assure himself that the set of rules and parameters he is using should be more robust in the future than those evolved from a single optimization run. If the system passes the walk-forward test with profit, consistency, and efficiency, it is a system that can be traded in real time with confidence. When considering using a trading system, always make sure it has satisfactorily passed a walk-forward series of tests. Most reputable developers will disclose this fact in their promotional information.

The Least You Need to Know

- Use technical analysis to anticipate the direction of the next move. Traders who wait for a move and then have to chase it will always be at a disadvantage compared to traders who get in before the move takes place.

- Market internals comprise a group of indicators and indexes disseminated by the various stock and futures exchanges that measure the health of the trend of the markets as a whole.

- The use of computerized trading systems can be valuable to many technical traders who want to eliminate the effect of emotions from their trading decisions.

- Successful walk-forward testing increases the chances that a particular trading system has predictive value and is more likely to perform well on future market data.

21

Pulling the Trigger

In This Chapter

- ◆ Entering and exiting positions
- ◆ Managing your trade
- ◆ Planning entries and exits
- ◆ Trading strategies

Buy low and sell high. What could be simpler? All it needs is a little expansion to include "cut your losses quickly" and "let your profits run." Of course, if it were that easy everyone would do it. However, this cliché sums up the key to trading success. The solution is simple, but the execution is not. This is where you put your knowledge of technical analysis to work. Entering the trade at a favorable position and exiting at an equally favorable point is what technical analysis is all about—that point where you believe you have the highest probability of success and the least chance of failure.

Go Up, Go Down, or Go Sideways

When you boil it down to the lowest common denominator, the business of trading comprises some very simple rules and goals. At a time of your choosing, you either buy or sell a piece of paper representing a number of shares of stock, or you buy or sell the right to own a specific commodity, or you buy or sell an option to buy a certain number of shares of stock or a commodity at an agreed-upon price before an agreed-upon deadline. If you sell that piece of paper at a higher price than you bought it, you make a profit and add that amount to your capital. If you sell it at a lower price than you bought it, you incur a loss and subtract that amount from your capital. The object of the process is to increase your capital. You are out of the game if you lose all of your capital.

The prices of the instruments traded in the markets in which traders operate can only do one of three things: go up, go down, or go sideways. Thus, the objective of technical analysis is to help the trader identify opportune points in price and time to buy, sell, or stay out. It is important to remember that no matter at what price you enter a trade, it is not the price at which you enter the position that makes you a winner or a loser; it is the price at which you exit the position that will determine whether you can add to or deduct from the profit column. In order to be on the winning side of the ledger, you must sell at a higher price than you buy, regardless of whether you buy before you sell or you sell short first and then buy it back later. In trading, an excellent exit on a mediocre entry will make you more money than a bad exit on a good entry.

Trading Discipline

Trading well consistently requires discipline to follow your method. Without discipline, you really have no method. You must have the mental fortitude to accept the fact that losses are part of the game and must be accommodated. There is no such thing as perfection in trading. Trading is like batting in the game of baseball. A good player may hit the ball 30 percent of the time. A really great player may get a hit 40 percent of the time. Keep in mind, that means that even the greatest players don't get a hit 60 percent of the time. It's the same with trading. You don't have to be perfect to win in the markets. However, you must work to keep your losses small. That's why you also need a good money management strategy.

> **Heads Up**
>
> Take positions with the market flow, not against it. It's more fun to surf the waves than to get eaten by the sharks.

Don't let small profits turn into a large loss because you were shooting for large profits. You might only want to hit home runs, but don't miss taking the singles and the doubles. Some people like to play the lottery. They buy lottery tickets in hopes of winning the jackpot, not $5 or $10. Don't pass up a small profit in hopes of scoring a larger one. Jackpot winners are rare, so don't let your profits slip away because they were not jackpot profits.

On the other hand, to trade well, you also need the mental fortitude to stay with a potentially big move that comes only 5 or 10 percent of the time. These are the ones that will pay you for all of your losses and your diligent efforts as a technical analyst and trader. Don't miss the big moves for reasons other than those defined by your clearly defined trading method. Don't arbitrarily limit yourself by exiting if your profit exceeds your normal range of profits. When the big trade finally does come along, you need the self-esteem to accept its full potential.

Timing Your Entries and Exits

So what is the process to follow to enter the market at just the right time and capture the big moves we often see on our charts? First of all, here are some general rules:

- Forget the news, remember the chart. No one is smart enough to know how news will affect price in every case. The chart already knows the news is coming.

- Execute positions based on numbers, time, and volume, not emotions. This discipline forces you to distance yourself from reckless gambling behavior. Through detached execution and solid risk management, I guarantee you will be more successful in your trading endeavors.

- Remember that participants in the markets echo similar patterns over and over again based on the infallible rules of human behavior. This knowledge and understanding gives you the power and confidence to build systematic rules to take advantage of these repeating patterns to generate profits and minimize losses.

Trading Breakouts

One of the best methods to enter a trade is on a breakout. A breakout move, also known as a momentum move, occurs when price breaks away from an extended period of sideways movement known as a congestion area or trading range pattern. As traders, we ideally want to buy or sell short shortly after the beginning of the momentum move, hold on through the move, and take profits close to the end of the move.

Unfortunately, that is often easier said than done. Price can respond in different ways to breakouts. The challenge to the technical analyst is to confirm, before making a trade, that the beginning of the breakout move is the beginning of a trending move that carries through successfully to higher levels and not a fake-out, or *whipsaw*, move that will quickly reverse back into the original congestion area or a false move that starts a trend in the opposite direction.

def•i•ni•tion

A **whipsaw** is a choppy price swing up and down through a support or resistance level. Whipsaws exhibit a tendency to trap traders who enter an apparent breakout move too quickly, only to find price reversing direction shortly thereafter, thus trapping them with a loss. Whipsaws tend to shake out weak hands and force prices back into the congestion area.

Just be aware that any position you take near a breakout level carries considerable risk, no matter how perfect a pattern looks (see Figure 21.1). Breakouts occur out of zones of conflict and uncertainty as to the direction of the next trend. Both sides of the market are very passionate at these turning points, but no one knows how much force is required to carry price into a sustainable uptrend or downtrend.

There are usually huge numbers of traders waiting to enter the market when price reaches key breakout levels. Once the price breaks out and these traders execute their trades, they are at the mercy of the market. Their profits depend on others seeing the breakout and jumping in behind them. False breakouts occur when this second crowd fails to appear.

Figure 21.1

Breakouts.

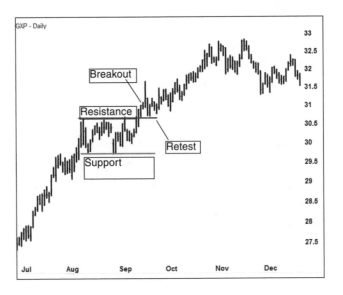

An overbought, one-sided market can drop quickly below a breakout level. This throws all the traders who bought the breakout into losing positions. Without the support of fresh buyers, a stock can fall from its own weight. Each incremental low triggers more stops and increases fear within the trapped crowd. Momentum builds to the downside, breaks key support, and invites fresh short-sale signals from a whole new batch of traders.

Figure 21.2

Whipsaws.

To minimize the risk of getting trapped in this kind of whipsaw situation (see Figure 21.2), traders often look for a 3 percent to 5 percent move outside of the previous trading range or pattern before they consider the breakout to be a valid indication of a continuation of the trend in the direction of the breakout.

> **TA Intelligence**
>
> Follow the path of successful traders and learn from their experience. You can break new ground when you are a seasoned trader, but in the beginning trust the wisdom of experienced traders.

Channel and Triangle Patterns

Breakouts can occur out of either horizontal channel patterns or triangle patterns. Triangle patterns also include wedges and pennants, as they all confine the price within a gradually shrinking range with the passage of time. All of these patterns were described in detail in Chapter 6. A rule of thumb for triangle-type breakouts is that the more the range of the bars in the pattern shrinks with time and becomes tighter, the further the subsequent breakout will travel and the less chance of a fake out or whipsaw occurring on the breakout. This price behavior successively shrinking price bars is referred to as "range contraction" and is inevitably followed by a period of range expansion.

A successful breakout from any of the channel and triangle patterns previously described, which constitute the "indecision phase," usually follows a series of steps. The first step is the "action phase," where price breaks through a resistance level accompanied by increased volume. Demand must exceed supply during the action phase in order to break free of the previous indecision phase within the channel or triangle pattern. Sometimes price expands a few points and then reverses as soon as buying interest fades. This starts the "reaction phase" in which a pullback into the previous breakout price occurs on much lighter volume. At this point, fresh buyers see a chance to get into the market at a price close to the breakout price. If all systems are go and new demand exceeds the available supply, then a second rally kicks in and carries price beyond the initial breakout high. This marks the "resolution phase," and the trend move continues from there. Whipsaws and false breakouts can occur if the supply-demand dynamics fall out of balance during any of the above phases.

Following the Trend (Momentum)

If you remember your high school physics, Newton's first law of motion teaches that an object in motion tends to remain in motion. Once the trending move is underway during the resolution phase, your potential profits depend on this well-understood mechanism. New trends can be very difficult to stop once they are underway. As with other objects in motion, trends tend to feed on themselves because they draw in fresh energy from cash and emotions on the sidelines. This energy drives prices toward your price target. However, no trend can last forever. New market forces and changes in the supply-demand balance will eventually stop or reverse this directional price movement. As the trend progresses, follow your oscillators (like MACD, Stochastics, Momentum, and RSI) for signs that the trend is slowing down and that it's time to tighten up your trailing stop orders or simply take your profits and await further developments for a new entry signal (see Figure 21.3).

Figure 21.3

Oscillator warning of trend slowdown or reversal.

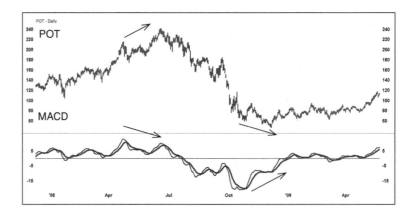

Info/Tips

Staying out of the market is an aggressive way to trade. All opportunities carry risk, and even perfect setups lead to very bad positions. Stay on the sidelines and wait for the opportunity to develop. There's a perfect moment you're trying to trade.

Trading Pullbacks

"Buy the first pullback from a new high. Sell the first pullback from a new low. There's always a crowd that missed the first boat." —Anonymous

If you missed entering the trend on the original breakout, the market will often give you a second chance to enter by pausing midtrend to pull back and "take a breath." Usually this first reversal of direction in the trending move after a breakout constitutes a tradable pullback that carries a high probability of continuing the previous trend after it shakes out the weak holders and takes on new buyers who did not enter on the initial breakout.

One of the lowest-risk and highest-probability trades you can take is to enter at the end of a pullback in anticipation of the return of the price from the pullback into the direction of the original trend (see Figure 21.4). The previous leg of the move has defined the overall direction of the longer-term trend. The termination of the pullback move has identified an excellent point at which to limit your risk by placing a stop-loss exit order slightly below the bottom of the pullback swing. Additionally, the length of the first leg added to the bottom of the pullback swing gives you a good estimate of the probable length of the new swing leg and allows you to calculate with a higher degree of certainty a potential profit target price. (See a more detailed explanation of this "measured move" technique in Chapter 6.)

Figure 21.4

Entering at the end of a pullback.

When planning a trend-pullback entry, keep in mind that prices within a pullback move often follow a 1-2-3 pattern. That is, they pull back somewhat, bounce, and then pull back again before finding support and breaking out in the direction opposite to the pullback. But be careful. The deeper the pullback corrects, the smaller the likelihood is that a break-out will take out the old trend high and develop into another significant wave move. Any pullback that exceeds 40 percent of the length of the previous thrust leg should be entered with caution. Preferably, only take entries after tight and small 1-2-3 pullback patterns of less than 40 percent.

When in a pullback, you can use very-short-term RSI or Stochastics oscillators to determine when the pullback has run its course and is in a position to resume the previous trending move. When these oscillators cross below the oversold level and subsequently cross back above the oversold level, it's time to make your move (see Figure 21.5).

Figure 21.5

Two-bar RSI signals end of pullback.

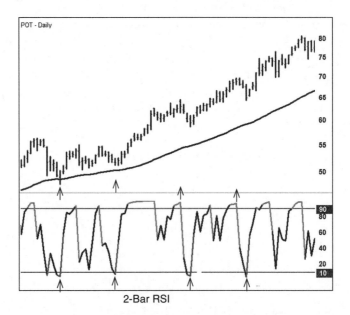

2-Bar RSI

After each pullback in a trend, the odds decrease that the trend will continue. Watch the oscillators, particularly the Stochastics, for divergent peaks in an uptrend or divergent valleys in a downtrend to give you a warning that the trend is running out of steam. (See Chapter 10 for a detailed description of this process.)

Follow-Through in a Trending Market

When prices are trending, one way to determine the likelihood of the trend continuing into the next day is to look for evidence of "follow-through," or the tendency of the market to continue in the direction of the existing trend into the next day of trading. In order to determine the existence of follow-through, look at the relative position of the daily close with respect to the high and the low of that day (see Figure 21.6). If we are in an uptrend, the close of the day should be relatively near the high of the day. Thus, the market is exhibiting a strong close—one that in all likelihood should follow through to the upside in early trading for the next day. On the other hand, if the close is nearer the low of the day, it is considered to be a weak close, which should lead to lower prices in early trading for the next day. This can serve as a warning of a possible pause in an ongoing uptrending move. The concept of follow-through is also important when combined with the concept of range contraction, which is described in the next section.

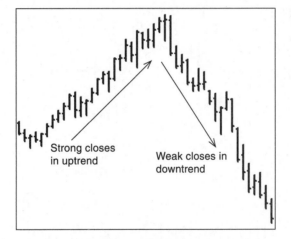

Strong closes
in uptrend

Weak closes in
downtrend

Figure 21.6

Strong close, weak close.

Trading Range Expansion/Contraction

"Average range" is a concept often used by technical analysts to decide when to pull the trigger. The range of a bar is the distance between the high and low of the price bar. The average range is the average of the range of a series of successive price bars. During a consolidation period, the average range of the price bars typically contracts as many participants move to the sidelines awaiting a signal of continuation or reversal of the existing trend. This behavior is referred to as "range contraction." When price ranges contract, they are building up energy for their next major move. Average range is often plotted as an indicator below the price chart to highlight the range behavior of prices (see Figure 21.7).

Technicians also look at the relationship of each bar's range to its neighbor. A tool that is often used to identify and analyze intrabar range contractions is called NR7. An NR7 bar is the narrowest-range bar of the last seven bars. Such a bar combination is considered comparable to a coiled spring and often precedes a significant range expansion. An ideal setup for a possible breakout trigger is an NR7 bar in close proximity to a sloping five-period exponential moving average and accompanied by volume contraction. If, in addition, the high and low of the NR7 bar are inside the high and low of the previous bar, the odds of the setup leading to a significant breakout are even higher. Figure 21.9 illustrates an NR7 bar that fulfills the preceding criteria as the last bar of the chart. The coiled spring is ready to break out.

Techniques used to determine future market direction out of range contraction include looking at the follow-through behavior of the narrow-range bars, studying the market internals, and examining the Arps fear/greed indicator for clues.

Figure 21.7

Range contraction.

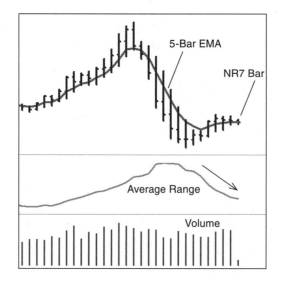

Trending moves out of range contraction during a consolidation period are generally followed by both range and volume expansion. Technical analysts are alert for such behavior. This is the type of setup that will provide solid entry points and quick results on the plus side of the P&L for the alert technical analyst/trader.

Conclusion

Over the very long run, stock markets have been upwardly biased. The problem is that it applies "over the long run." There is a famous saying, "Over the long run we'll all be dead." One of the objectives of technical analysis is to strive to make money consistently, regardless of whether markets as a whole are moving upward, downward, or sideways. There will always be opportunities to trade using technical analysis. Pretty much all you need to survive and thrive as a trader and technical analyst, no matter if the markets go up, down, or sideways, whether the economy is growing or we are in the midst of a great depression, are chart setups to look for, markets that best fit that particular setup, and a set of rules to apply to that setup.

Perhaps this book has opened your eyes to an entirely new approach to investing and trading. I hope that with the contents of this book, you will have learned a number of useful, practical methods of improving your investment and trading performance. If you have gotten this far along, I believe you have the will. Don't think of this as the ending but as a new beginning. So go out and practice what you have learned from this book and then return in a year or so and see if the concepts don't mean even more to you the second time around.

During your trading and investing lifetime, you will have winners, and you will have losers. Hope for the winners but do expect losers as well. Accept it as part of the business. So until the next time we meet in these pages, just remember, "The chart is the truth. It tells all."

The Least You Need to Know

- ◆ Technical analysis helps you identify the best entry and exit points of a trade.

- ◆ Trading success requires discipline.

- ◆ Planning your entry and exit points based on what the charts say takes emotion out of trading.

- ◆ Follow proven trading strategies for the best probability of success.

Glossary

accumulation   Purchases of large quantities of shares in anticipation of a major rise in the price of the stock. This is done by those with superior knowledge of the company who believe the stock is greatly underpriced.

ascending triangle   A stock price pattern characterized by two or more tops at the same approximate level and two or more bottoms, with each successive bottom being higher than the preceding bottom. A line drawn across the tops will be met by the ascending line drawn across the bottoms. These two lines form an upward slanted wedge.

ask price   An offer to sell a security at a specified price. The ask price is the lowest price any seller is prepared to accept.

at the market   A term used in entering a buy or sell order that tells the broker to buy immediately at the best available price from any seller or to sell immediately for the best available price to any buyer.

bar   Used on charts to plot the price action during a single time period, including its constituent high, low, opening, and closing prices.

bar chart   A type of chart constructed out of bars that reflect the price activity occurring during a specified time period.

basing action   Extended sideways trading at recent historic low price levels. Prices form a base at lower levels from which they will eventually break out.

bear   An investor who believes the price of a stock is going to decline.

bear market   A period (usually from six months to several years) during which stock averages trend lower and lower, and any upward price movement is relatively short in duration.

bid price   An offer to purchase a security at a specified price. The bid price is the highest price any buyer is prepared to pay.

blowoff   A blowoff move is characterized by extreme optimism by the general public leading to a strong and rapid upward movement of prices.

bottom   A succession of prices that fall to a low point and then rise from the low point for at least several days. The lowest point in this sequence of prices is called the bottom.

bottoming out   The process by which an extended downtrend is converted into an uptrend. This change in direction can occur in one day or it can take several days to complete. Usually, however, the bottoming-out process involves the formation of a double bottom, a triple bottom, an inverted head-and-shoulders, a triangle, a rectangle, or a rounding bottom.

bounce   A term used to describe the reversal of a downtrend at a point of resistance.

box   The area of a point-and-figure chart into which the technician places one X or O, representing a given amount of price increase or decrease.

box size   The box size is the minimum price movement in a point-and-figure chart. It is the distance the price has to move to create a new X or 0. The technician decides what minimum price change to use for the chart.

break   A rapid drop in price.

breakaway gap   The movement of price into a new range that leaves an area on a chart at which no trading occurred.

breakout   The point when the market price moves either up or down out of a trend channel or congestion area.

Bretton Woods system   An international monetary agreement adopted by most of the world following World War II. One of the key features was a commitment by countries to tie the exchange rate of currencies within a few percentage points of the value of gold.

bull   An investor who believes the price of a stock is going to rise.

bull market   A period of time (usually from one year to several years) during which stock averages trend higher and higher, and any downward price movement is relatively short in duration.

cancel   An instruction to disregard an order that you previously entered but no longer want.

cancel/replace   An instruction to cancel an existing order and place instead a new order for the same symbol that has adjustments made in the price, action, quantity, and/or duration.

channel   A pair of lines that contain prices throughout a trend. A channel can be a straight-line channel or a curving channel. A breakout of a channel can be a signal to buy or sell.

commission   The amount of money paid to a broker for executing a transaction.

congestion area   An area of the price chart where price movement trades sideways within a relatively narrow trading range for an extended time period. *See also* consolidation.

congestion market   A congestion market is a period of market action when prices are basically going sideways.

consolidation   A market that has undergone a sustained trend will "pause" to catch its breath or move into a consolidation phase. This means price action on the charts turns more sideways and choppy. An area of consolidation is also sometimes referred to as a "congestion area."

continuation pattern   A price pattern that interrupts a trend and implies a continuation of the trend (rather than a trend reversal) when the pattern is complete. Triangles, pennants, and flags are examples of continuation patterns.

contract   In futures trading, a standardized agreement that, because of its uniformity, makes the buying and selling of its obligations easier and more liquid. It is comparable to the concept of a share in stock market parlance.

correction   When a market has seen a sustained price trend, it will often make a shorter move in the opposite direction. This is called a correction, or pullback. Odds favor the eventual resumption of the trending move after the correction runs its course.

cover   The buying back of a share of stock or a futures contract that was sold short earlier.

crossover   A crossover occurs when an indicator moves through an important level or a moving average of itself. It is used to signal a change in trend or momentum.

cycle   A repetitive pattern in price or time.

day order   An order that is to be executed, if possible, during one day only. If the order cannot be filled during the day specified, it is automatically canceled at the close.

day trader   A trader who is in and out of one or more trades during the course of a day.

day trading   The practice of making multiple trades that you plan to open and close within the same trading day.

delayed data Continuously updated price and volume information that lags real-time data by a specified interval, usually 15 or 30 minutes, because it is usually offered as a free service. Delayed data is adequate for nontraders or long-term traders who do not require that their data and information be up-to-the-second.

demand The total volume of orders to buy shares or contracts at any specific point in time. The amount of this volume varies continually. When the demand is substantially greater than the supply, there is upward pressure on the price of the stock.

descending triangle A stock price pattern characterized by two or more bottoms at the approximate same level and two or more tops with each successive top being lower than the preceding top. A line drawn across the bottoms will be met by the descending line drawn across the tops. These two lines form a downward slanting wedge. The third side of the triangle is not drawn because it does not serve to define the boundaries of the price fluctuation.

distribution Sales of large quantities of shares of a stock in anticipation of a major decline in the price.

divergence A deviation between the directions of prices and indicators. In technical analysis, the term often is used to mean that a technical indicator is failing to corroborate or confirm the direction of price.

double bottom The pattern formed when the price of a stock that has been in a down-trend has made one bottom, rises, then declines again to the same approximate level, and then rises to begin a new uptrend.

double top The pattern formed when the price of a stock that has been in an uptrend peaks once, drops, then rises again to the same approximate level, and then retreats once more.

downtrend line A line drawn through two or more descending tops.

drawdown A reduction in account equity as a result of a losing series of trades.

Elliott wave theory A pattern recognition technique, published by Ralph N. Elliott in 1939, that holds that the stock market follows a rhythm or pattern of five waves up with three waves down in a bull market and five waves down with three waves up in a bear market to form a complete cycle of eight waves.

end-of-day data Data based on the closing price for the day. Often these data contain the open, high, and low for the day as well.

envelope Another name for a price channel.

exchange A central location for the buying and selling of stocks, futures, or options. An exchange can be a trading floor where buyers and sellers interact face to face, or it can be a "virtual" trading space where traders interact via Internet connections.

exchange-traded fund (ETF)   Similar to mutual funds except they trade on stock exchanges just like stocks. Each ETF represents an equity (or bond) index and allows investors to trade sectors, sections, or the broad market.

exponential moving average (EMA)   A type of moving average that is more sensitive to recent changes in price than to earlier changes in price.

fill   An executed order; sometimes the term refers to the price at which an order is executed.

flag pattern   A short-term congestion pattern usually consisting of at least five bars that appears as a small consolidation within a trend. The upper and lower boundaries of the flag should be contained in parallel sloping trendlines; if the lines converge, forming a small triangle, the pattern is referred to as a "pennant."

floating supply   The outstanding shares that are available to be traded in the open market, as opposed to shares that are closely held by organizations or individuals who want to maintain their ownership in the company.

floor pivots   A set of predicted intraday support and resistance levels for the current trading day based on mathematical calculations utilizing the previous day's high, low, and closing prices.

fundamental analysis   A method for calculating the value of a company's shares by analyzing the sales, earnings, and value of its assets, along with an estimate of the future growth in earnings of the company. This theory holds that stock prices may be predicted by looking at the relative data and statistics of a stock as well as the management of the company in question and its earnings.

futures   Contracts that obligate the owner to deliver a specific commodity or financial instrument by a certain date at an agreed-upon price. Futures facilitate a more stable market for the producers and consumers of commodities. In addition to agricultural products such as cattle, wheat, and soybeans, futures contracts are traded on metals such as copper, gold, and silver, as well as many financial instruments such as Treasury bonds, stock indexes, and foreign currencies.

gap   On a price chart, a time period where adjacent price bars do not overlap.

head-and-shoulders   A chart pattern often interpreted to mean a trend reversal may be imminent. This pattern forms when the price of a stock rises to a peak, declines, then rises to a second peak higher than the first, declines again, and then rises to a third peak that is lower than the second peak. This sequence of prices gives the rough appearance of a left shoulder, a head in the middle, and a right shoulder.

index   A statistical composite that measures changes in the economy or in financial markets, such as the S&P 500 Index or the Dow Jones Industrial Average.

inside bar   A price bar in which the high and low of the bar stays within the high and low of the previous bar.

intraday   Trading periods that begin and end within a one-day time frame.

intrinsic value   Intrinsic value is an analytical judgment of the real value of a company based on projected earnings and other perceived characteristics inherent in the investment, such as quality of management, brand name, and uniqueness of product, that are often difficult to calculate. Different fundamental analysts use different techniques to calculate intrinsic value.

Japanese candlesticks   A unique charting method, originally from Japan, in which the high and low of a given time period is plotted as a single vertical line referred to as the shadow. The price range between the open and the close is plotted on top of the shadow as a narrow rectangle and is referred to as the candle body. If the close is above the open, indicating an up day, the body is white. If the close is below the open, indicating a down day, the body is black. The portions of the shadow appearing above and below the candle body are referred to as wicks.

key reversal   A one-bar reversal pattern that occurs when a market makes a new high (or low), preferably a spike high (or low), and then reverses to close at or near the low (or high) of the price bar. The implication is that the market has experienced an extreme intraday sentiment change, and a reversal of trend direction is likely.

lag   The number of data points that a filter, such as a moving average, follows or trails the price data.

leverage   The use of borrowed money with invested funds to increase returns. The effect is to magnify profits or losses and increase the amount of risk.

limit order   A price set by a buyer or seller that a filling broker must equal or better in the execution of his or her order.

line chart   A type of chart that connects successive closing prices with a line that moves up and down sideways as prices move up and down.

liquidity   The characteristic of a financial instrument to be quickly and easily converted to cash. A share of stock listed on a stock exchange is usually considered to be highly liquid, whereas an apartment building would be considered to be relatively illiquid.

long   The state of actually owning a security, contract, or commodity. If you go long in the market, you are buying.

long liquidation   Selling that occurs either when traders take profits from long positions or when weaker longs exit the market if it appears to be exhibiting weakness. Long liquidation usually occurs when a market has been in a sustained uptrend and many bulls feel that the market is vulnerable to a downside correction.

main thrust The main thrust of an up move is the strongest leg of a major move in prices and usually follows a pullback in price.

margin A brokerage account in which purchase of stock may be partially financed with money borrowed from the brokerage firm.

market A public place where buyers and sellers make transactions, directly or via intermediaries.

market maker The brokerage or bank that maintains a firm bid and ask price in a given security by standing ready, willing, and able to buy or sell at publicly quoted prices.

market on close (MOC) A market order that can be filled only within the closing range.

market order An order that does not specify a price; rather, it instructs the filling broker to execute the order "at the market," meaning at the best price available on receipt.

market-if-touched (MIT) A type of order that becomes a market order if and when the stock hits a price you specify. Like limit orders, buy MITs are entered at or below the current market, and sell MITs are entered at or above the current price. Unlike limit orders, there are no limitations placed on the floor broker as to fill price; the broker will execute the order at the best available price, the same as any market order.

momentum The rate of change in prices over a fixed period.

moving average An average price calculated for a specific number of price bars. For each new price bar, a new average is calculated and plotted on a price chart for the stock. Moving averages are a way to smooth the random oscillations on a price chart.

Moving Average Convergence/Divergence (MACD) An oscillator based on the difference between two moving averages of different length. Technicians often use the crossing of this value over the zero line to signal buying or selling opportunities.

neckline The line that can be drawn through the two bottom points of the two valleys between the head and shoulders of a head-and-shoulders formation.

odd lot A quantity of shares that is not a multiple of 100.

open The first trade price of the day (or other time period). In futures markets, the open is a representative price of the first minute of trading. In stocks, the open is the first recorded trade price.

open interest A concept used in futures trading. It represents the number of open contracts outstanding at any specific point in time.

order cancels order (OCO) An order that is also called "one cancels the other." This order consists of two separate buy or sell instructions to the filling broker, who will execute whichever portion of the order he is able to do first and then automatically cancel the alternate instruction.

oscillator A technical indicator that oscillates between a minimum and maximum level. Well-known oscillators include the Relative Strength Index (RSI), MACD, and Stochastics indicators.

outside bar A price bar in which the high and low of the bar exceed both the high and the low of the previous bar.

outstanding shares The total number of shares held by investors, including restricted shares owned by management but not including shares repurchased by the company.

overbought A high oscillator value level above which buyers are considered to be very aggressive in purchasing a stock or futures contract.

oversold A low oscillator value below which sellers are considered to be very aggressive in selling a stock or futures contract.

paper trade To make simulated transactions with no real money, to practice or test theories.

penetration The action of a stock price when it breaks through from one side of a boundary or trendline to the other side.

pit A specially constructed arena on the trading floor of exchanges where trading is conducted. Some exchanges call these areas a ring rather than a pit.

pivot A price swing high or swing low. A pivot represents the extreme price at a chart peak or valley where prices reversed direction.

pivot price The average of the high, low, and closing prices of a specific trading period such as a day, a week, or a month.

point-and-figure A charting method using columns of X's and O's that plots price swing moves without regard to time. When prices are rising, a rising column of X's is formed. Each X represents a user-defined fixed price increment. When prices are falling, a new column of falling O's is formed, where each O represents the same fixed price increment. Each column continues until the movement direction is reversed by a given amount and a new column starts.

position A term used to describe a current open trade. For example, if you bought 100 shares of XYZ, your position would be long 100 shares of XYZ.

protective stop   To limit losses on an open position, traders place a protective stop order to close the position at a predetermined level if prices go against them.

pullback   A short-term countertrend move. Pullbacks offer opportunities to enter existing trends.

range   The highest value minus the lowest value of a price bar on a chart.

real-time data   Trade-by-trade price data that is transmitted instantaneously as it happens.

Relative Strength Index (RSI)   An indicator used to ascertain overbought/oversold and divergent price behavior.

resistance level   The price level at which rising prices have stopped rising previously and either moved sideways or reversed direction. Frequently history will repeat itself, and the price will stop rising if it returns to this level.

retest   Occurs when the price encounters resistance, pulls back, and then again tries to cross through the resistance level. If the price is unable to break through the resistance level, it is referred to as a failed retest. If price does break through the resistance zone, it is referred to as a successful retest.

retracement   Price movement in the opposite direction of the prevailing trend.

reversal pattern   Any of several patterns that form while the direction of price movement is changing from upward to downward or from downward to upward. The price approaches the pattern from one direction and exits the pattern in the reverse direction.

reversal stop   A stop order that, when hit, is a signal to reverse the current trading position.

reward-to-risk ratio   The potential profit involved in a position as compared to the amount of risk. Divide the maximum expected profit by the potential loss if wrong. A risk/reward ratio of 1 or better means the potential profit is higher than the potential loss. Most skilled traders look for a reward-to-risk ratio of 3 to 1 or better.

risk   A measure of the possibility that an investment will lose money.

risk of ruin   The chance that, by using a given system or method, one will deplete one's funds to zero over time.

risk tolerance   A way to judge how much risk you are willing to take to achieve an investment goal. The higher your risk tolerance, the more risk you are willing to take.

rounding bottom   The saucer-shaped curve that develops when a downtrend in a stock price gradually changes into an uptrend over a period of several months or longer.

rounding top   The upside-down, saucer-shaped curve that develops when an uptrend in a stock price gradually changes into a downtrend over a period of several months or longer.

sensitivity setting   A term used to describe how aggressive or conservative a technician is when determining what conditions must be met for the chart to indicate a significant action.

short   The state of having borrowed a security in order to sell it or, in the case of a futures contract, entering into an agreement to sell a particular commodity at a given price at a specific time in the future. If you are short the market, you are a seller and will make a profit if prices go down and you rebuy (buy to cover) your short position later at a lower price than where you sold it short.

short covering   Traders who have established short positions decide to close out their positions by buying shares or contracts. Short covering may occur either when traders decide to take profits from existing short positions or to exit the market if it appears prices are going to rise.

short selling   A trade in which you sell a security that you do not own in anticipation that the price is going to fall. In the case of stocks, your broker borrows the stock from another client. You sell the stock and put the money in your account. If you are correct, you buy back the stock at the lower price and pocket the profit. The original owner then gets the stock back.

slippage   The difference between the anticipated cost and the actual cost of a transaction.

spike   A quick up-and-down price movement that has the appearance of an upright spike on a price chart.

Stochastics   An oscillator measuring the position of closing prices compared to the trading range over a set period of time. %K refers to the fast Stochastics line; %D refers to the slow Stochastics line.

stop (stop order, stop-loss order)   A buy order placed at a predetermined price above the current price of the market or a sell order placed at a predetermined price below the current price of the market. If the price touches the stop level, an order is automatically placed to be executed at the current market price. Stops are often used as protective orders to exit a losing position in order to limit the amount of loss incurred.

stop close only (SCO)   A stop order that can be triggered and executed only during the market's closing range at the end of the trading day.

stop limit   A variation on the simple stop that instructs the filling broker to fill an order at a specified price or better, if possible, once the stop is triggered. This gives the trader more control over the fill price. If, however, the market runs past the stipulated price before the broker is able to execute it, the order is not filled unless the price returns to the specified limit price.

supply   The total volume of shares or contracts available for sale at any specific point in time. The amount of this volume varies continually. When the supply is substantially greater than the demand, there is downward pressure on the price of the stock.

support level   A price level, lower than the current price, where the price previously stopped going down and reversed to the upside. Frequently history will repeat itself, and the price will stop declining if it returns to a previous support level.

swing   A price move defined by a valley of a given magnitude and an adjacent peak of an equivalent magnitude. A swing chart is a zigzag chart that displays successive upswings and downswings.

symmetrical triangle   A triangle formation that is formed when price fluctuations result in two or more consecutive descending peaks and two or more consecutive ascending valleys. A straight declining line drawn across the tops will be met by a straight ascending line drawn across the bottoms. These two lines form a wedge-shaped figure. The third side of the triangle is not drawn because it does not serve to define the boundaries of the price fluctuation.

technical analysis   The analysis of price and volume behavior over time as the basis for making investment decisions. The rationale for this approach is that the price and volume information at any point in time reflects all that is known about the company by all the interested parties who have bought or sold that investment vehicle. Since a price chart summarizes and displays the net result of all these buy and sell decisions, it is the best single resource for making rational investment timing and selection decisions.

technician   A person who practices technical analysis is often referred to as a technician.

thrust   A swing move in the direction of the prevailing trend. This is in contrast to a pullback, which is a swing move against the direction of the prevailing trend.

tick   The minimum price fluctuation of a tradable. For example, a tick in most stocks is 1¢, while the S&P 500 index trades in 25¢ ticks.

ticker   A scrolling display of current prices and volume as the trades occur in real time.

top   A top is formed when a succession of stock prices rise, reach a high point, and then decline for several bars, creating a peak. The highest point in this sequence is called a top.

trading   The act of buying and selling financial instruments such as stocks, bonds, futures contracts, and Forex.

trading volume   The daily trading volume is the number of shares traded in the course of the business day. These figures are published in most daily newspapers.

trailing stop   A stop order that is raised (in a rising market) or lowered (in a declining market) to follow an open position and lock in profits.

trend The current general direction of movement for prices.

trendline A line drawn through two or more ascending bottoms or through two or more descending tops. The former line will trend upward, and the price is said to be in an uptrend. The latter line will trend downward, and the price is said to be in a downtrend.

triple bottom A pattern formed when prices fall, then rise and fall again, and stop falling at the same approximate level at least three times in a row.

triple top A pattern formed when the prices rise, then fall and rise again, and stop rising at the same approximate level at least three times in a row.

true range A volatility calculation developed by Welles Wilder that modifies the standard range calculation by accounting for gaps between price bars. True range is defined as the largest value (in absolute terms) of today's high and today's low (the standard daily range calculation), or today's high and yesterday's close, or today's low and yesterday's close. Average true range (ATR) is simply a moving average of true range calculated over a fixed number of days. True range and average true range are common volatility measurements.

uptrend line A line drawn through two or more ascending bottoms of similar strength.

V-shaped bottom A price pattern that occurs when a sharp downtrend suddenly changes into a sharp uptrend.

volatility A measure of the degree of stability of the price of a stock, index, or futures contract. Wide price swings within a given time interval signify a high degree of price volatility.

volume The number of transactions that took place within a specified trading period; a measure of trading activity during that period.

whipsaw Losing money on both sides of a price swing.

wide-range bar A bar whose range is much greater than that of the preceding price bars or, alternately, one with a range much greater than the average range over a fixed number of days.

Further Information About Technical Analysis

The following resource lists are not exhaustive, but they are sources reviewed and recommended by the author.

Recommended Books on Technical Analysis

All of these books can be ordered from www.invest-store.com/janarps/.

Aby Jr., Carroll D., Ph.D. *The Complete Guide to Point & Figure Charting.* Greenville, SC: Traders Press, Inc., 1996.

Achelis, Steven B. *Technical Analysis from A to Z.* Chicago: Probus Publishing, 1995.

Appel, Gerald. *Technical Analysis: Power Tools for Active Investors.* Upper Saddle River, NJ: Financial Times Prentice Hall, 2005.

———. *The Moving Average Convergence-Divergence Method.* Great Neck, NY: Signalert, 1979.

Brooks, Al. *Reading Price Charts Bar by Bar.* Hoboken, NJ: John Wiley & Sons, Inc., 2009.

Carter, John F. *Mastering the Trade—Proven Techniques for Profiting from Intraday and Swing Trading Setups.* New York: McGraw-Hill, Inc., 2006.

Cassidy, Donald L. *It's When You Sell That Counts.* New York: McGraw-Hill, 1997.

Covel, Michael W. *Trend Following: How Great Traders Make Millions in Up or Down Markets.* Upper Saddle River, NJ: Financial Times Prentice Hall, 2006.

Crane, John. *Advanced Swing Trading—Strategies to Predict, Identify, and Trade Future Market Swings.* Hoboken, NJ: John Wiley & Sons, Inc., 2003.

Dorsey, Thomas J. *Point & Figure Charting.* Hoboken, NJ: John Wiley & Sons, Inc., 1995.

Droke, Cliff. *Technical Analysis Simplified.* Columbia, MD: Marketplace Books, 2000.

Elder, Alexander Ph.D. *Come Into My Trading Room—A Complete Guide to Trading.* Hoboken, NJ: John Wiley & Sons, Inc., 2002.

———. *Trading for a Living.* Hoboken, NJ: John Wiley & Sons, Inc., 1993.

Hardy, C. Colburn. *Trader's Guide to Technical Analysis.* Columbia, MD: Marketplace Books, 2000.

Jenkins, Michael S. *The Geometry of Stock Market Profits—A Guide to Professional Trading for a Living.* Greenville, SC: Traders Press, Inc., 1992.

Kaufman, P.J. *Technical Analysis in Commodities.* Hoboken, NJ: John Wiley & Sons, Inc., 1980.

Kindleberger, Charles P. *Manias, Panics, and Crashes—A History of Financial Crises.* New York: Basic Books, Inc., 1978.

Lefevre, Edwin. *Reminiscences of a Stock Operator.* Hoboken, NJ: John Wiley & Sons, Inc., 1994.

Mackay, Charles. *Extraordinary Popular Delusions and the Madness of Crowds.* New York: Farrar, Straus and Giroux, Inc., 1932.

Miner, Robert C. *High Probability Trading Strategies.* Hoboken, NJ: John Wiley & Sons, Inc., 2009.

Murphy, John J. *Charting Made Easy.* Columbia, MD: Marketplace Books, 2000.

———. *Technical Analysis of the Financial Markets.* New York: New York Institute of Finance, 1999.

Nison, Steve. *Japanese Candlestick Charting Techniques.* New York: New York Institute of Finance, 1991.

———. *Beyond Candlesticks: New Japanese Charting Techniques Revealed.* Hoboken, NJ: John Wiley & Sons, Inc., 1994.

Prechter, Robert B. *The Wave Principle of Human Social Behavior and the New Science of Socionomics.* Gainesville, GA: New Classics Library, 2006.

Pring, Martin J. *The Successful Investor's Guide to Spotting Investment Trends and Turning Points.* New York: McGraw-Hill, 2002.

Schwager, Jack D. *Getting Started in Technical Analysis.* Hoboken, NJ: John Wiley & Sons, Inc., 1999.

Steenbarger, Brett N., Ph.D. *The Psychology of Trading—Tools and Techniques for Minding the Markets.* Hoboken, NJ: John Wiley & Sons, Inc., 2003.

Toppel, Edward Allen. *Zen in the Markets.* Chicago: Samurai Press, 1992.

Woods, Steve. *Float Analysis—Powerful Techniques to Exploit Price and Volume.* Columbia, MD: Marketplace Books, 2005.

Recommended Periodicals for Technical Analysts

- *Investor's Business Daily,* www.investors.com
- *Technical Analysis of Stocks & Commodities,* www.traders.com
- *Futures Magazine,* www.futuresmag.com
- *Active Trader* magazine, www.activetradermag.com
- *SFO Magazine,* www.sfomag.com

Recommended Websites for Market News and Analysis

- www.Bloomberg.com
- www.YahooFinance.com
- www.MarketWatch.com

Recommended Web-Based Charting Services

- www.StockCharts.com
- www.ProRealTime.com

Recommended Technical Analysis Websites

- www.TraderPlanet.com
- www.TradingMarkets.com
- www.TradersWorld.com
- www.BigTrends.com
- www.FloatCharts.com
- www.WallStreetWindow.com
- www.Infowire.net/td
- www.JanArps.com

Index

handle, 79
projected price target, 80
currency exchange rates, 219
custom-built computers, 205
cutting losses short, 264

D

data
graphic display, 5
information vs., 4
interpretation, 5
price information, 5
data feed, 205–207
data feed services, 202
caution, 206
decision, 206
end-of-day data, 206
real-time streaming price data, 206
server farms, 205
types, 206
user fee, 206
day orders, 237
deep dip double divergence, 132
delayed streaming data, 206
DIA, 217
discipline, 284
distribution, 59, 171
distribution day, 162
divergence, 129
buy signal, 133
chart of types, 138
confusion, 131
deep dip double divergence, 132
identification, 134
intermarket, 138
neural networks, 138
normal divergence patterns, 131
oscillators, 129
crossing signal, 135
downtrend, 130

false signal, 132
most common, 132
oscillator bumps, 130, 132
Stochastics oscillator, 130, 134
uptrend, 132
ways to use, 129
pivot, 131
problem with analysis, 132
pure deep dip double example, 133
signals, 131
software, 138
trader objectivity, 133
trend divergence, 136–137
triple-bump divergence, 135–136
valid, 132–133
divergent trend reversal, 222
doji, 31
doji bar, 222
Donchian channel, 95–97
dot.com markets, downtrends (2000–2003), 76
double bottoms, 63, 146
double top pattern, 63
Dow, Charles, 5, 22
Dow Jones indexes, 218
Dow Jones Industrial Average, 187, 217
Dow Theory, 22–23
downside breakout, 143
downtrends, 75, 88

E

efficient market hypothesis, 14
Elliott wave pattern, 62
EMA. *See* exponential moving average
emotions
basic, 13
behavior and, 8

capital and, 265
crowd, 21
facts vs., 7
float boxes, 175
impact of on trading, 186
managing, 244
money management and, 251
price movements and, 85
removing, 265
supply and demand and, 17, 56
end-run around problem, 261
entry orders. *See* orders
equal-tick bar chart, 42–43
equal-volume bar chart, 42–43
equity curve, 278
equity index, 193
ETFs. *See* exchange-traded funds
exchange-traded funds (ETFs), 193, 215, 217
advantage, 217
commodities, 217
DIA, 217
first, 217
index-based, 217
international, 217
leveraged, 217
NASDAQ 100 index, 217
pricing, 217
QQQQ, 217
supply and demand, 217
exhaustion gap, 72
exit plan, 239–240
exit position, 265–266
exit rules, 245
exponential moving average (EMA), 102–103
Extraordinary Popular Delusions and the Madness of Crowds, 21

W– X– Y–Z